MAXIMILLIAN MALONE

CUT-OUT
CURIOSITIES
BOTANICA

A COLLAGE BOOK

Smith Street Books

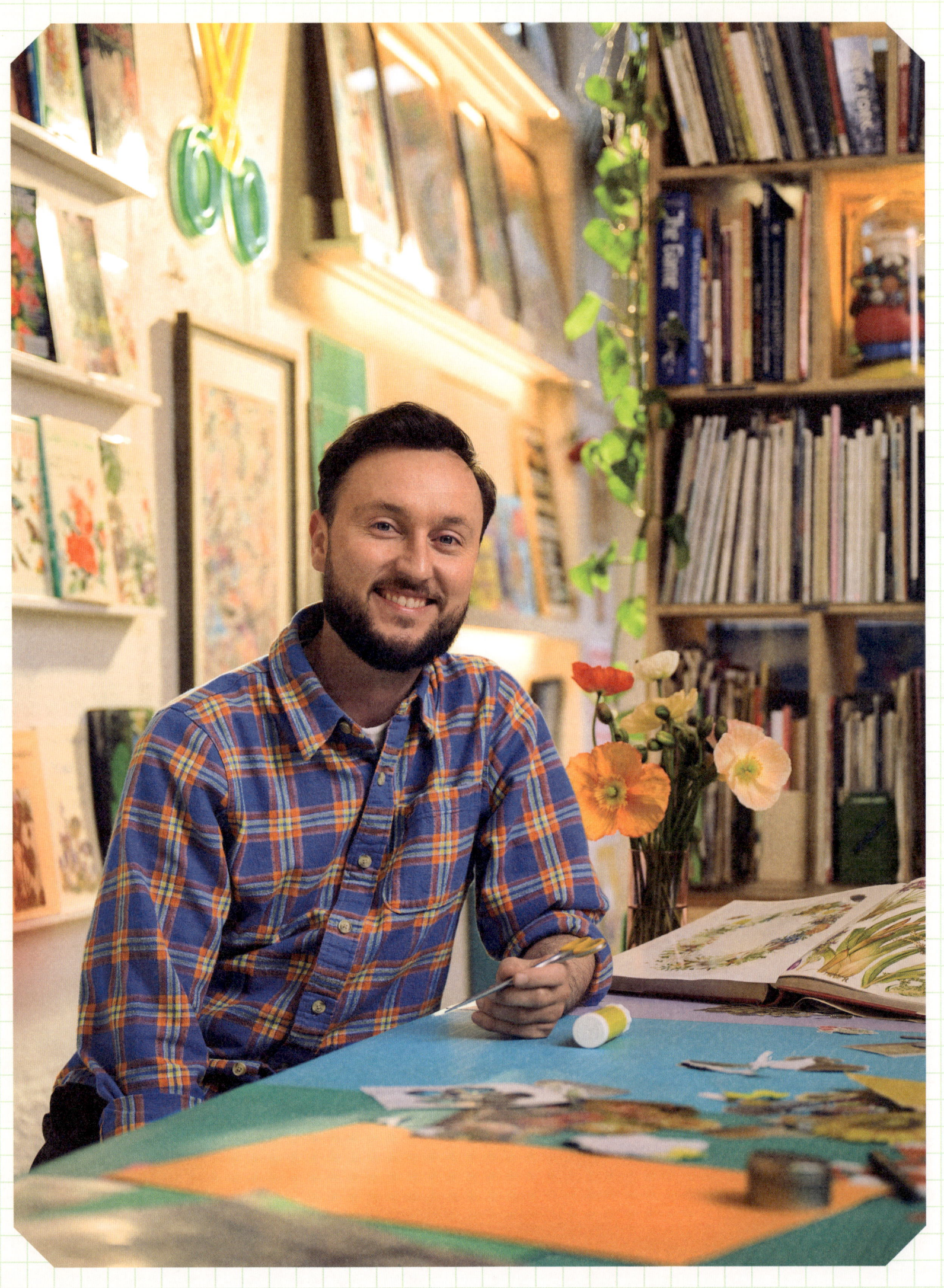

INTRODUCTION

—

I'M MAX, an artist with a fascination and, if truly honest, near obsession with the world of collage.

I gather old books, magazines and other ephemera from flea markets, vintage fairs, junkyards and even bins! Then, I repurpose these flaking papers with crumbling inks into new works of art. It's what I love to do! The process of cutting, ripping and combining images into new ideas and creations brings me so much joy.

My personal journey with collage goes back as far as I can remember. As a child, I was naturally creative and curious, either making things with cardboard boxes or concocting mud pies in the garden. I loved collecting stickers, decorating my skateboards, personalising my schoolbooks and sewing patches onto my backpack: I was forever adorning, embellishing and layering onto things. As I entered my teens, cutting and pasting became a new way that I expressed myself. Collaging was my tool to help me discover and understand my particular tastes and interests.

Fast-forward to the present day, and I'm as passionate about collage as ever, designing my life around it. I now live in a home studio, named That Paper Joint: a magical place dedicated to collage, making art and running workshops. It is filled with an amazing array of vintage books, postcards, comics and illustrations from around the world. This art studio, home and gallery all rolled into one has a wonderful shopfront facade where any passerby can peer into this world of collage filled with plants, vibrant colours, treasures and trinkets, and of course, a lot of paper!

But why collage – why not painting or drawing? Well for me, collage is limitless, unbound by technical skills. You can reuse and build upon what already exists, repurposing and reinventing anything with such immediacy and impact. Collage is this democratic and accessible process that anyone can try. It has long been my passion, and I believe it can be a passion for you too! Whether you've attended art school or consider yourself creative, most of us can wield a pair of scissors to make something, regardless of experience and expertise. In this book, I hope to inspire you with the potential of collage, and to welcome you to this world of amazing possibilities.

When choosing a theme for this book, botanicals came to mind instantly! I love the natural world and draw a lot of inspiration from trips out into the wilderness, walking with my partner and my dog. So I truly hope you enjoy this book filled with natural visual delights!

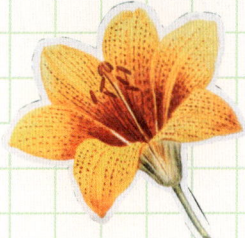

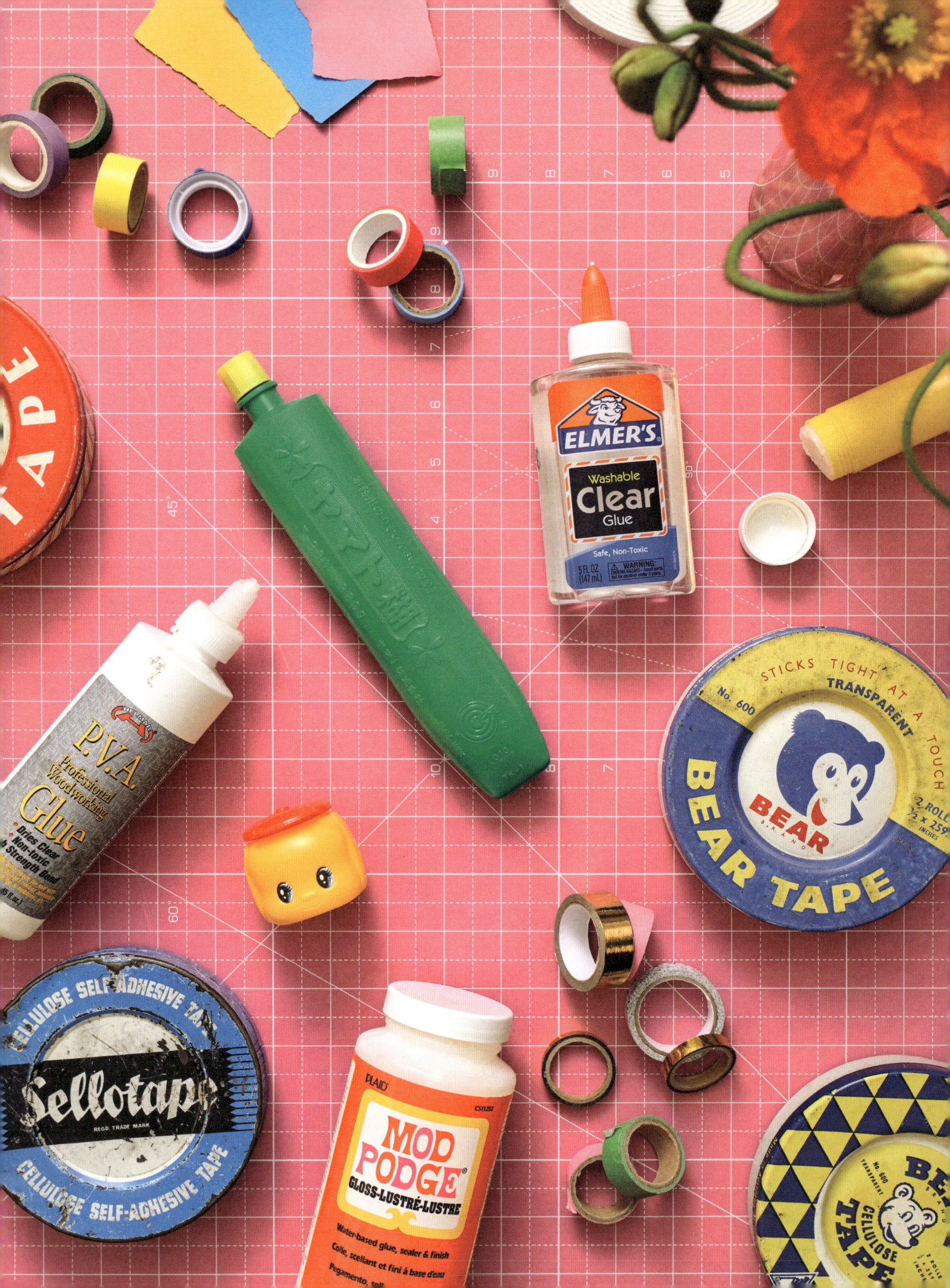

WHAT YOU'LL NEED

Aside from this book, here are the tools you'll need
to get started on your collage journey.

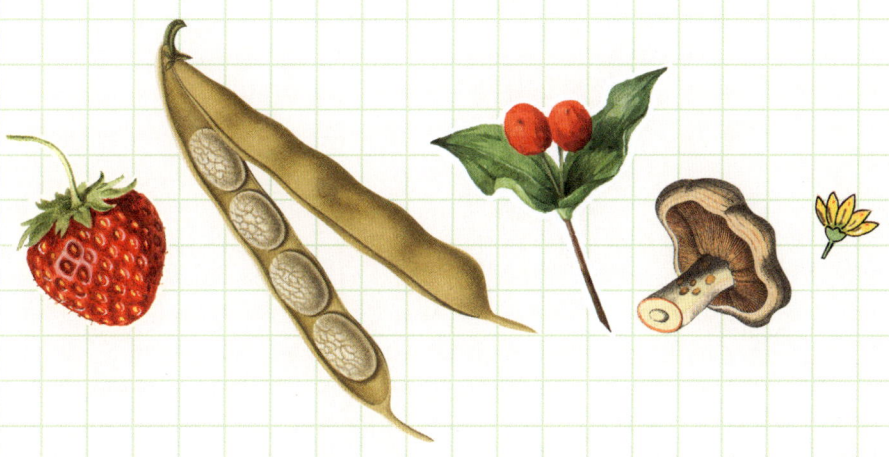

SCISSORS

A trusty pair of scissors is a must. These days, I'm obsessed with my Japanese-made scissors, which are high quality and super sharp! You don't need an expensive pair though: any old pair you have at home will work. I've tried and tested so many different shapes and sizes to find my favourites. Over time, you'll find pairs that suit you. Once you do, keep them safe and use them only for paper.

Try adding pairs of decorative scissors to your collection too. They may look like they're just for kids, but they can help you to create interesting and dynamic outlines.

GLUE

Glue choice is really down to personal preference, and what you like to work with. My go-to recommendation is a simple, quality, acid-free glue stick: a clean, easy-to-use option that can be taken wherever you go.

Glue sticks won't create the most durable results, though, so for long-term preservation of collages, more hardy options like gel mediums are recommended (see page 22). To find whether you prefer to work with PVA, wallpaper paste, spray adhesives, tapes or another option, practise with a range and be ready to make mistakes. While you explore different options, try using a rubber roller to smooth down your cut-outs: this helps avoid air bubbles.

CRAFT KNIFE AND MAT

To create more-advanced artworks, you'll need a craft knife/scalpel and a cutting mat. Craft knives allow you to 'pluck' imagery from within a page with exacting precision. If you're using one, you'll need a self-healing cutting mat to protect your table: always cut on mats, rather than directly onto tables. It's helpful to have plenty of spare blade tips handy.

BACKGROUNDS

'What should I glue onto?' is a common question. It depends. You may choose to use some of the pages from this book as your base layer, but for a sturdier result, fix your collage onto a heavier weight paper, piece of wood or canvas. I love using old book covers: their marks and imperfections add history and texture, which results in artworks that feel more organic and original.

EXTRA FUN BITS

If you're committed to exploring collage further, seek out paper punches, deckled edge rulers, tweezers, stencils, stamps, paints, pens, and anything else you'd like to use. There's a world of tools available that will help you add personality and an extra dimension to your collages.

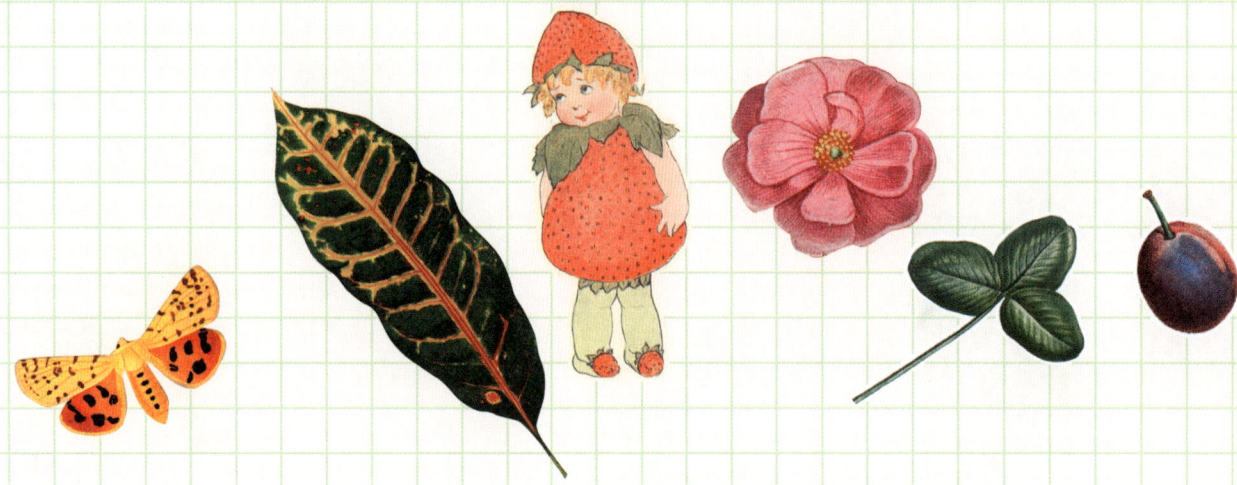

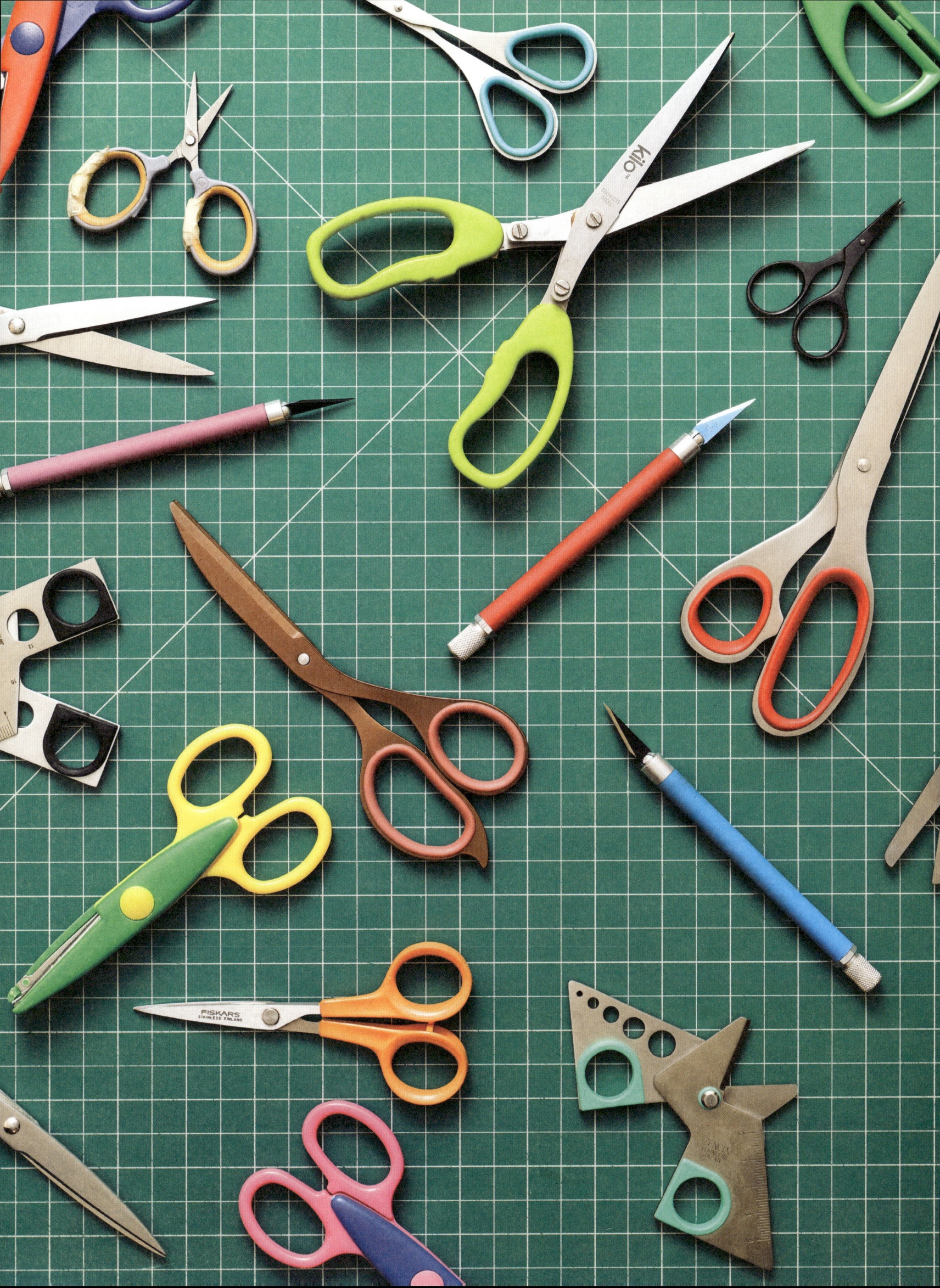

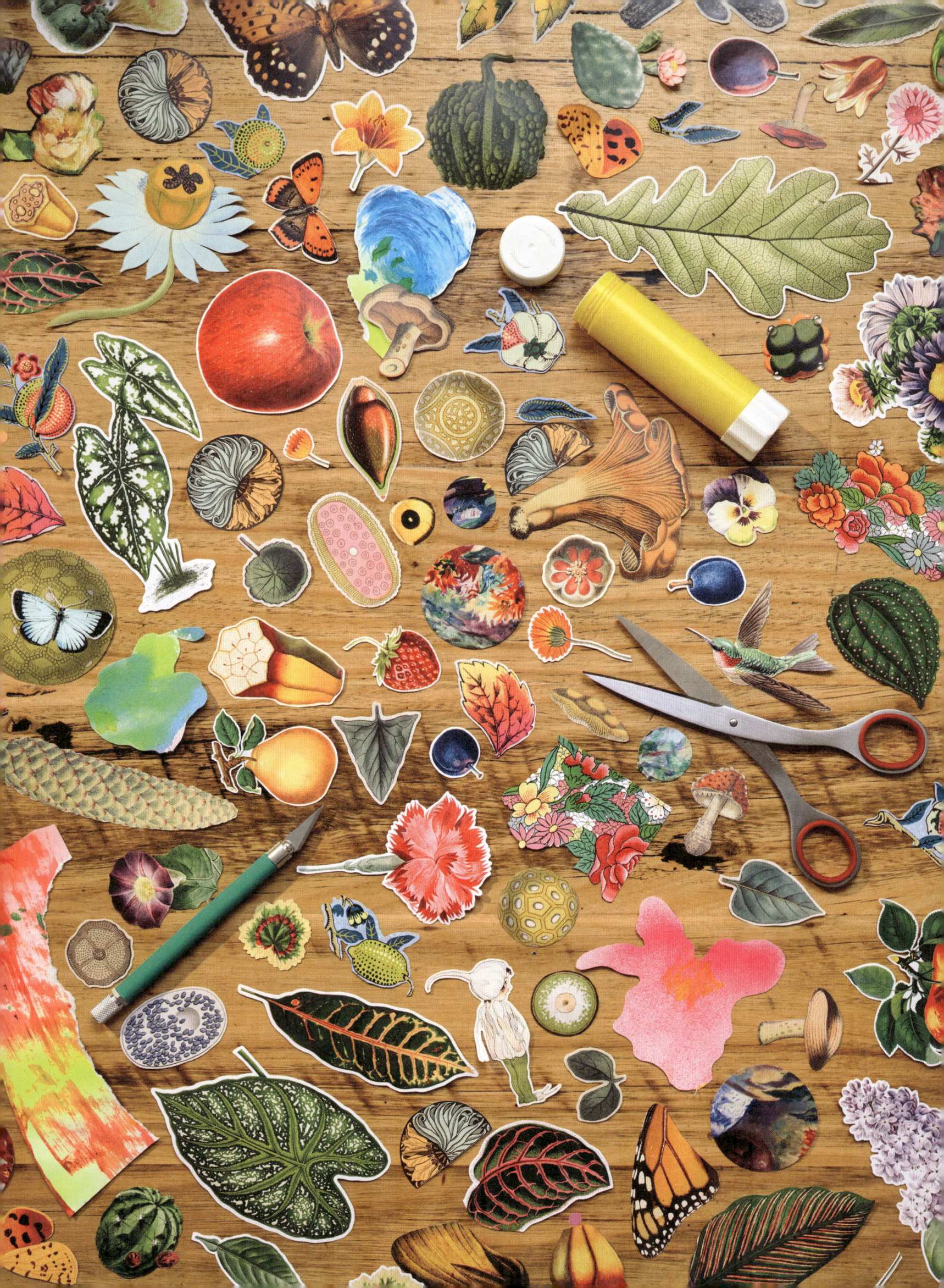

PROCESS

There is no right or wrong way to collage or to use this book. Some of you may keep it intact for reference, but many of you (myself included) will enjoy chopping it into a hundred pieces and collaging it into something new. It's all about experimenting and having fun.

WHILE THERE'S NOT ONE DIRECT METHOD TO FOLLOW, HERE ARE A FEW IDEAS THAT MAY HELP YOU ON YOUR COLLAGE JOURNEY:

Firstly, you could dedicate a little corner of your home to your art. The more space you can take over, the better! Whether this is in your bedroom or on the lounge-room floor, enjoy making a mess and embrace the cutting chaos. You don't need a lot of space to get started, but be warned: collages can expand exponentially, taking up far more space and time than you planned for. If this feels overwhelming, begin simply: cut out a few elements you like and don't overthink it. Just keep snipping.

Let's be honest, we're not always in the creative mindset. At times like these, just enjoy the act of cutting and don't pressure yourself to make art. Lean into the meditative nature of putting scissors to paper. There are so many gorgeous images in this book, so start on something relatively easy and cut cut cut! If you can dedicate a good chunk of time to cutting with a podcast or show to keep you company, it really can be very relaxing. I find cutting things out to be highly addictive. Once you start, sometimes you just can't stop! If the sun is shining, perhaps take things outdoors, but keep paper weights handy.

Once your pile of cut-outs has grown, lay them out so that you can admire your handiwork: well done! Give your cramped hand a rest and sit back and observe your collection. This is where things start to get exciting, as you're now ready to consider the possibilities.

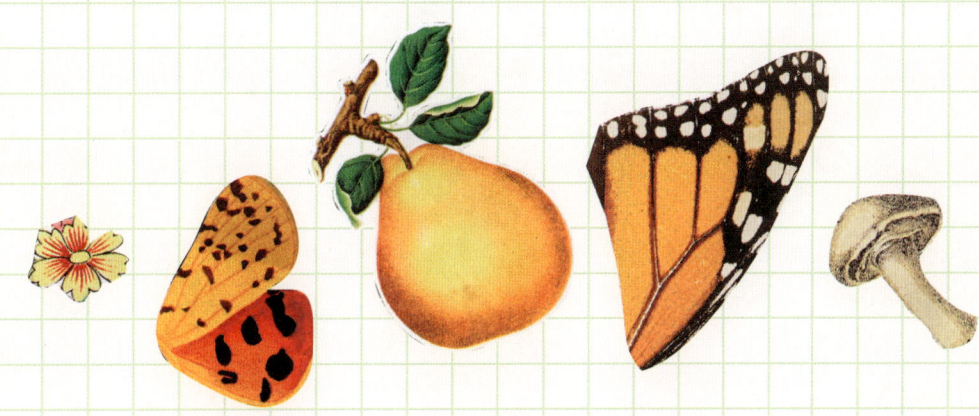

Your subconscious will often do more than you realise when your cut-outs are visible, formulating potential groups and unlikely ideas. Try observing your pieces upside down and back-to-front. Think outside the box: you can use them literally, but also abstractly. Try matching complementary images with similar vibes or play with juxtapositions and contrasts. Blend old with new, big with small: mix things together and take your time. The more you allow yourself to explore combinations, the more likely a lucky opportunity will present itself. Collage is often about chance. There's an element of serendipity when seemingly random elements come together to tell a new story.

In the collage workshops that I host at That Paper Joint, it's very common for people to want to try and tell a particular story. However, this can be tricky, as the elements you have on hand might not match the idea you have in your head. Sometimes a narrative can get in the way of creative experimentation and play.

If you like to have a plan, that's fine too, but my usual advice is to 'let the pieces lead the way'. Let the story/meaning evolve organically. Let your subconscious guide the direction. It's totally okay if your work doesn't have a strong, immediate message. Many of my favourite artworks that I've made are open to interpretation. If you allow yourself time to freely experiment, you'll be amazed at what you come up with.

Your collage can be simple, with just two pieces, or it can be wildly complex, with multiple layers woven together. Minimalism and maximalism are equally fun to try. Collage can go in many directions and that's what keeps it exciting. Sometimes finished pieces will express a poignant message, but collage can go totally the other way and be incredibly silly, completely random and downright bizarre! Make works that are quick and impulsive, as well as slow and thoughtful. This book contains the beauty of nature, so let that be a starting point for inspiration.

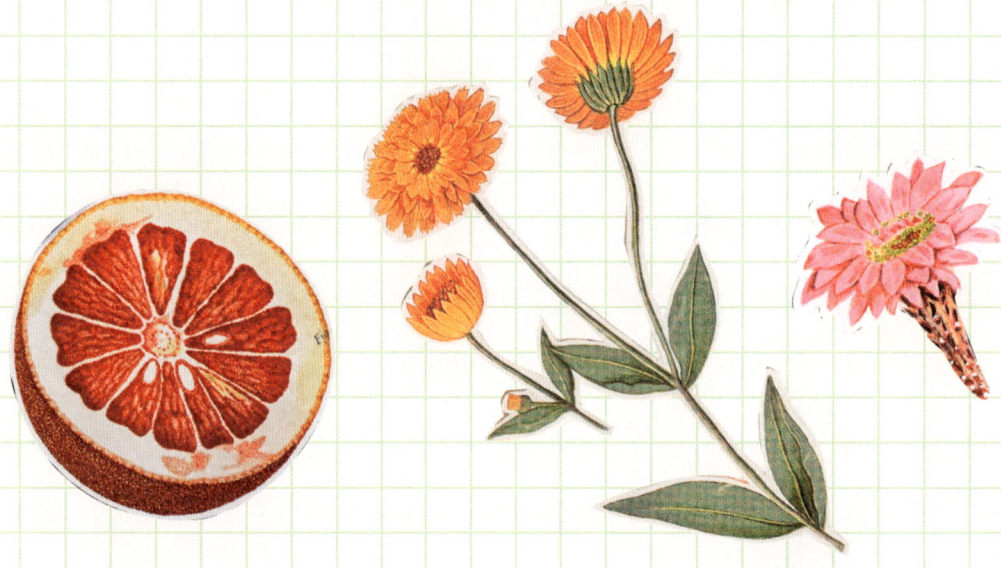

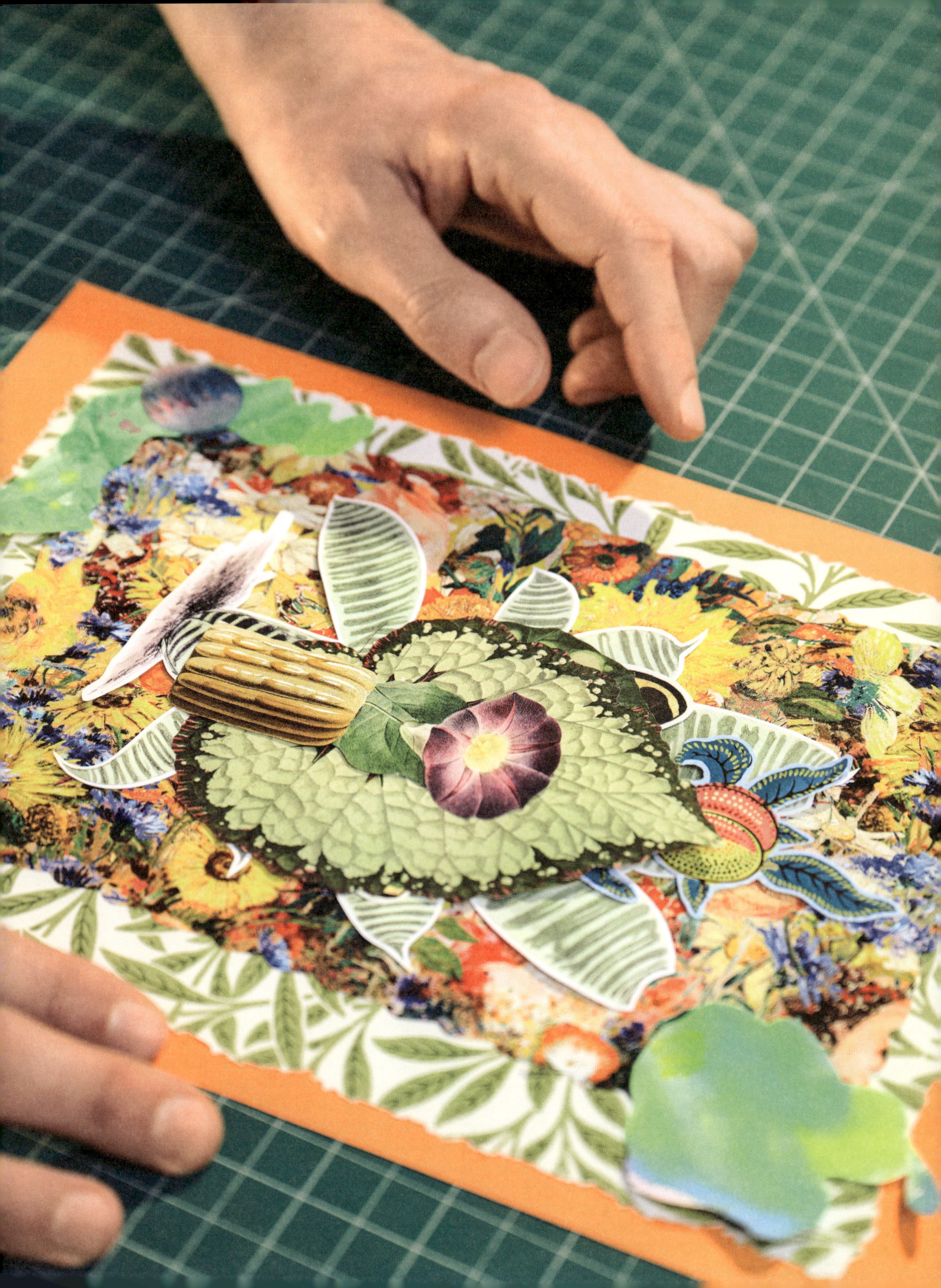

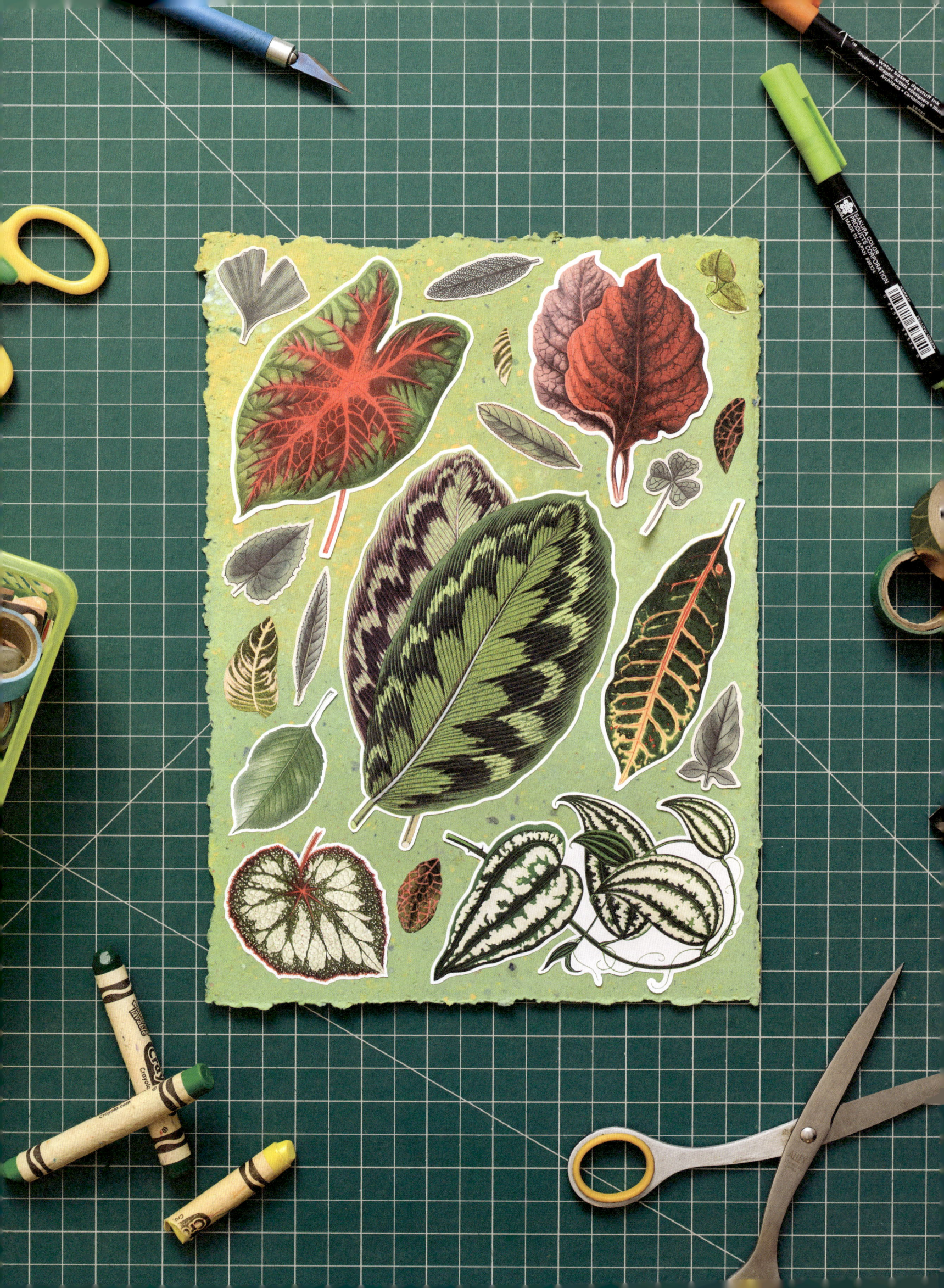

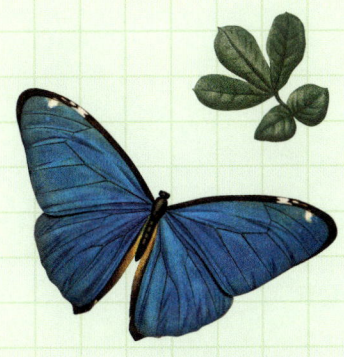

APPROACH

IN FOUR PARTS

—

If you want help getting started, I'll explain how to break down the collage process into my four recommended steps: Research, Cutting, Arranging, and Gluing and Finishing. Or, if you wish, skip my suggestions and just go for it!

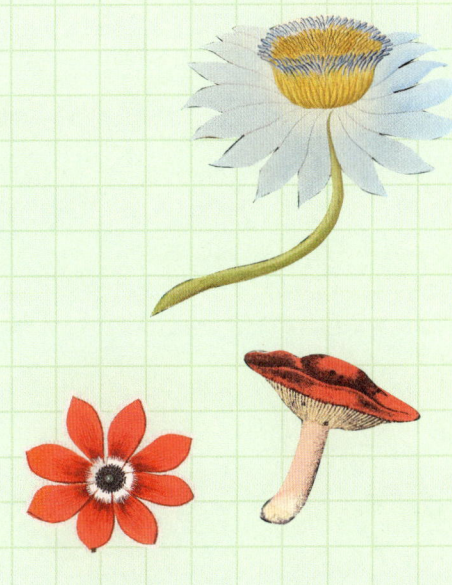

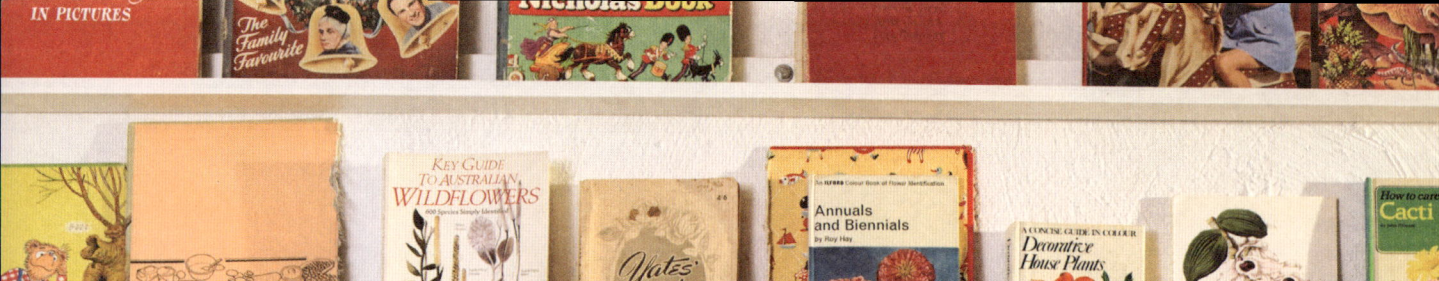
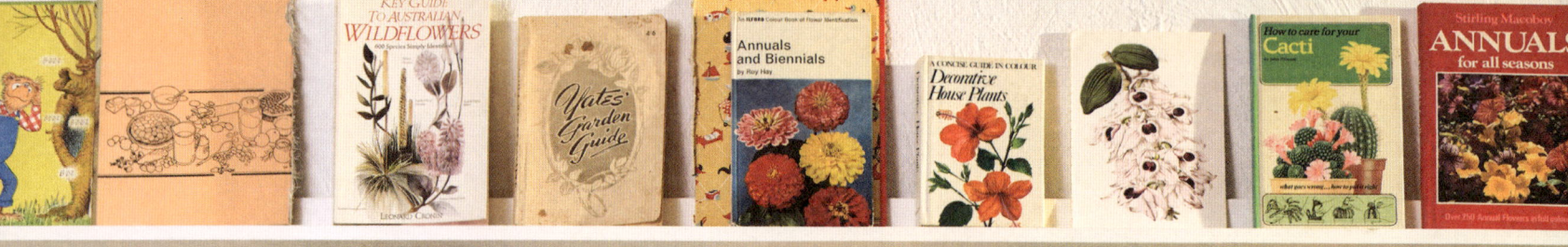
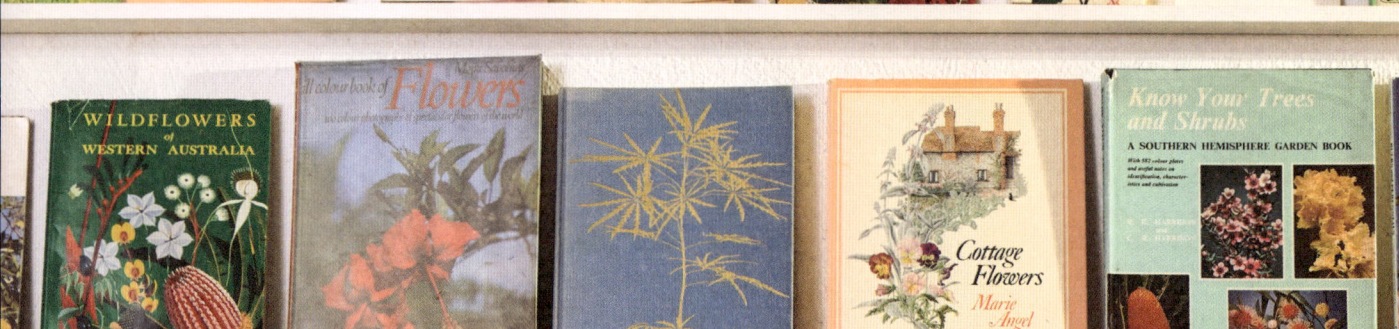
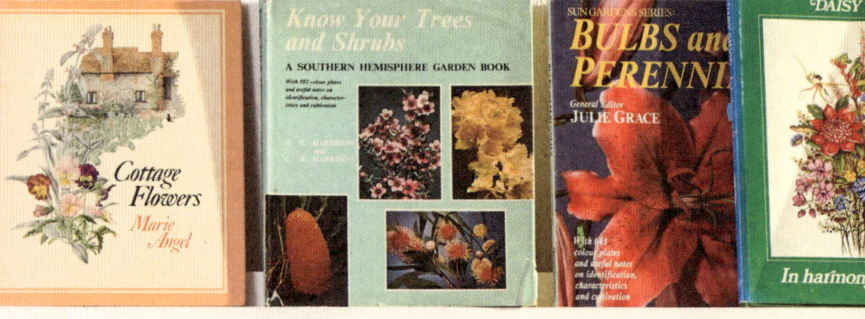
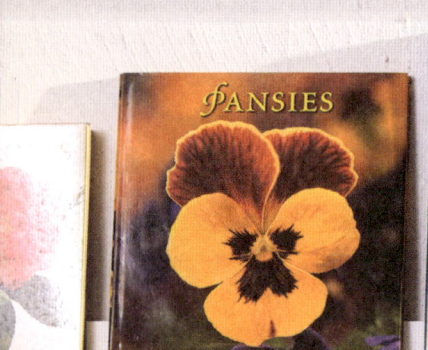
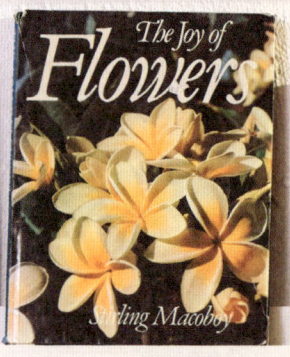
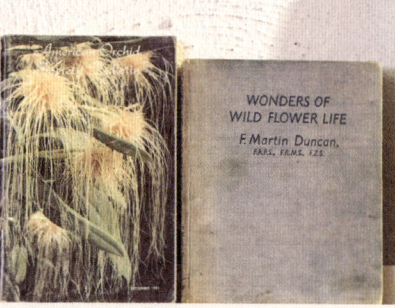
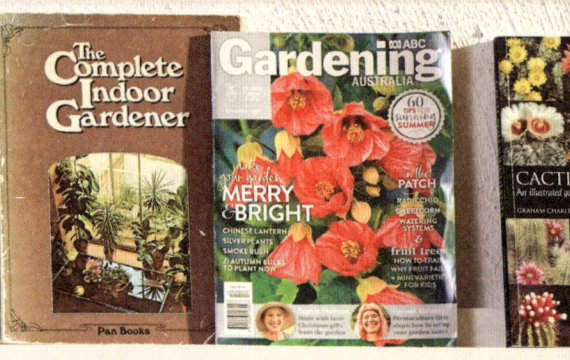
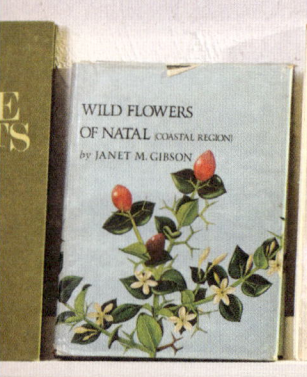
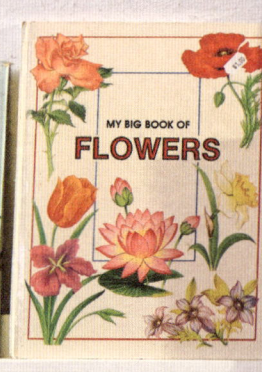
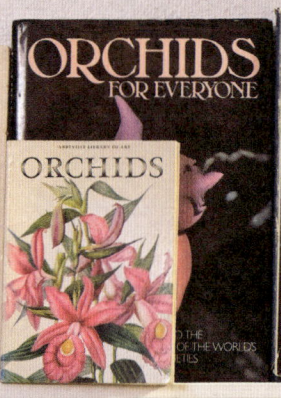
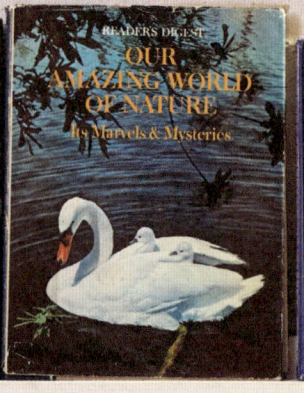
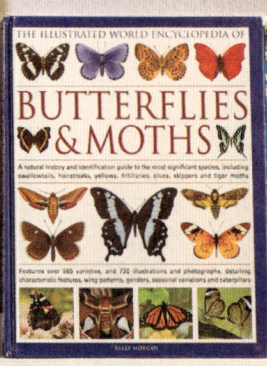
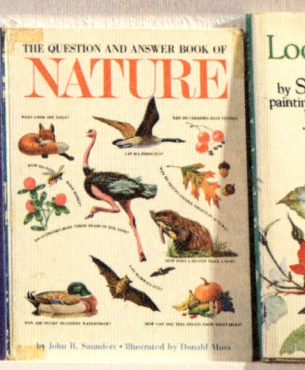
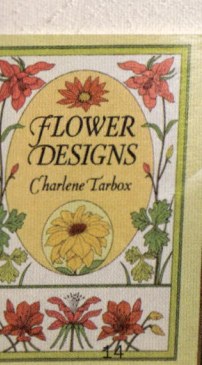
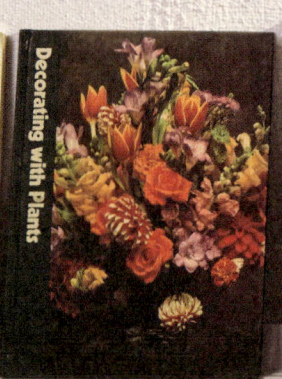
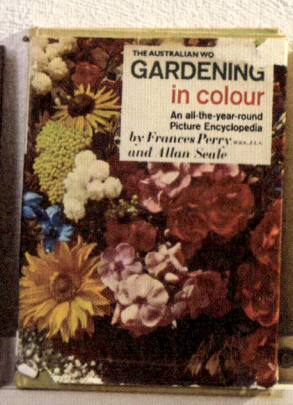
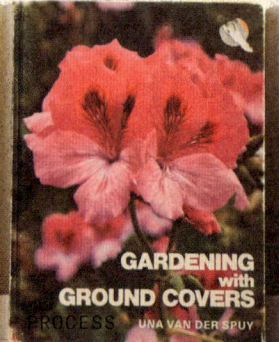
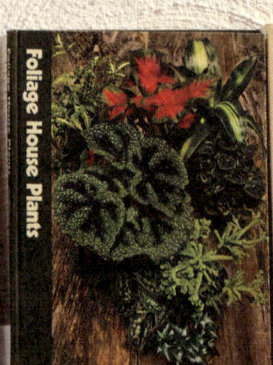
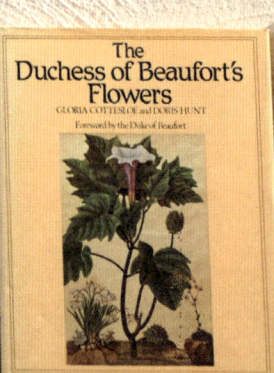

1

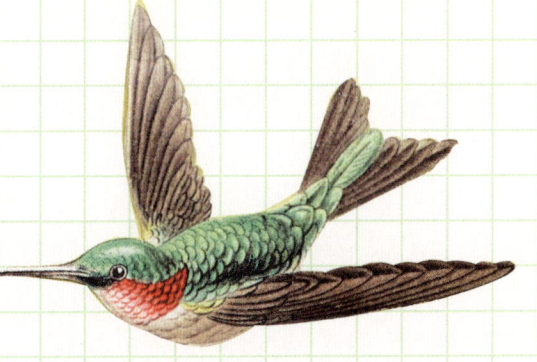

RESEARCH

Luckily, a lot of the hard work of this step has been done for you, as we've curated a world of gorgeous botanicals for you to use. This collection has everything you'll need to create a wonderful masterpiece featuring plants, birds, butterflies and more.

As you flick through the book, what catches your eye immediately? What excites you? Start there. Follow your intuition and begin with what you're naturally drawn to.

Compile your favourites: no need to know what you're going to do with them just yet.

While you consider your collage, I highly recommend starting a collage stash. Along with the images you find in this book, consider growing your collection by saving old magazines, envelopes, postcards, train tickets, paper and cards.

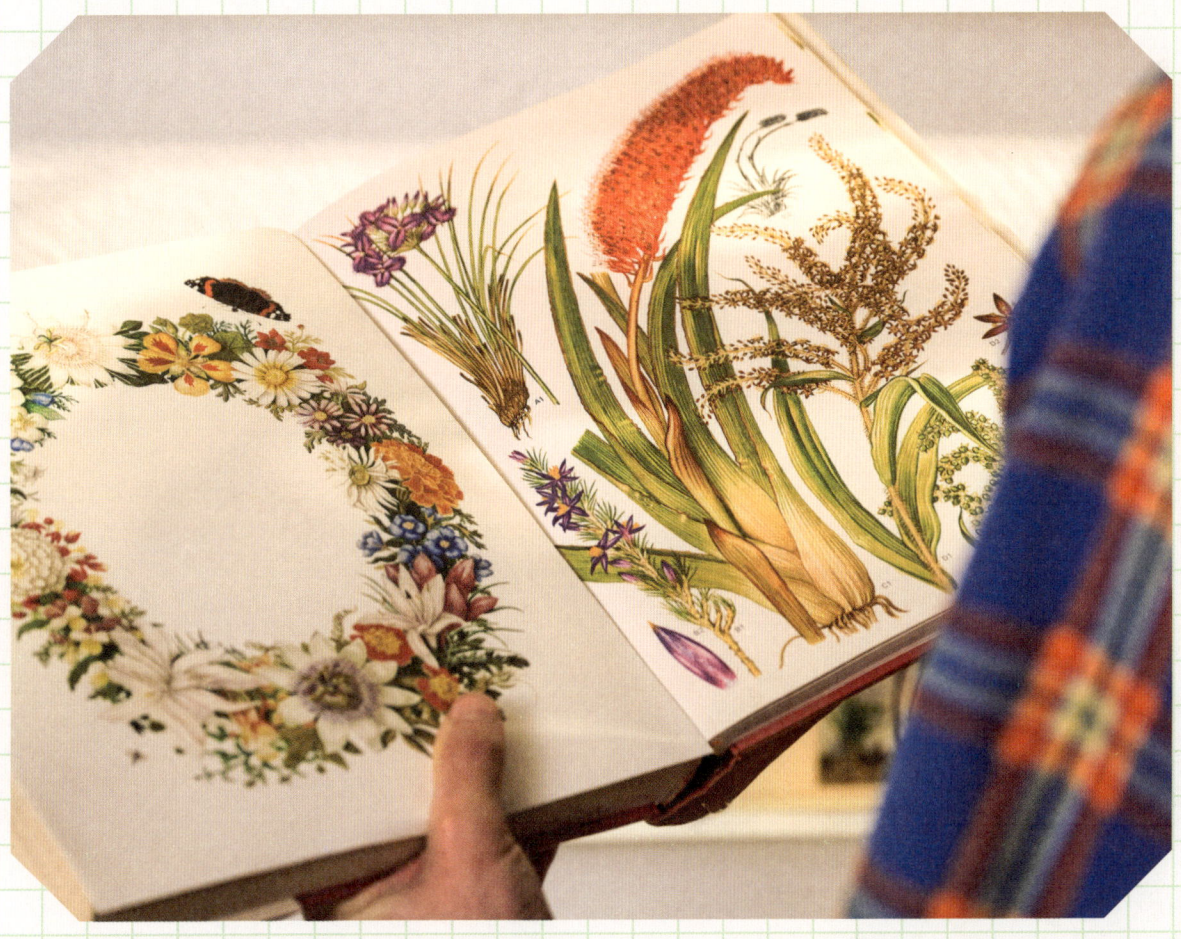

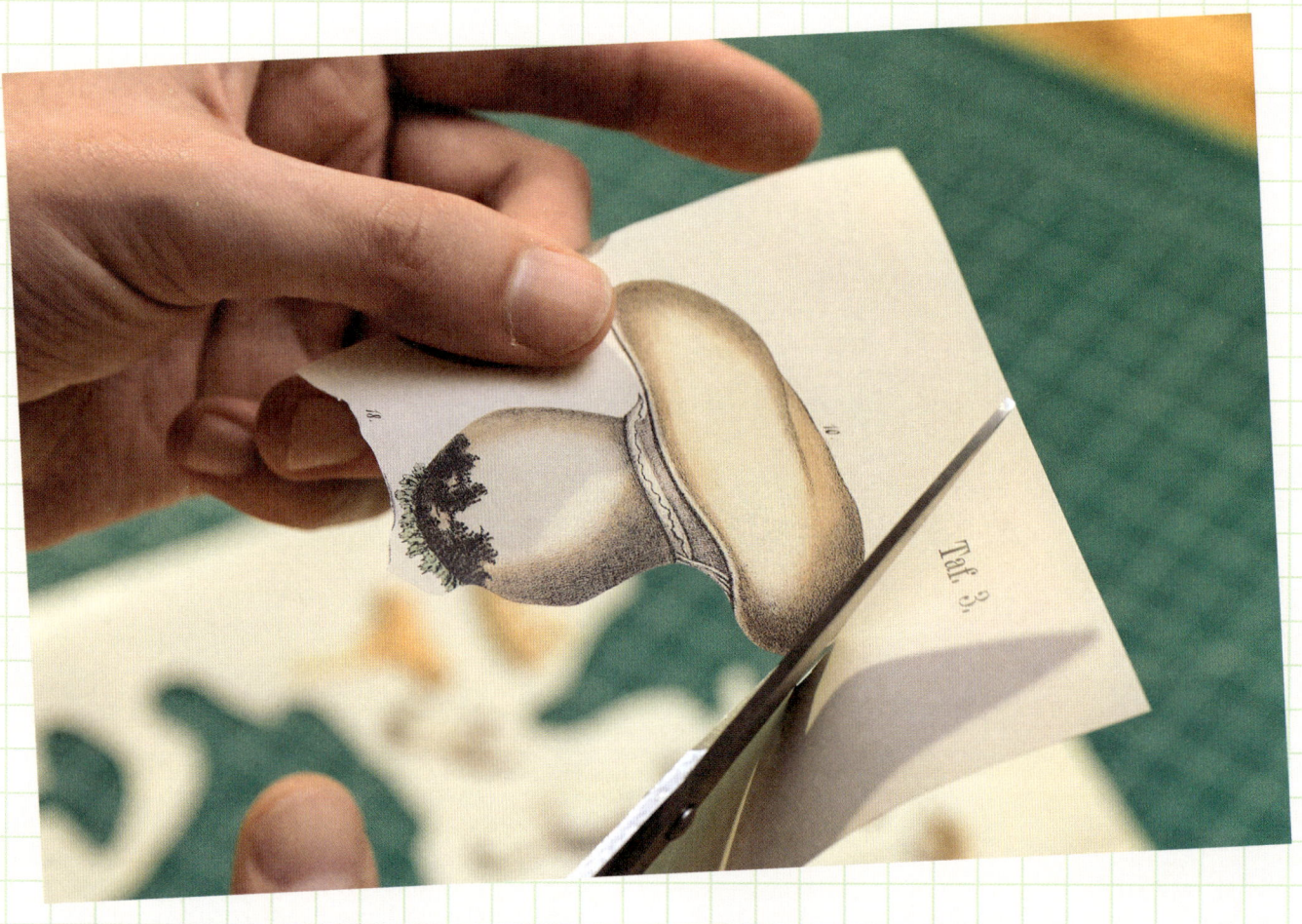
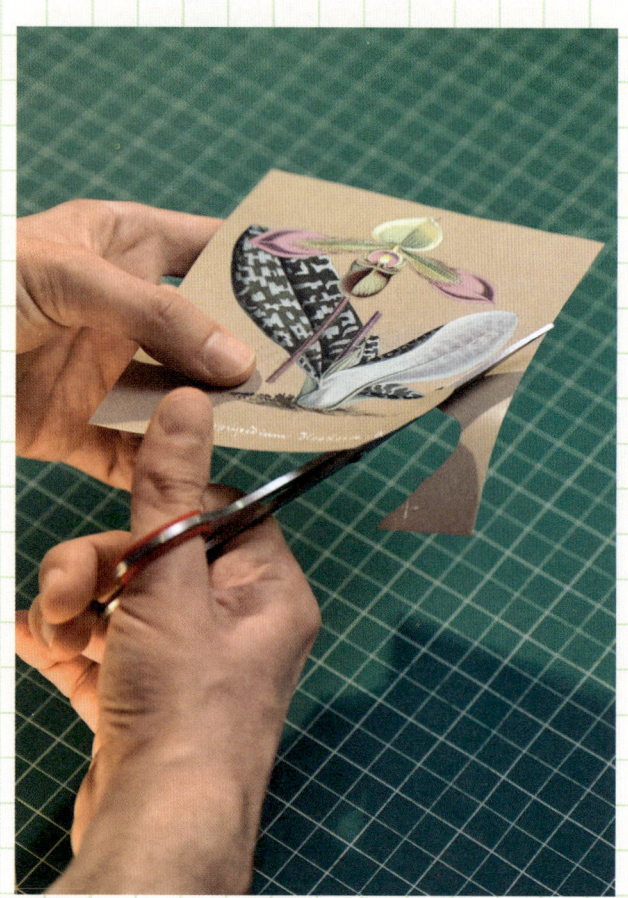
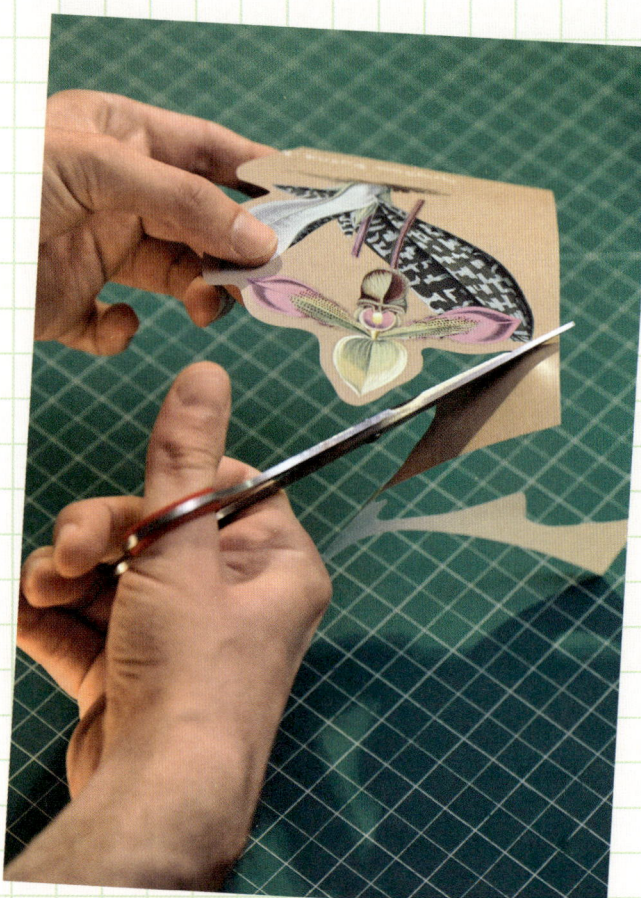

2

CUTTING

Don't overthink it, just start cutting. This part takes practice, so be kind and patient with yourself. Practise your scissor technique around tight corners and odd angles. It's more about turning the paper than the direction of your scissors: both hands should be working.

The obvious approach is to cut things out 'neatly and literally' by carefully following the objects' outlines. By paying close attention and dedicating time to cleanly removing a subject from its background, you'll end up with a wonderful and very useful cut-out.

But while we all love superbly trimmed leafy trees, these take ages! Start with objects that have clear and simple silhouettes.

Another option is to leave a consistent border around your subject's edge. This can allow it to stand out more on a collage, and it will vary your cut-out collection. Change up the thickness of your borders, from intricate to thick and chunky.

Also try cutting things into fragments. Sometimes separating the best images into smaller parts is useful: cut a butterfly into four smaller wings; divide a flower into individual petals; or break up a pattern into repeated shapes. Don't be too scared to chop things up, as with no risk, there's no reward. Some of the example artworks in this book contain images divided into many smaller pieces.

Over time, seek out less obvious ways to cut. Make a game of finding multiple uses for an image. Look longer, search harder. Try turning the page upside down or sideways to gain a new perspective.

HELPFUL TIP

If an outline is very fiddly and tricky, it's okay to give your subject a haircut by cutting into it a little. Make life easier for yourself and simplify outlines.

CUTTING WITHOUT A PLAN

The wildest, most uncommon way to cut is by creating your own outline. Cut intuitively, based on feeling and instinct. This can feel the most unnatural, especially to begin with. However, some of the most fascinating cut-outs happen when you cut with less logic, letting your scissors dance with reckless abandon! Create fluid shapes and abstract shards or try tearing and ripping scraps.

Tearing is often an overlooked technique, but it can be quite liberating. The rugged, natural texture created contrasts wonderfully with precise cuts. Depending on which way you rip, you'll get different results.

Finally, always keep your scraps. The leftovers on the floor can often come in handy and be surprisingly interesting. The shapes you'd never intentionally make might be useful later on.

USING A SCALPEL TO CREATE OPPORTUNITIES

With a fresh craft knife and a cutting mat, you can have so much fun. Be warned: scalpels are very sharp, so please use with caution. Hold the knife the same way you'd use a pencil and draw it along the image where you'd like to cut. It takes practice and patience. Test your technique on scrap paper before cutting your favourite image.

Find spots on subjects where you can create a simple, one-line incision: along a stem, tree trunk or on a tulip. Now you've got an opening to tuck and layer with more complexity. Adding incisions creates depth. Once you've created a slot, you can play with positioning other cut-outs in front or behind, creating a 'peek-a-boo' moment. Finding opportunities to create these pockets is a lot of fun.

When you use a cutting knife to entirely cut out an image, you will be left with an opening, or window, on a page. This creates a two-for-one opportunity. You will get the positive cut-out you were after, but you will also be left with your cut-out's negative, which may be just as interesting, if not more.

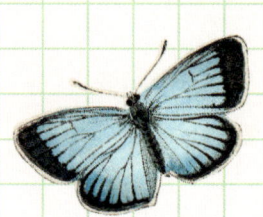
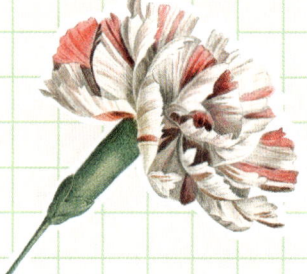
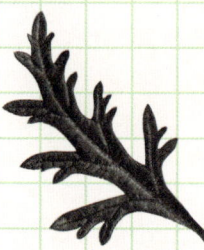

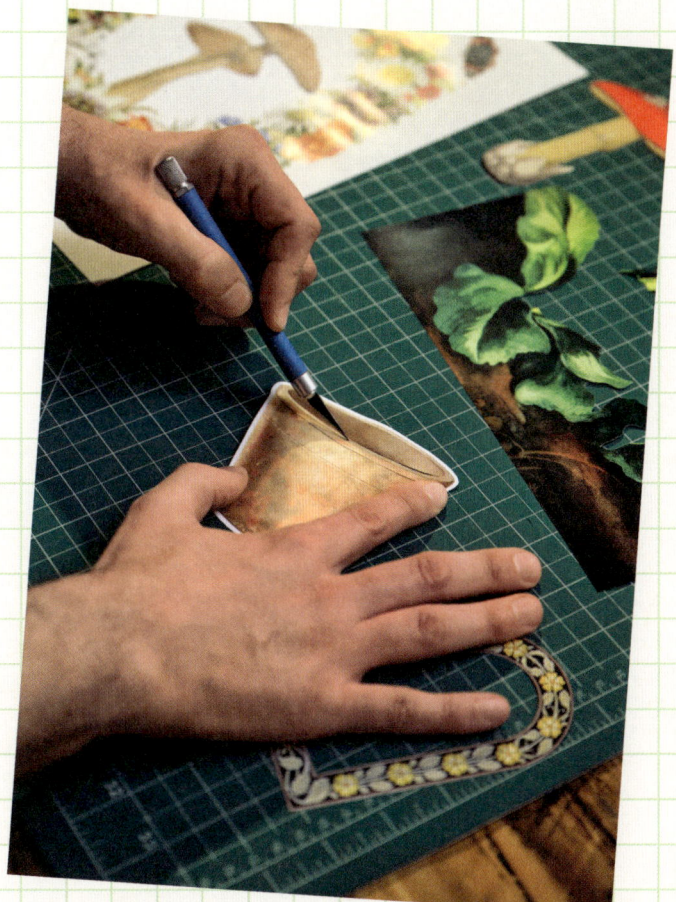
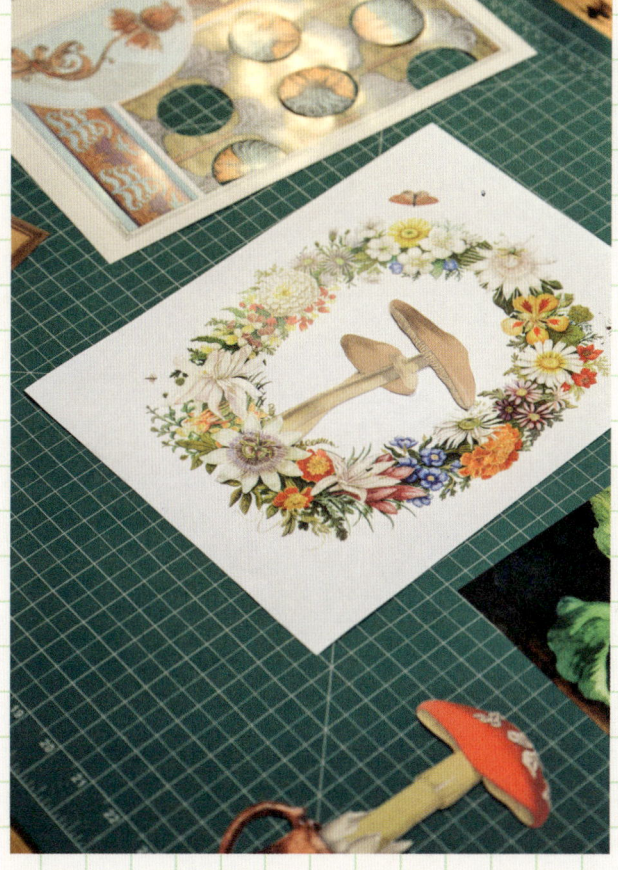
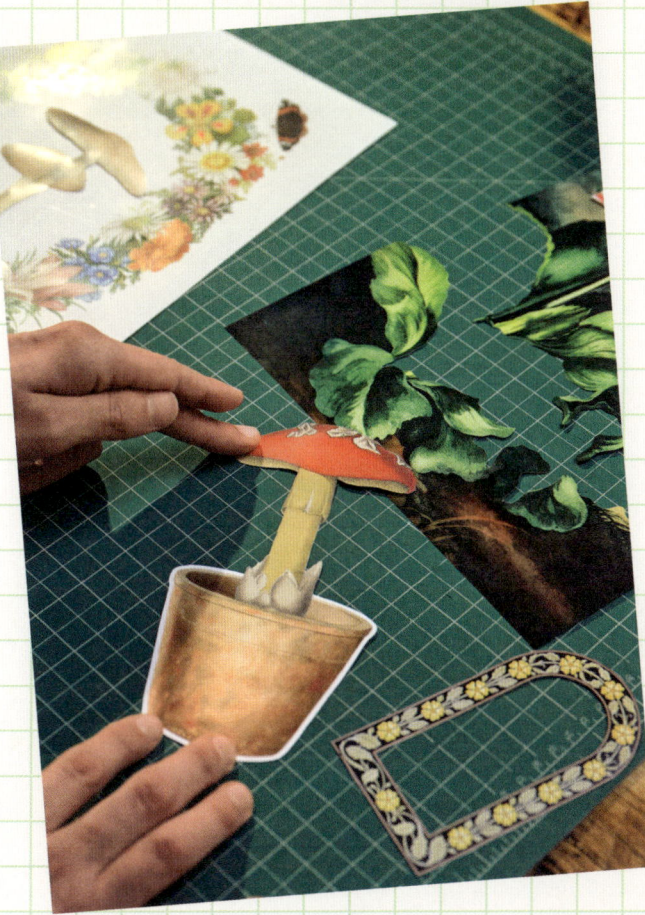

APPROACH

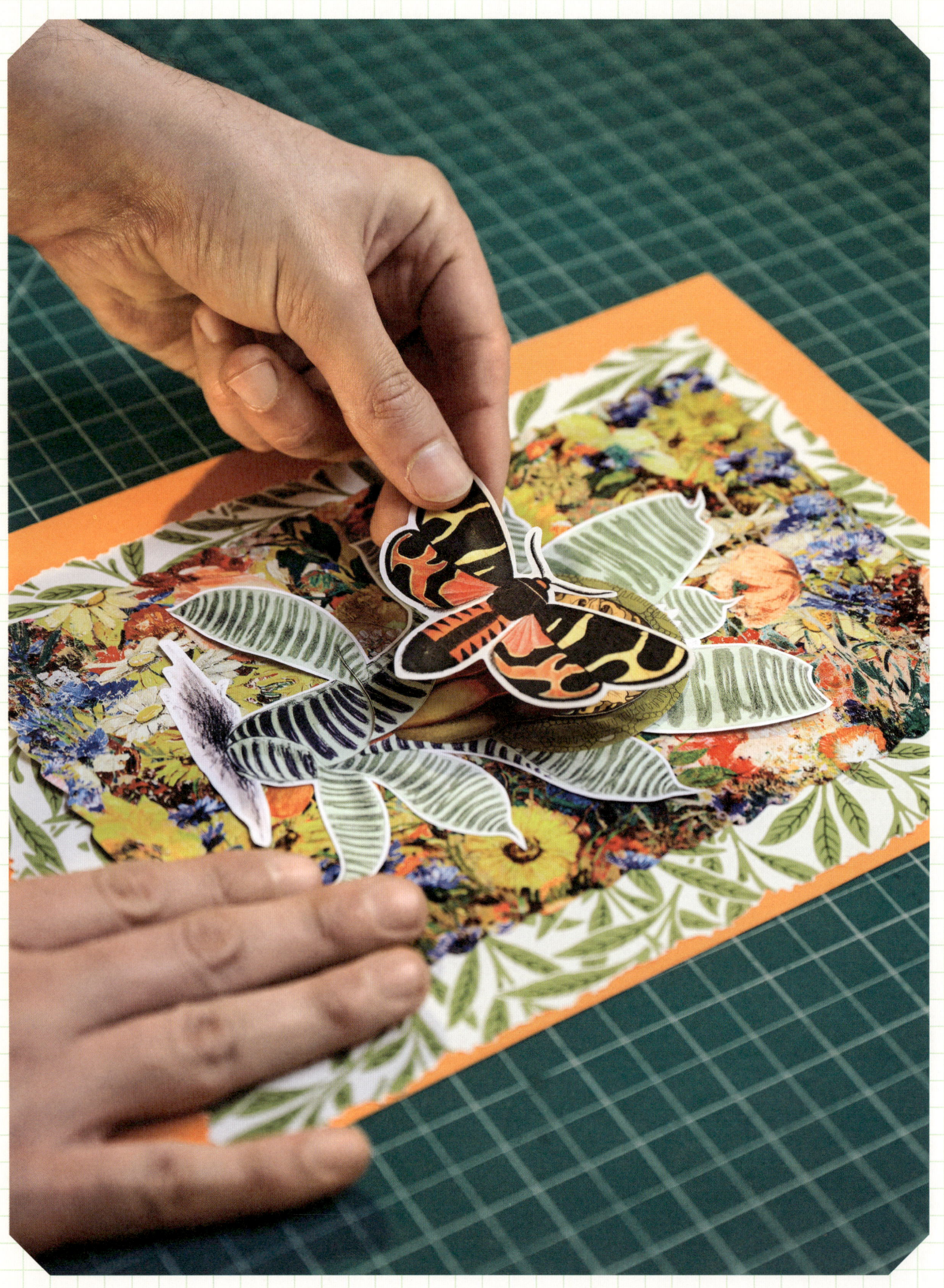

3

ARRANGING

Once you've got a library of cut-outs, you can play around with your pieces. Remember, you can make meaningful collages, but you can also make silly and fun ones: there are no rules!

Arranging uses an entirely different part of your brain than cutting, requiring problem solving through trial and error. This is one of the most exciting parts of collage making, but it can also be daunting! Again, be patient and kind to yourself. I like to work on multiple ideas at once, rather than getting too laser-focused on one idea. As soon as a project feels like it has reached a dead-end, I move on to something else, and revisit it later with fresh eyes.

You might find that an organised approach is best, with your selection of clippings categorised into distinct collections. This may help inform your ideas, but sometimes you have to lean into making a proper mess and allow your clippings to get jumbled up.

To begin with, I don't limit 'where or what to arrange onto'. Test composing your collage within a blank space, or change it up and work within a defined location or scene.

The overall format and shape of collages can vary: you can work small or go expansive. Sometimes an artwork may need a lot of breathing space, while other times, it may want to be compact and tightly framed.

Try partially covering the most interesting parts of your collage: layering creates intrigue and mystery. Make choices about what to reveal and hide. Create captivating collages by leaving the viewer guessing about what's hidden behind layers. Masking can help leave your work open to the viewers' interpretation.

Take the process in other directions, by adding other materials and medias like pencil marks, pens, paint, ink, fabric. Go nuts, add nuts?! There are no wrong answers.

Failure is a friend that you can learn from. Experimentation is key for every creative practice. Try out new ideas and consider what doesn't yet exist! Fight the obvious and consider alternative options. Change direction if you have to. Good things can come from happy accidents.

I've created a list of arrangement styles for you to try – just flip to page 26. You can refer to these arranging styles for inspiration.

4

GLUING AND FINISHING

*ONCE YOU'VE CREATED SOMETHING YOU LOVE,
NOW COMES THE STICKY PART… FIXING IT DOWN.*

There are many schools of thought when it comes to gluing, and over time, you'll find a method that suits the specific projects that you're working on.

My usual preference is an acid-free glue stick, as they're easy to use, affordable and clean to apply, not to mention very easy to travel with! Carrying a glue stick means you're always set for collaging adventures. Glue sticks, however, are not the most long-lasting, heavy-duty option.

If you're looking to make something that'll truly stand the test of time, you'll need gel mediums and even varnishes to sturdily attach your collages to a base. There are many options out there, from matt to gloss finishes. Some glues will be incredibly viscous and are easier to use once watered down.

There is something meditative about loading your brush up with a small amount of glue and taking the time to carefully apply it. But I'll be real with you: gluing is often my least favourite part of the collage process. It's fiddly, messy and, on occasion, your artwork won't glue down the way you first imagined. Acid-free tape is a quick and easy option, but it's unforgiving if you're not happy with the placement: once stuck, your pieces will be hard to adjust.

But prior preparation can help prevent poor performance! Get set up for success. First, have a piece of paper under the cut-out you're applying glue to. This sheet will stop you getting glue on your table or cutting mat.

Practise gluing your scraps first, adhering them onto differently weighted backgrounds to see how they take. If you are gluing paper to paper, you don't need a lot of glue: using too much on equally thin pieces of paper will lead to warping. To avoid ripples, your base needs to be thicker than the cut-outs you're applying.

Once you feel like you're ready to start gluing your masterpiece, take a photo of your loose arrangement first, so that you can remember how it looked.

At my studio, I often use digital scanners to capture loose arrangements, rather than gluing them down. If you don't have a scanner, you can do something similar by using your phone to photograph your work in a well-lit area. The benefit of working ephemerally is that you can reuse your cut-outs on another project. Maybe go wild and make a stop-motion animation!

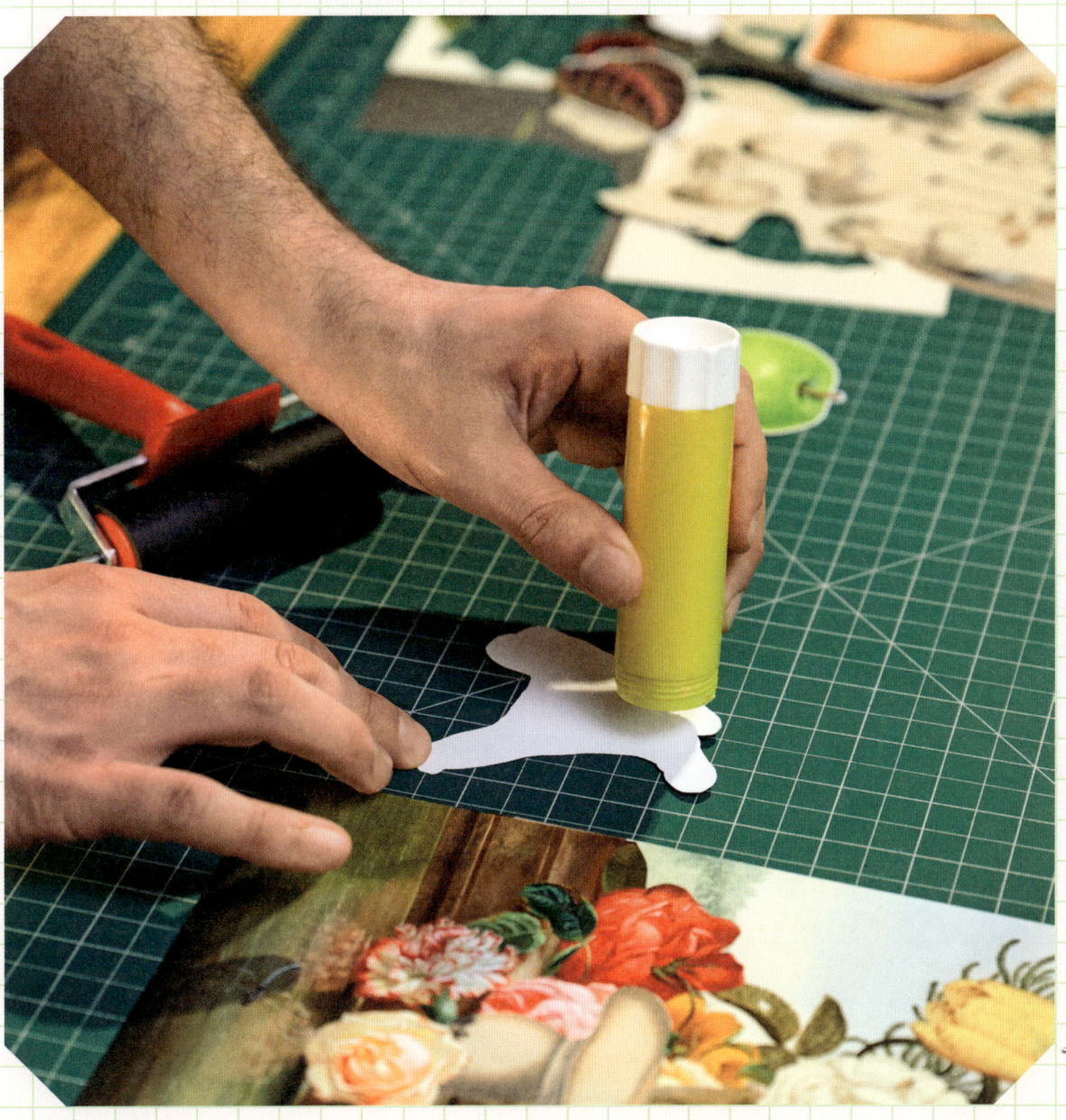

REMEMBER TO HAVE FUN

I'm so excited to see what you create with this book. I really hope you find use and creative potential within every single page (even with the scraps and leftovers!). My final words to you are to be open-minded, playful and kind to yourself. Creativity should be fun and without pressure or expectation! May your art inspire long walks out in nature, adventurous camping trips and a renewed love for all things Mother Nature.

    Much thanks to Dodgy Paper for the wonderful handmade paper sheets that feature as backings on many of the pages, and thank you to Hound & Bone Studio for their meticulous job scanning.

    Thanks to my partner, Zoe, always there to help, support and encourage me.

    This book wouldn't have been possible without assistance from my dear friends Conrad, Holly and Steph who spent evenings cutting things out while I had a fractured wrist, and wasn't able to work as quickly as I'd hoped.

ARRANGEMENT STYLES

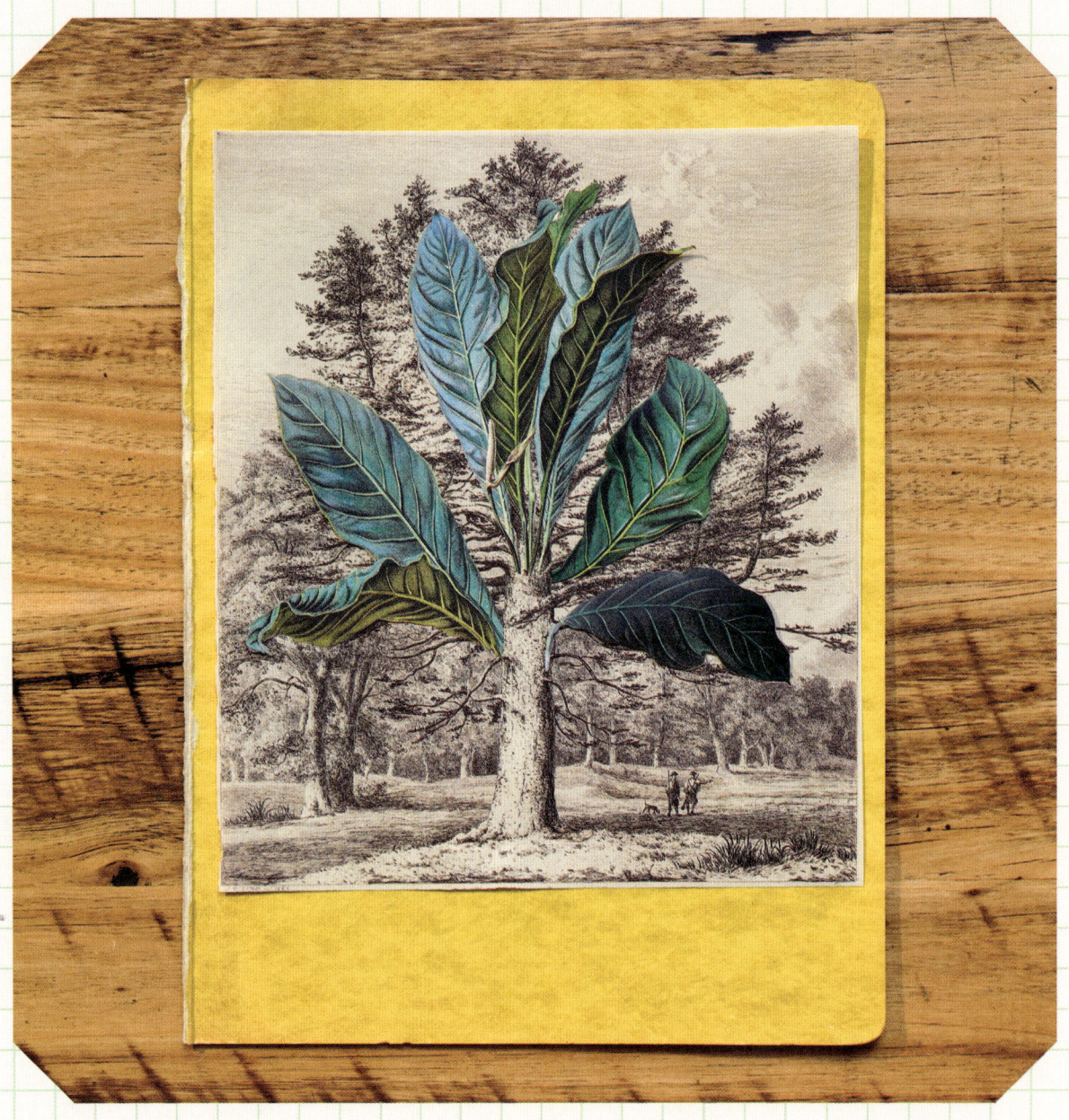

LESS IS MORE Minimalism looks effortless, but it can be tricky to achieve! Play with contrast: for instance, pair black and white imagery with colour. Or blend similar objects together, until it's hard to tell where one ends and another begins. This style can take time and patience. If you spread out your collection of cut-outs, you may spot potential combinations. I love it when just a few pieces of paper come together and create a whole new story.

STACKING This can be a simple, satisfying way to play! Pretend you're balancing weighted objects, one on top of another. To lean into some realism, consider the shadows on your pieces, and how this shading may influence the placement of the next piece. Stacking can be a warm-up game! How high can you make your stack? Try a pyramid, an archway, even a domino-like arrangement.

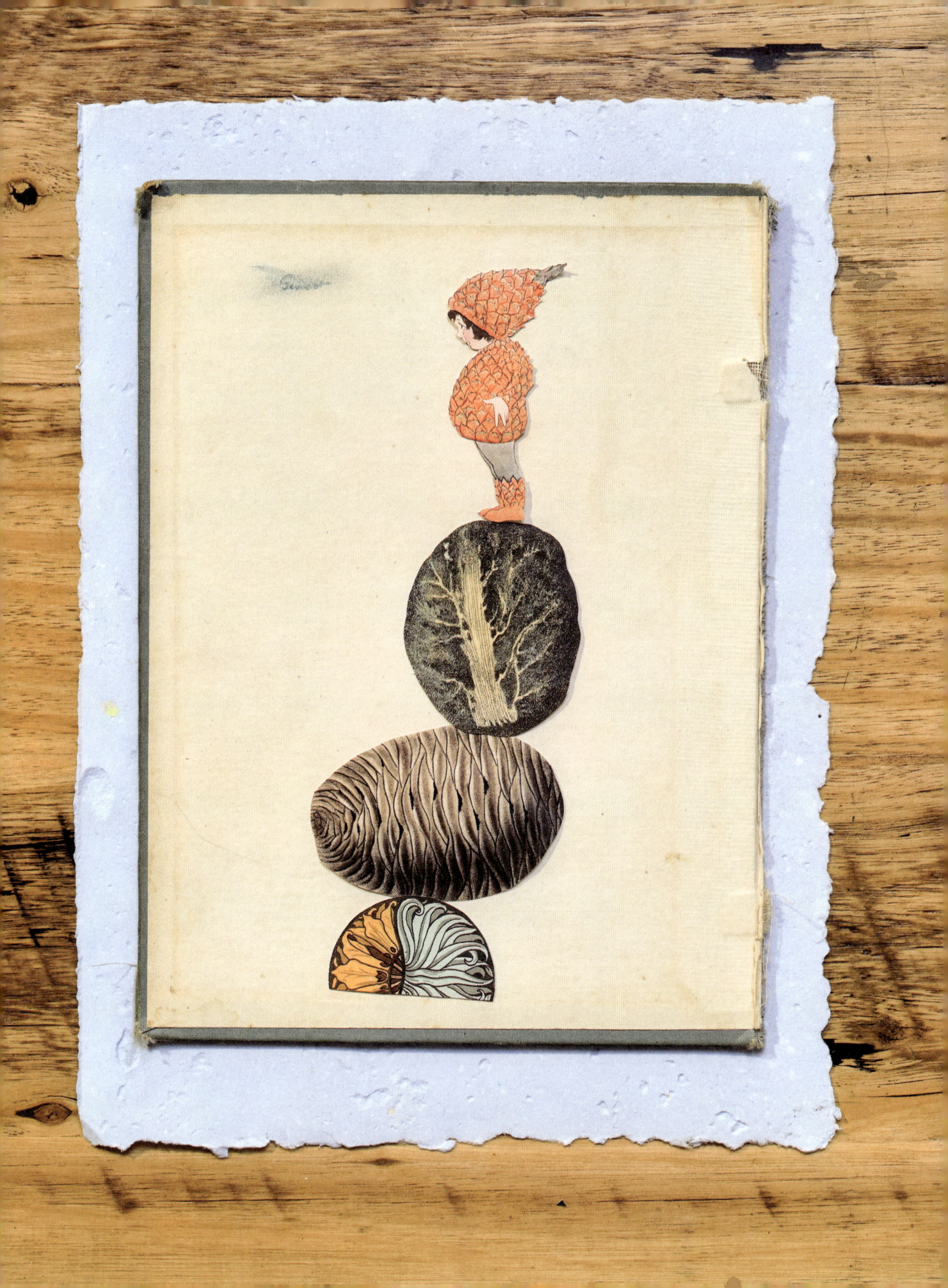

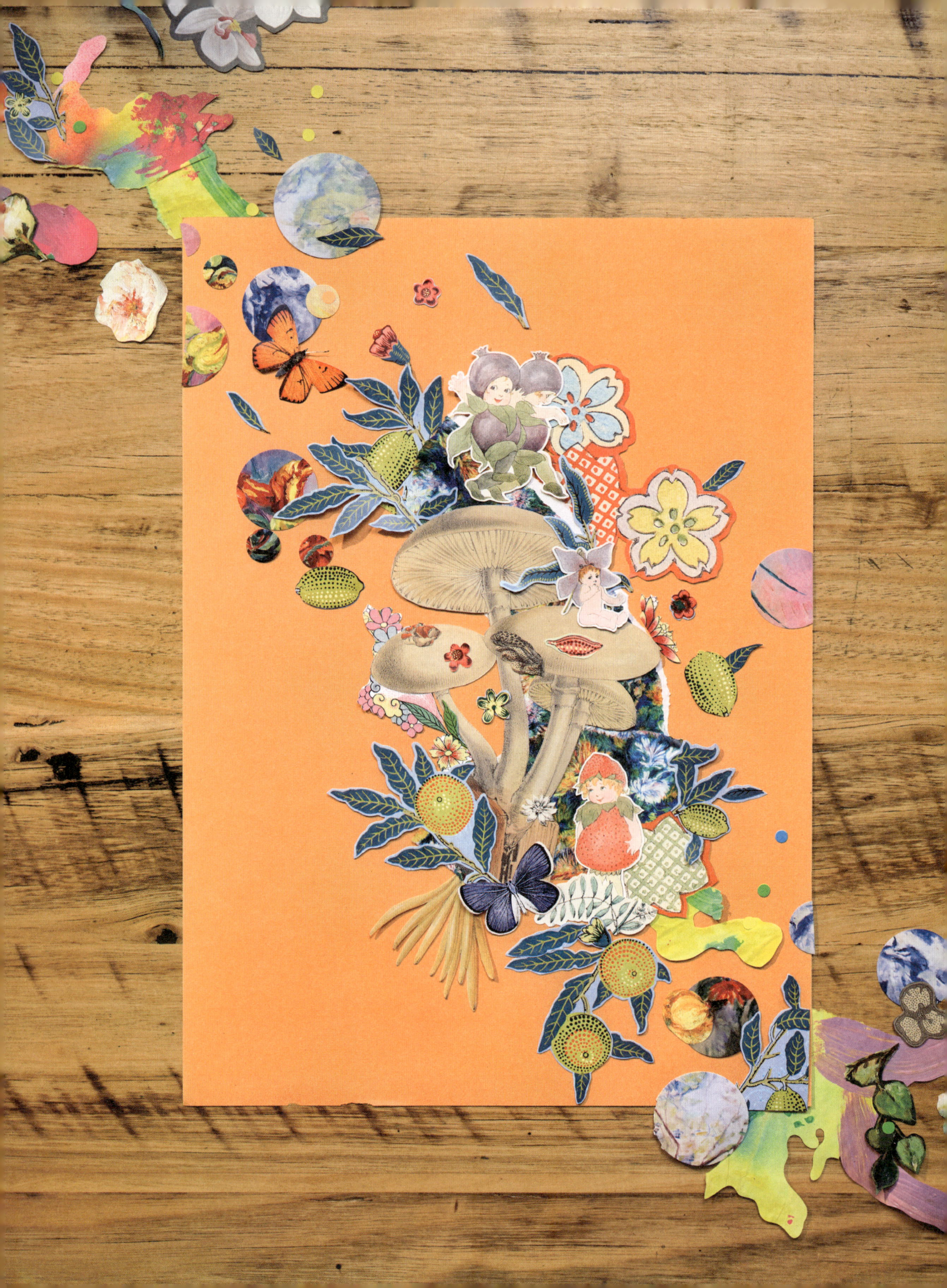

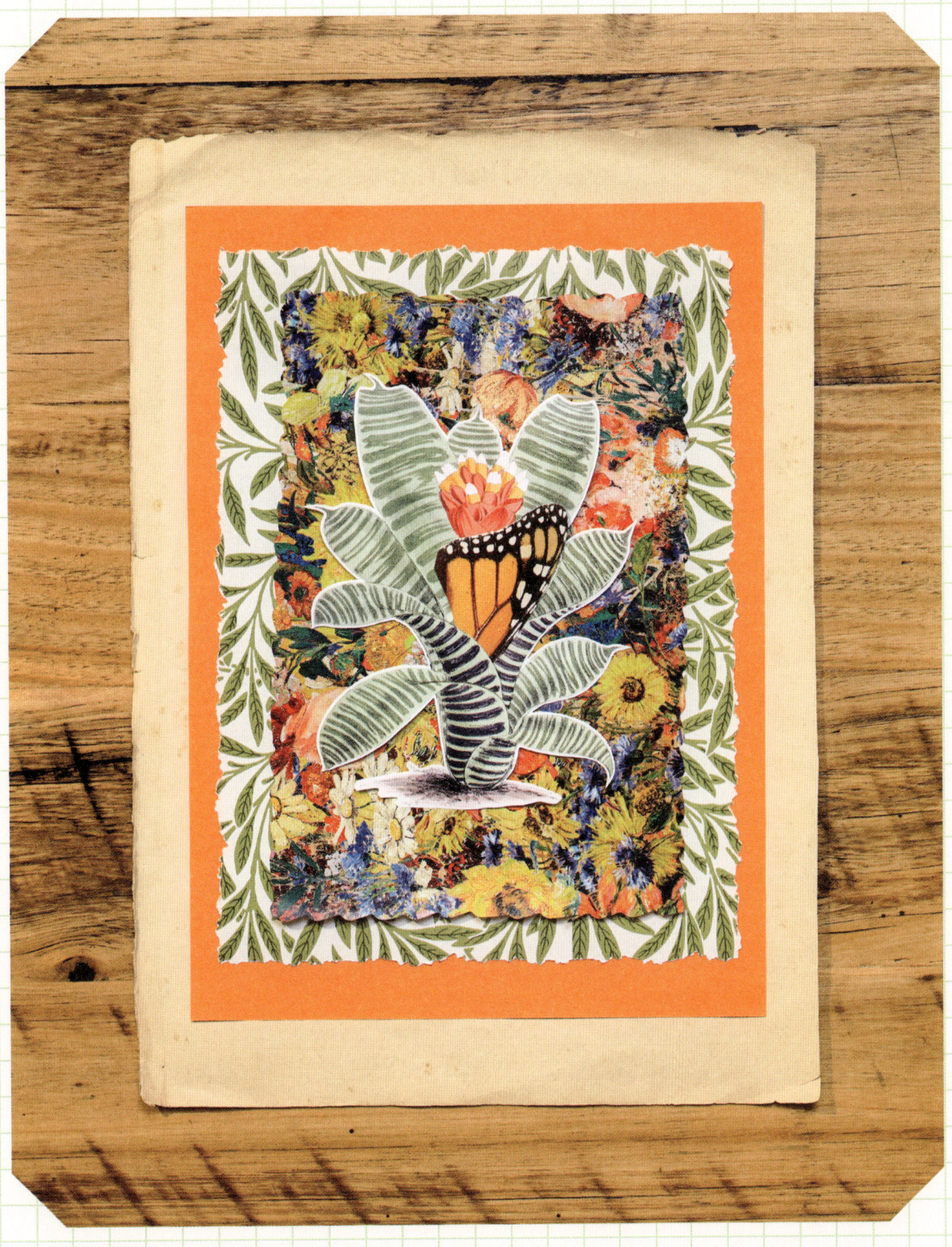

GO WITH THE FLOW Compare this style to a river, in which cut-outs flow one into the next. In a serpentine-like pattern, allow your creation to twist and turn. Go with the flow and see where it takes you! Try to make a collage that appears to be blowing in the wind, or one that looks as light as a feather. You could complement this approach with delicate images, such as petals and leaves.

LAYERING To try this style, place your biggest piece first and then place a slightly smaller cut-out on top, and repeat. In my example, I've simplified this process by placing each piece centrally. I've also used a craft knife to tuck the butterfly wing behind a leaf.

ARRANGEMENT STYLES

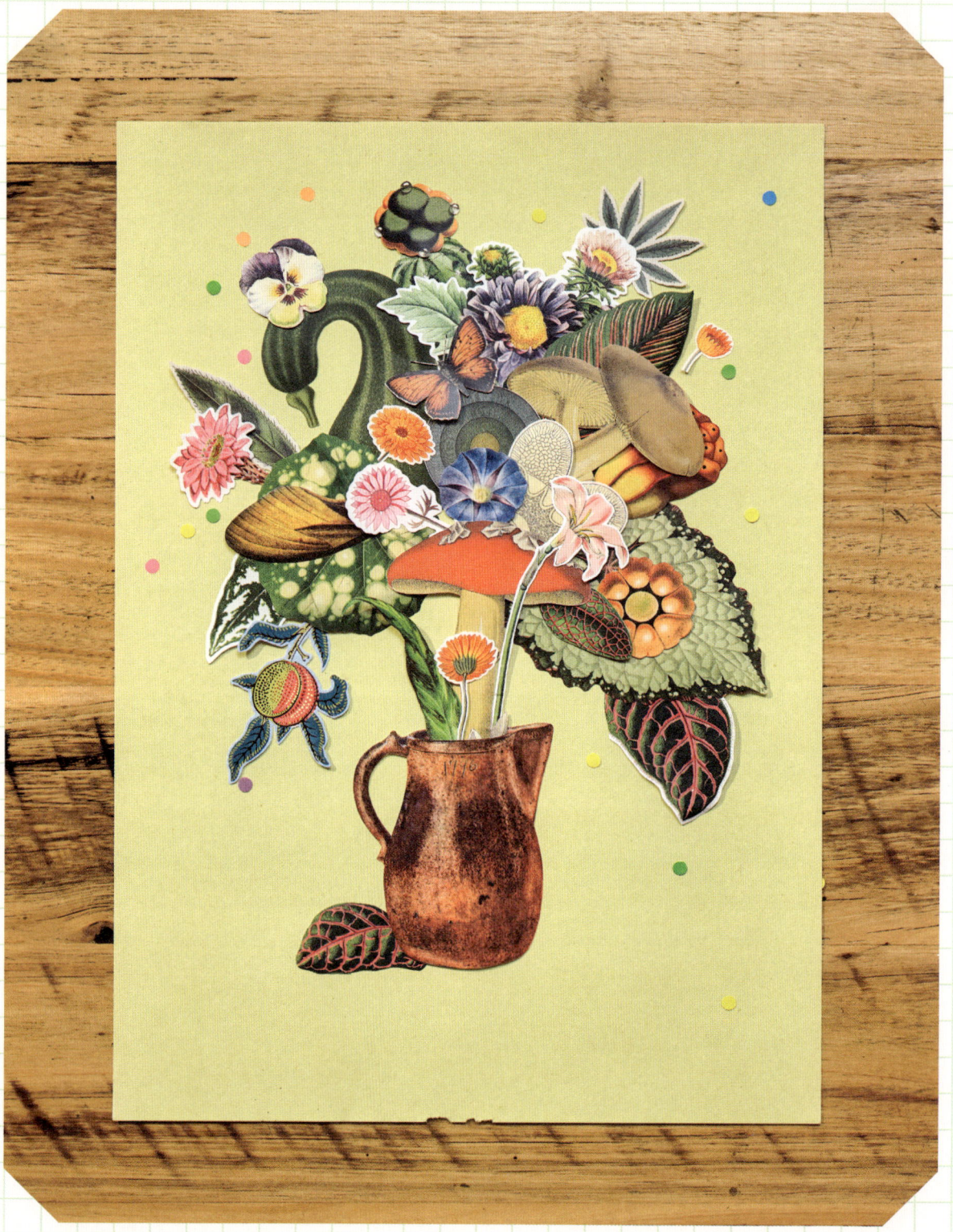

BOUQUET To create floral arrangements, experiment by clustering your cut-outs relatively compactly, with pieces growing this way and that way. Not everything needs to be a flower: try adding more unusual additions. Leave a border on some pieces to help them stand out more clearly from afar. Your collage doesn't have to be realistic: bits may appear to float away. An added character, animal or bird can change the scale of the vase, making it appear gigantic. While the examples included here have a decent amount of negative space, try adding a drop shadow or place your bouquet onto a background. And a final tip: a few sprinkles of colour can make the scene a little more magical!

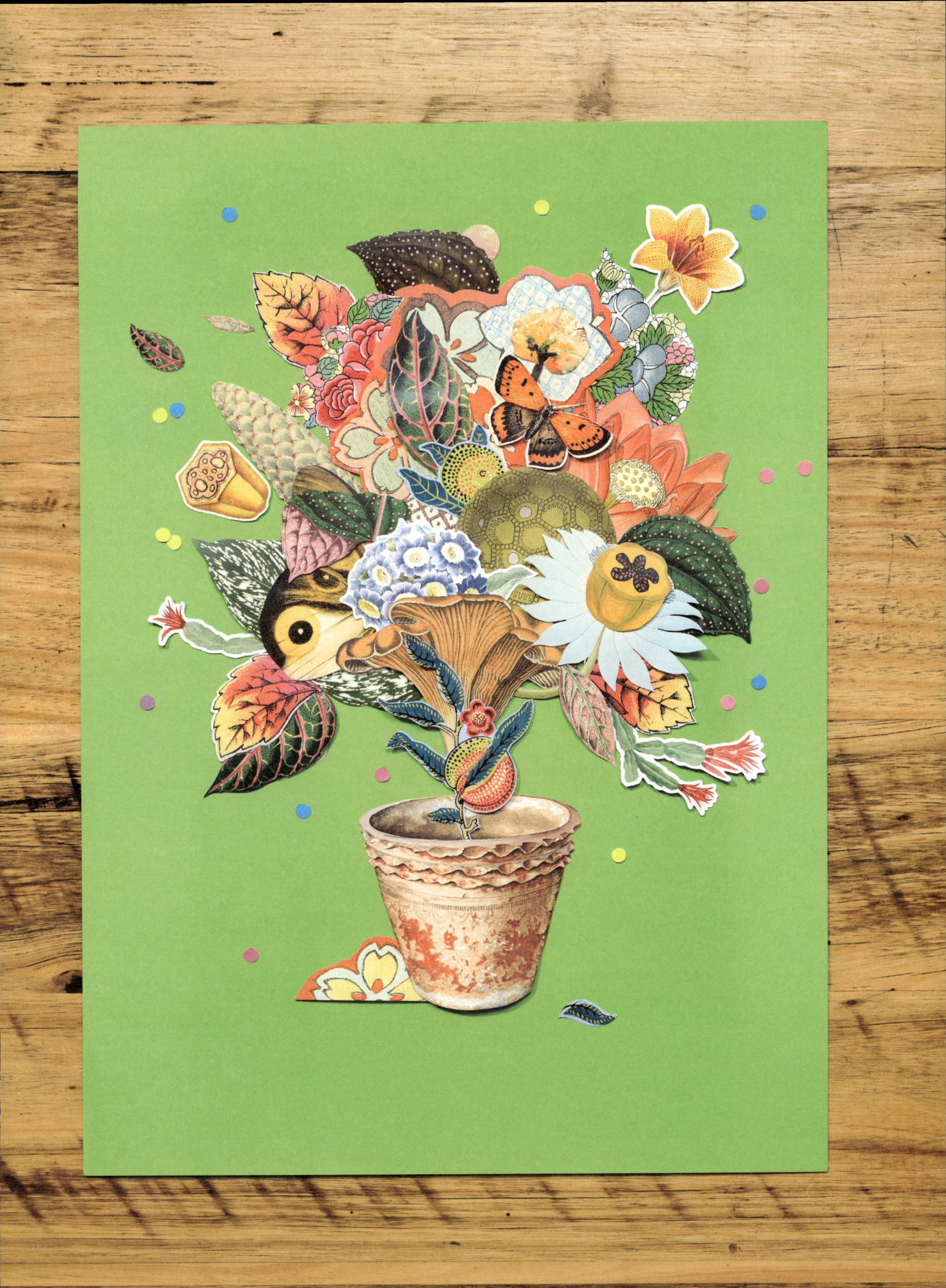

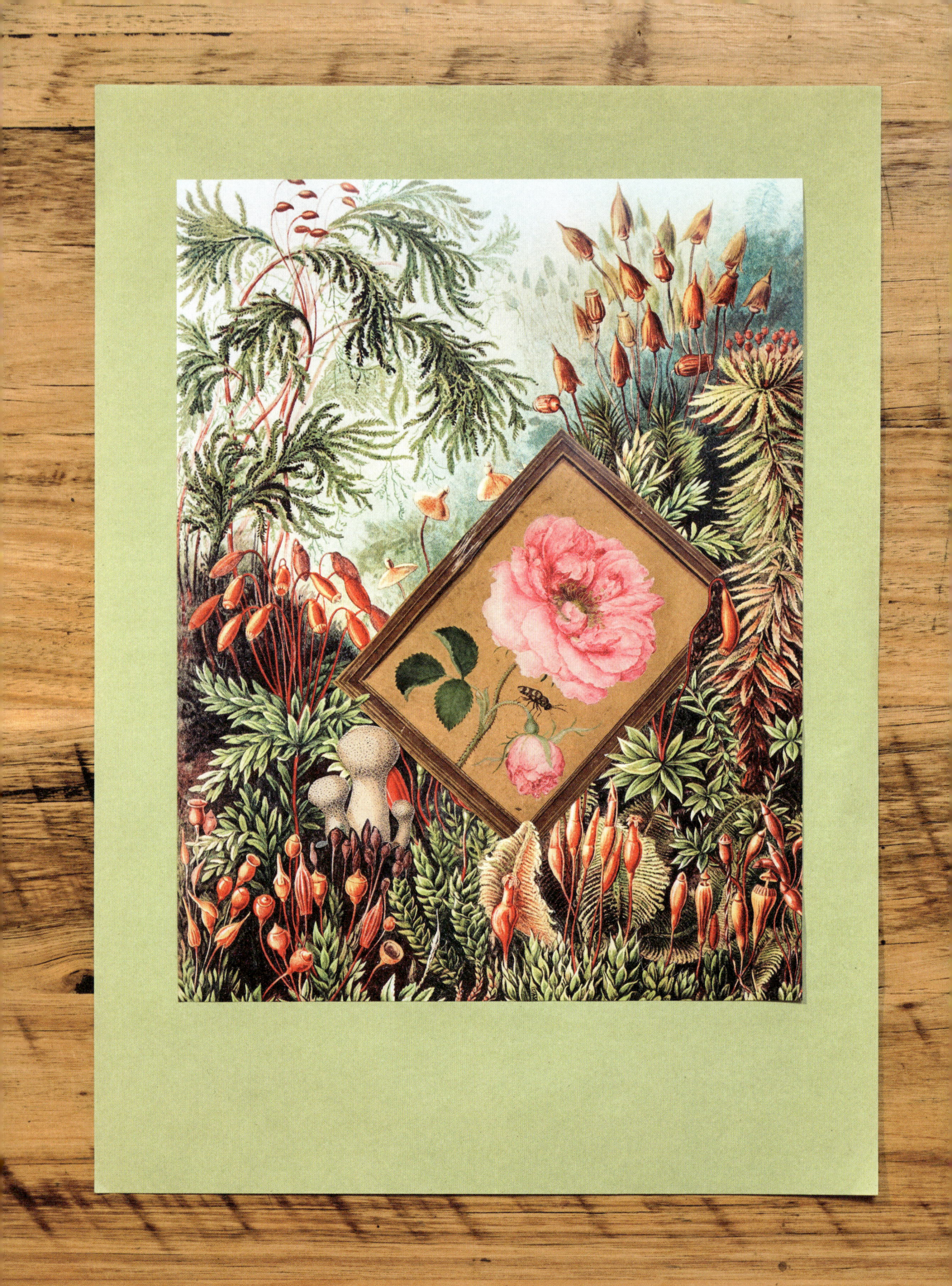

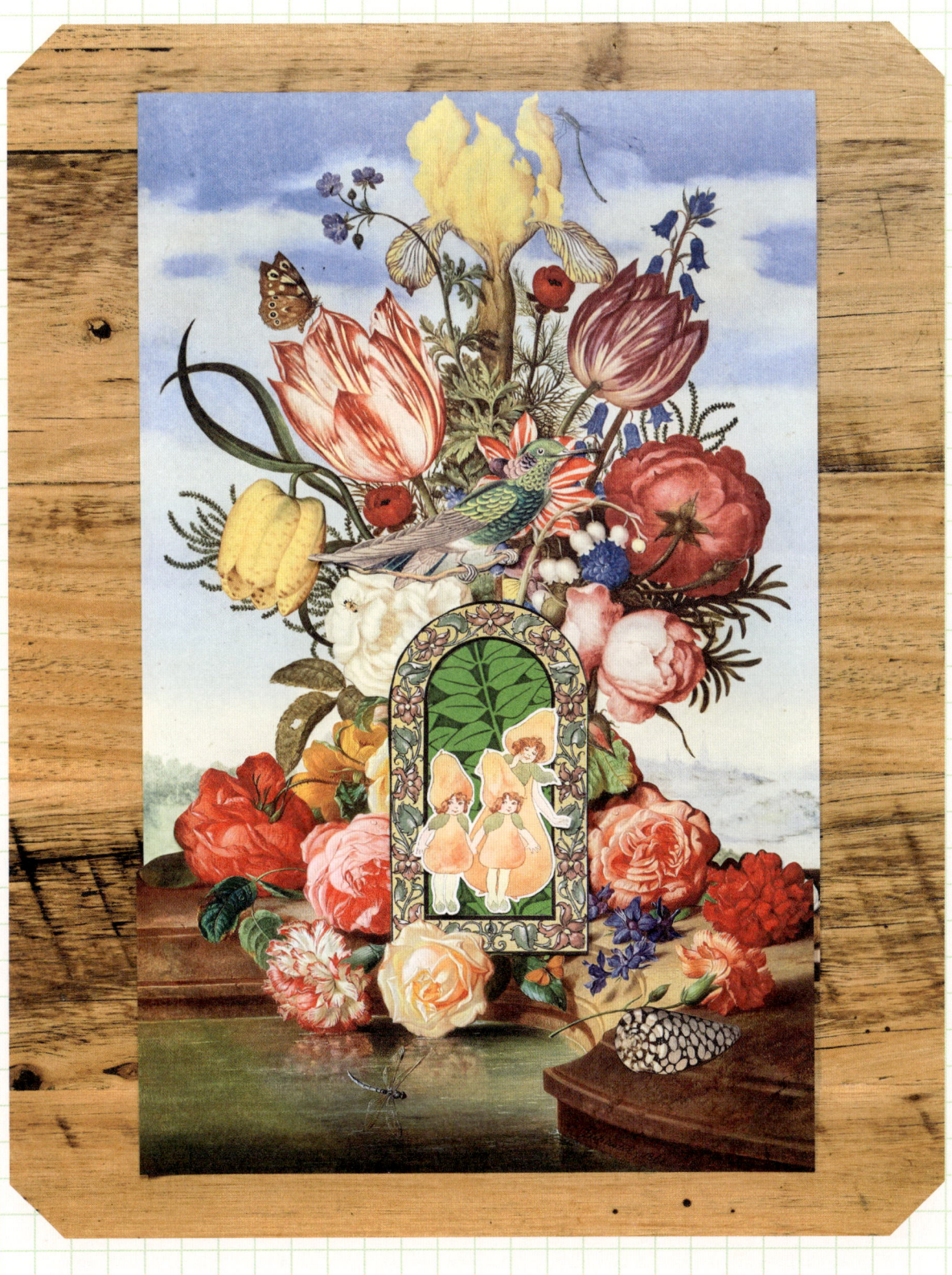

POCKETS AND WINDOWS With a craft knife at the ready, you can take your collages to the next level! Cut pockets into the page, which will allow you to tuck one piece behind another to create a sense of depth and distance. For the example on the left, I've added two small pockets, which allowed me to tuck the framed painting edges into the bush scene; this makes the painting feel submerged in the background. This example also stealthily integrates a mushroom that I added. Once you understand pocket opportunities, you'll notice them everywhere! You can also try cutting windows/openings into an image (see the next pages). This allows you to layer images underneath others.

ARRANGEMENT STYLES

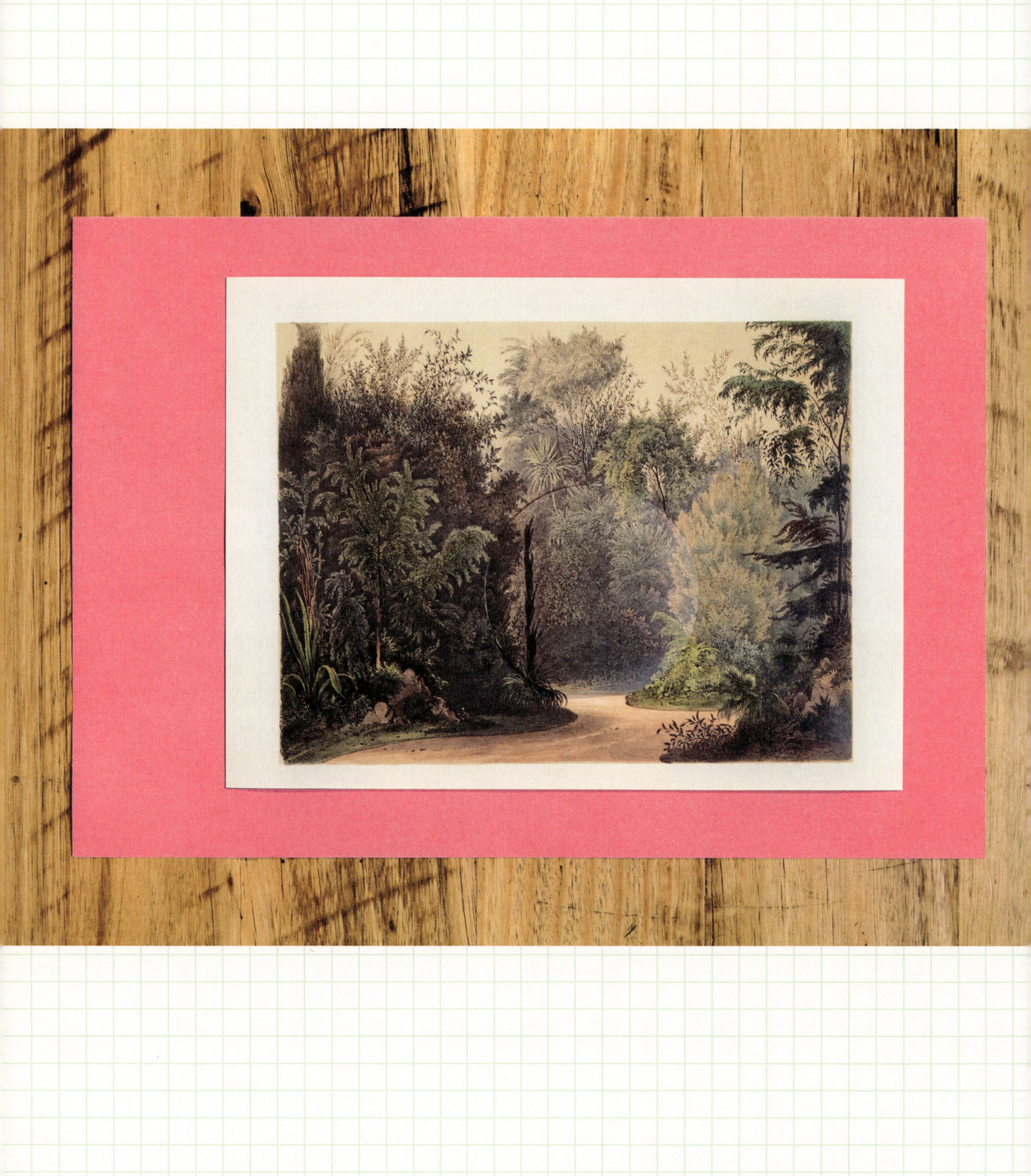

ARRANGEMENT STYLES

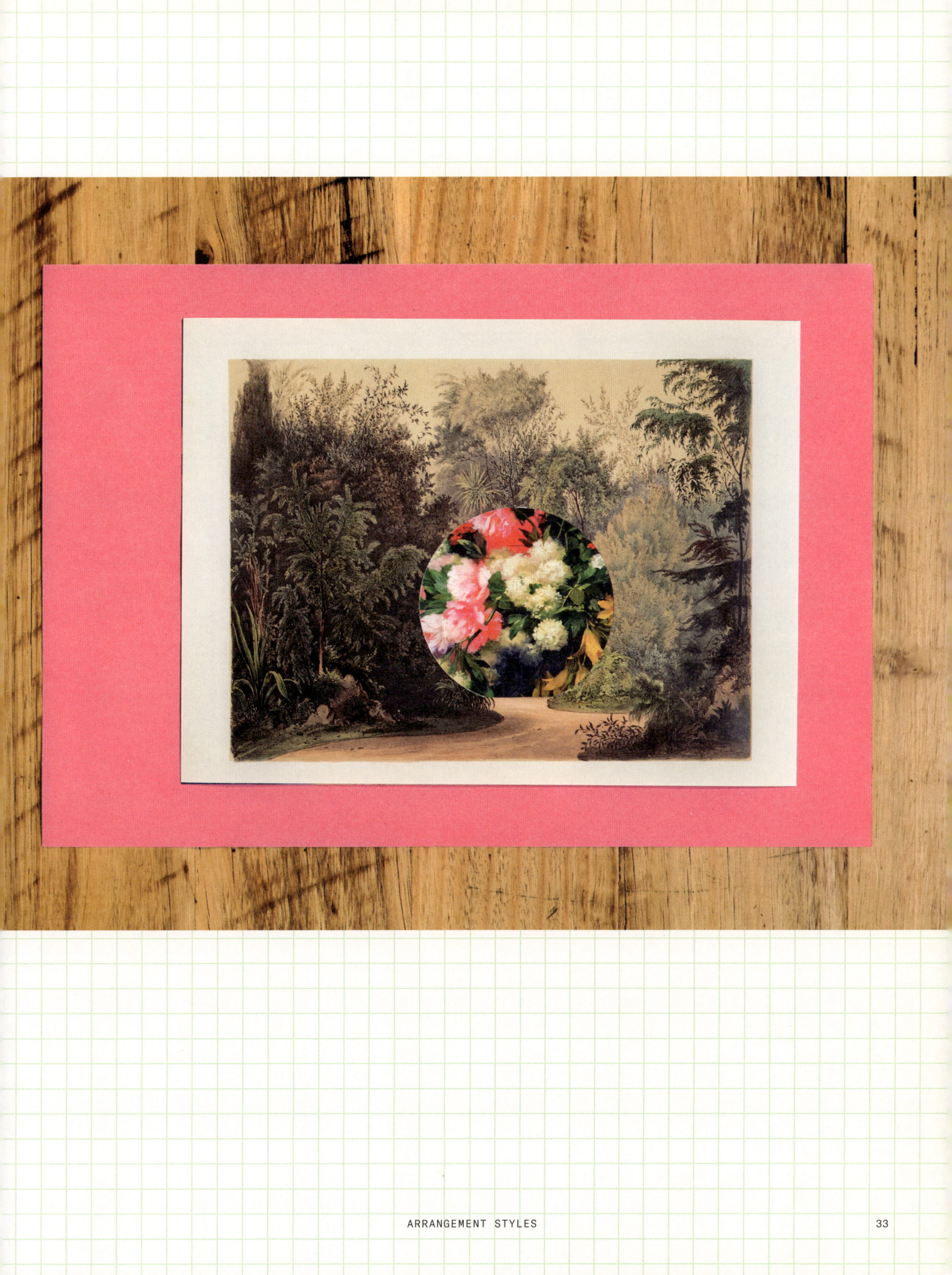

ARRANGEMENT STYLES

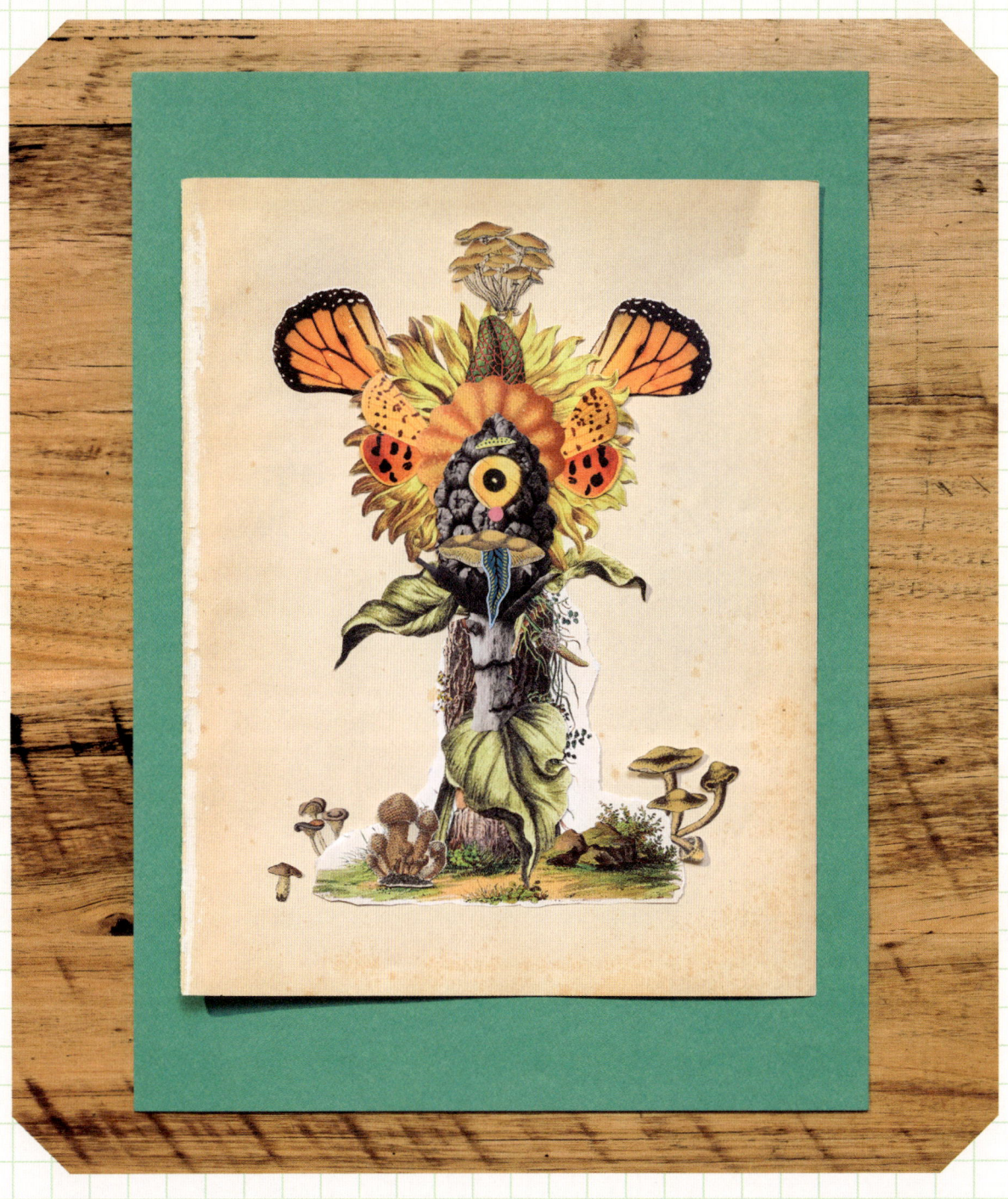

OTHERWORLDLY CREATURE Turn a leaf into a tongue, a wing into an eye or a bunch of fungi into a marvellous mullet! Get wild turning cut-outs into something from a make-believe new world, like a green giant from this book's leaves and green veggies!

MORE IS MORE Try leaning into creating something explosive, with loads of pieces! This may end up looking like a hot mess, but if you have a few guides in place, you can test the limits. Try adding a focal point, which is clear from a distance. If you add too many hero pieces, your collage may feel crowded. You can also try a limited colour palette, to create harmony. The examples include painting experiments I chopped into abstract pieces.

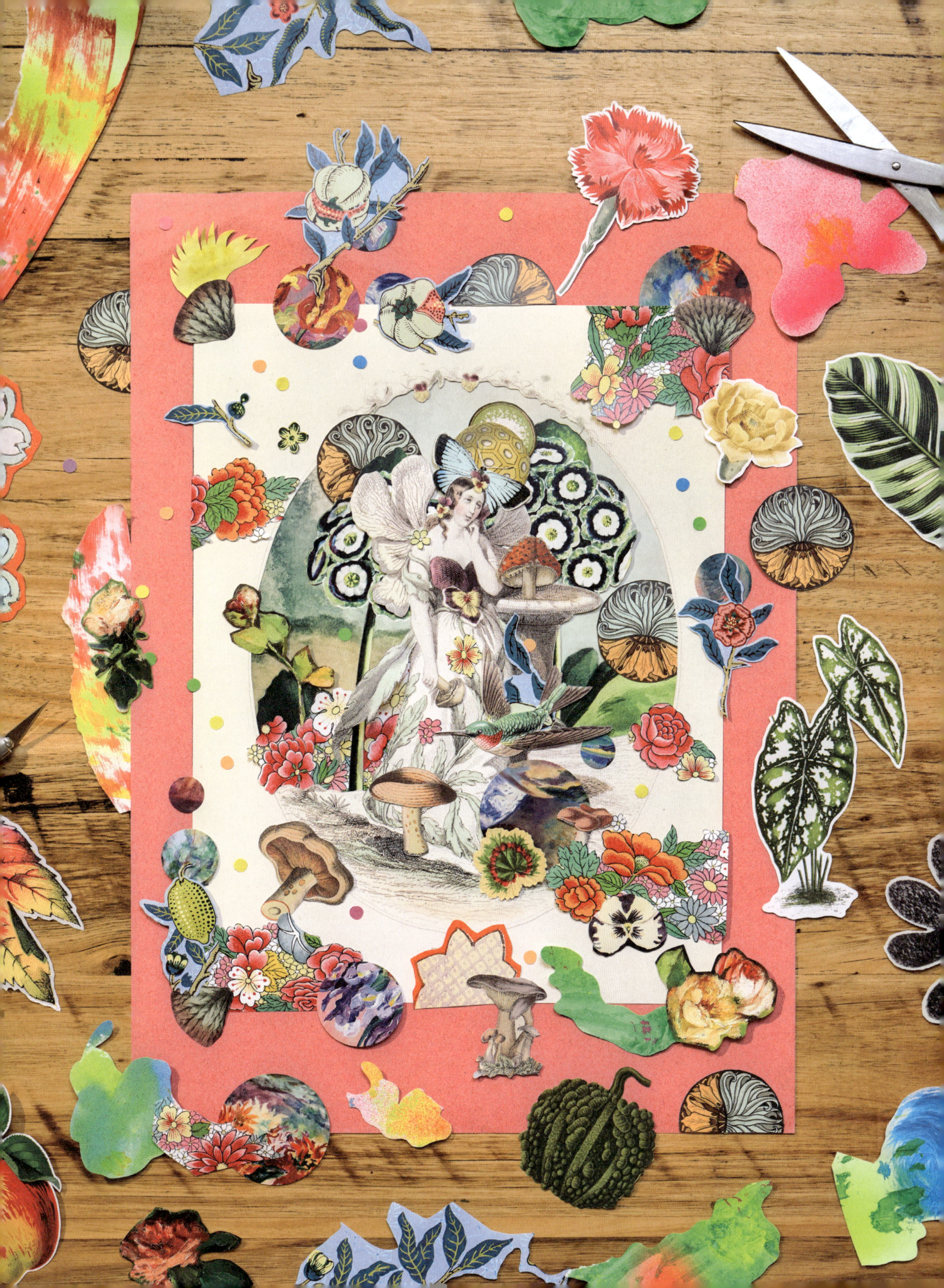

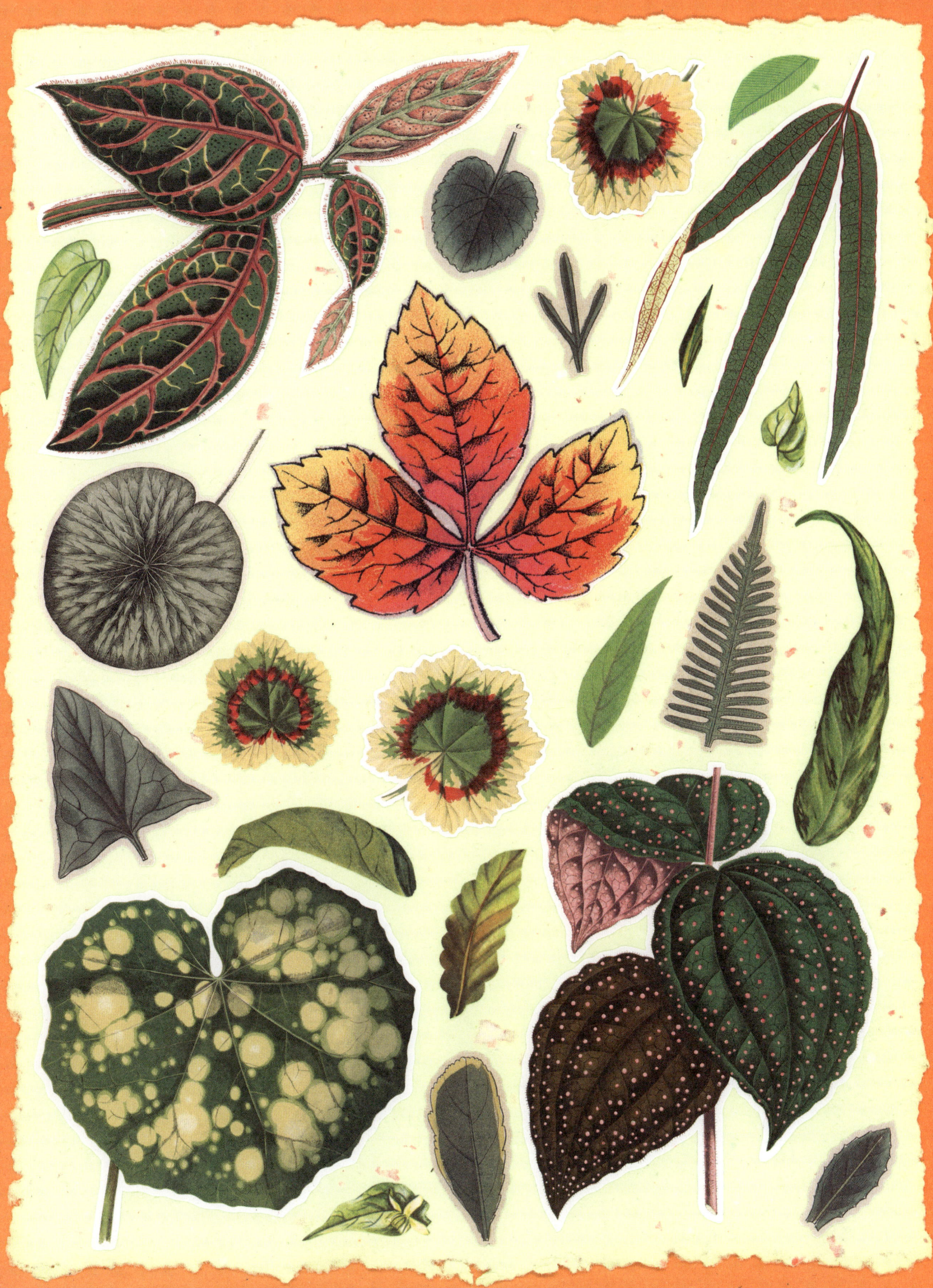

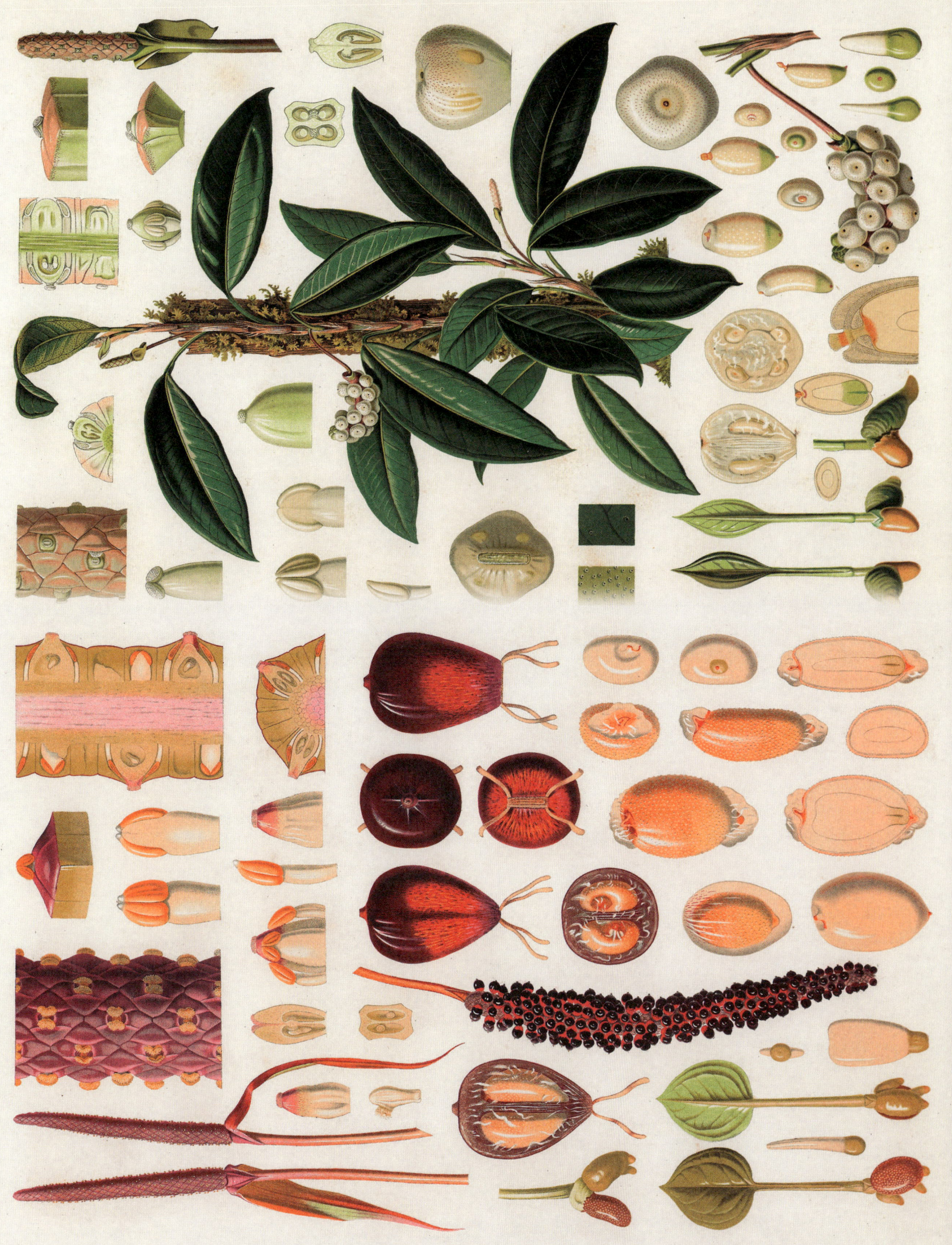

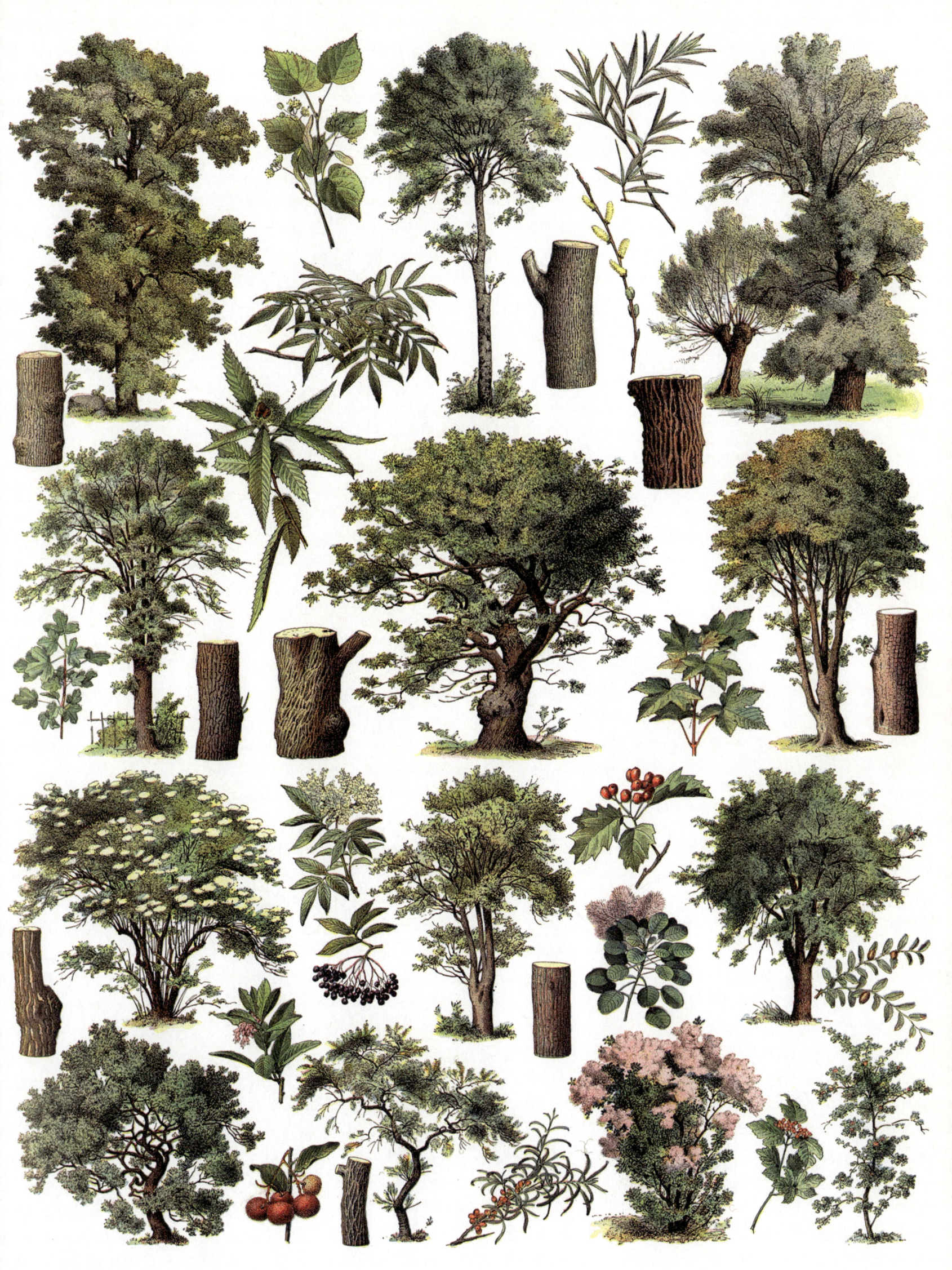

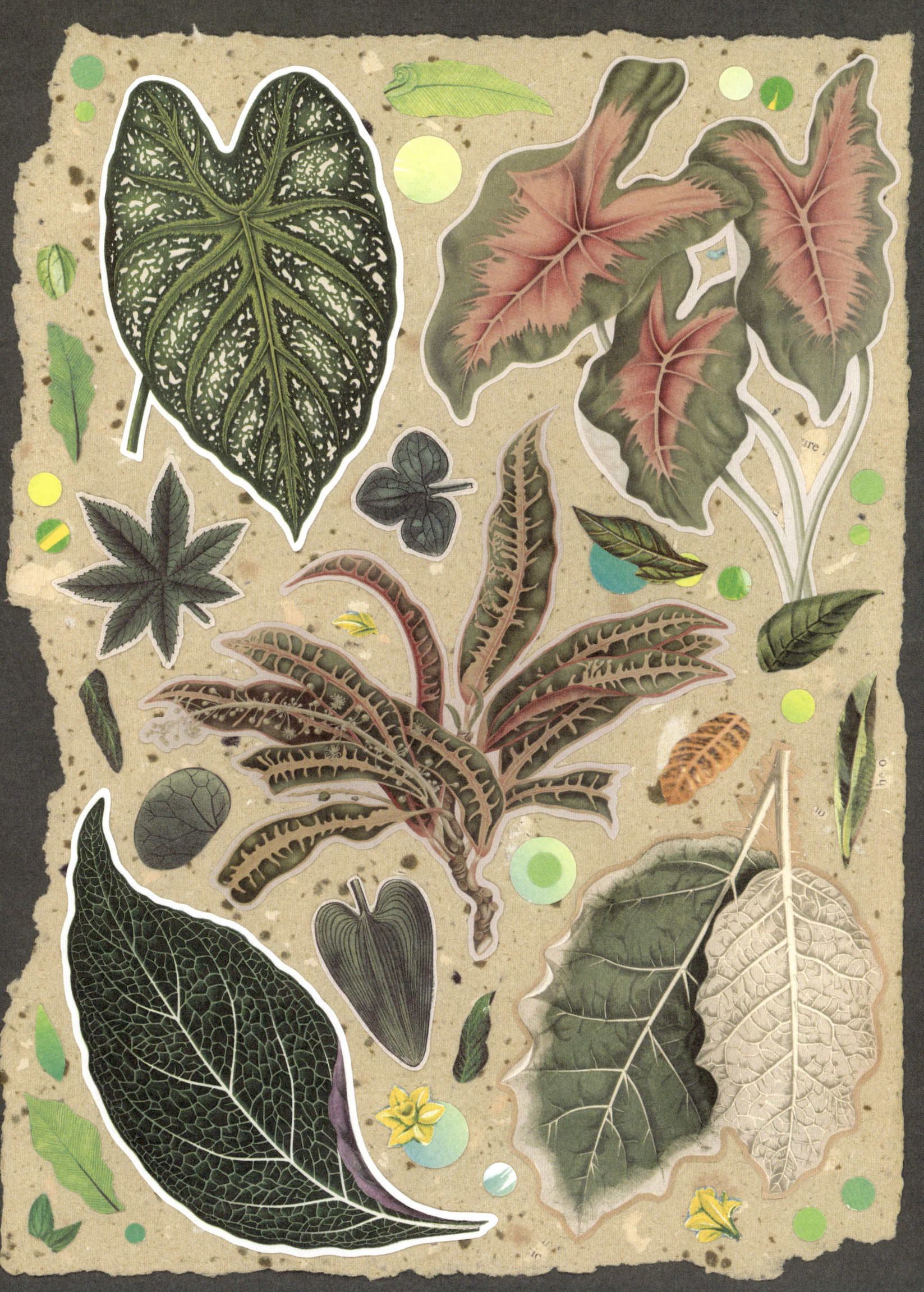

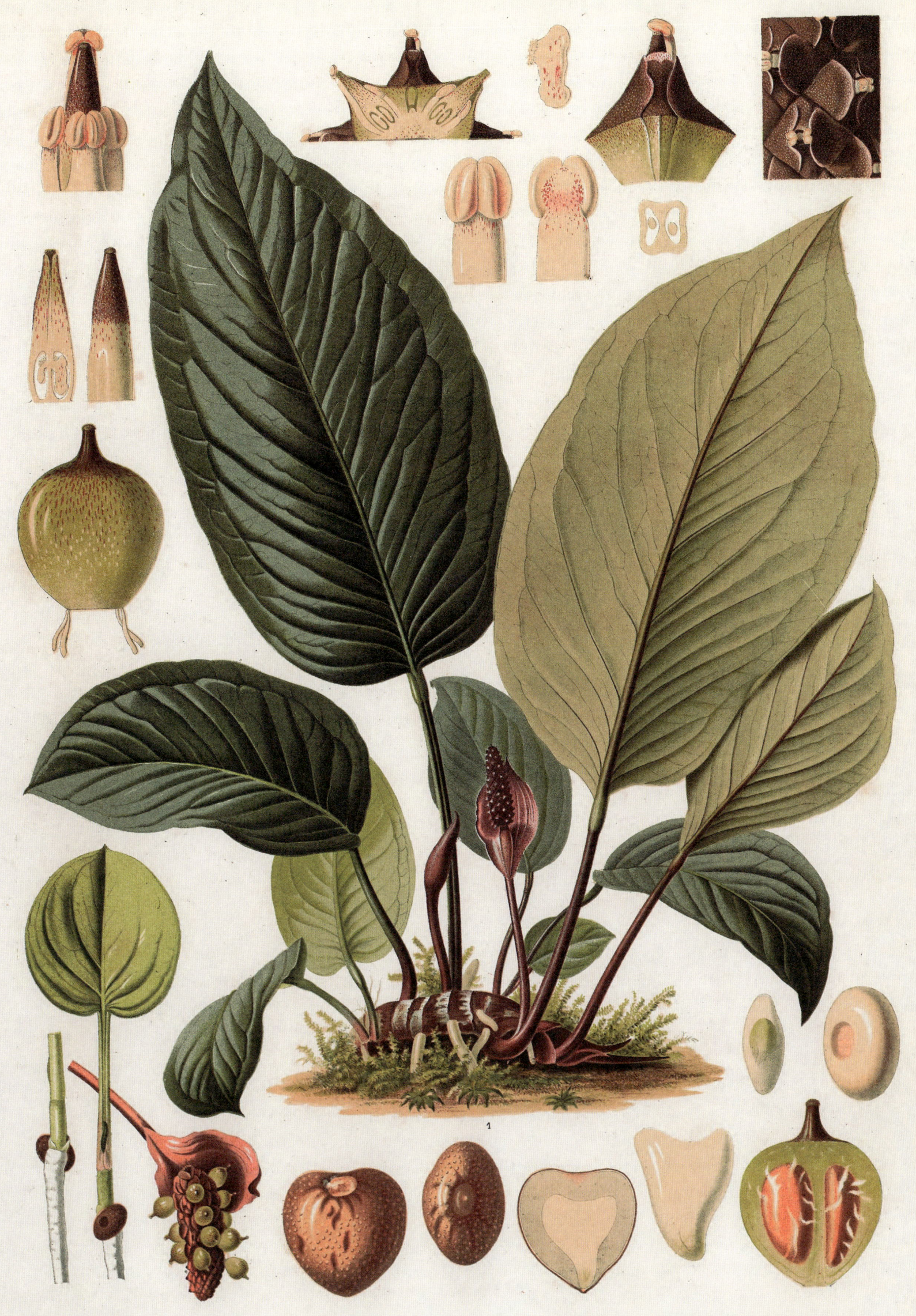

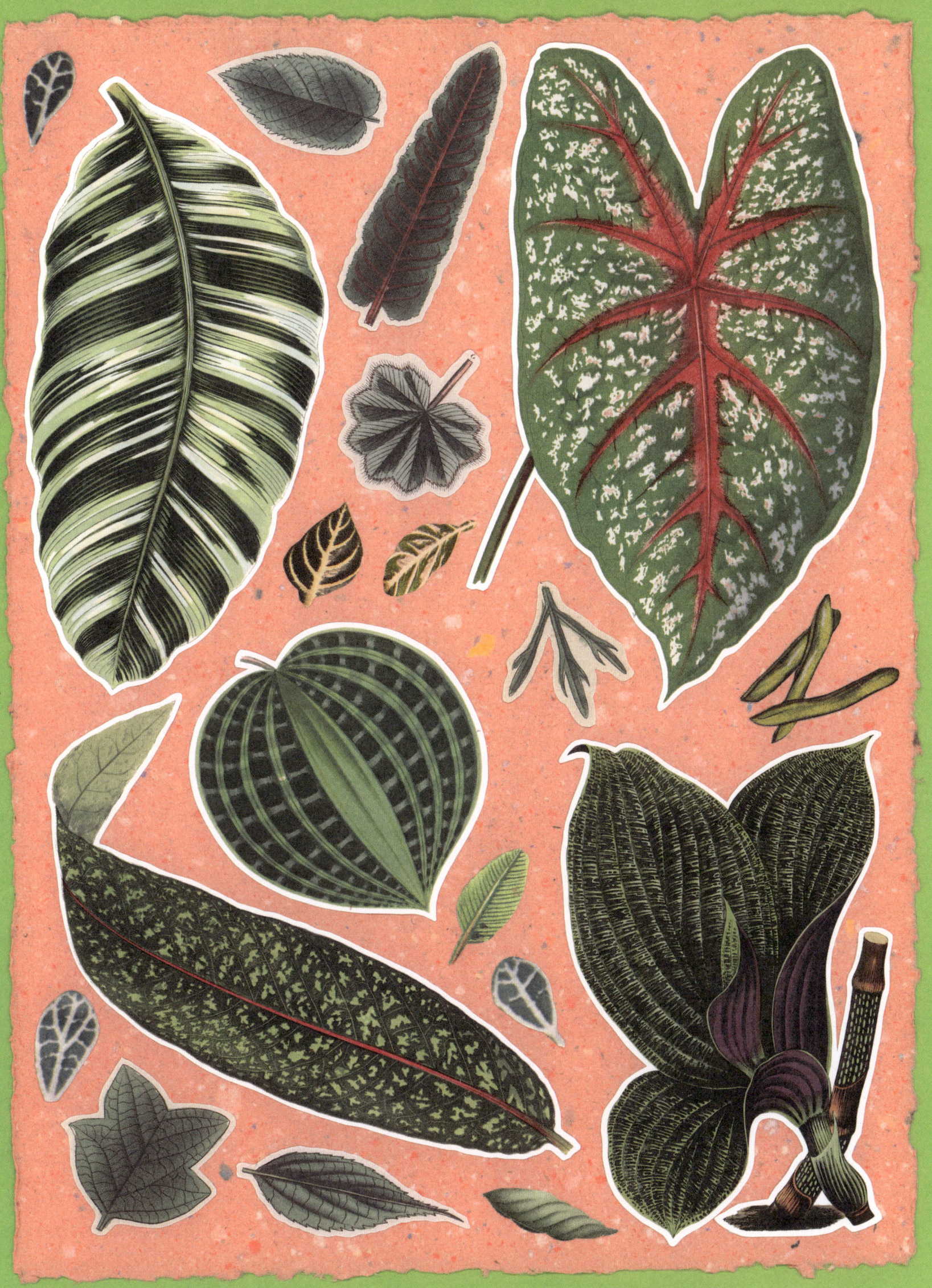

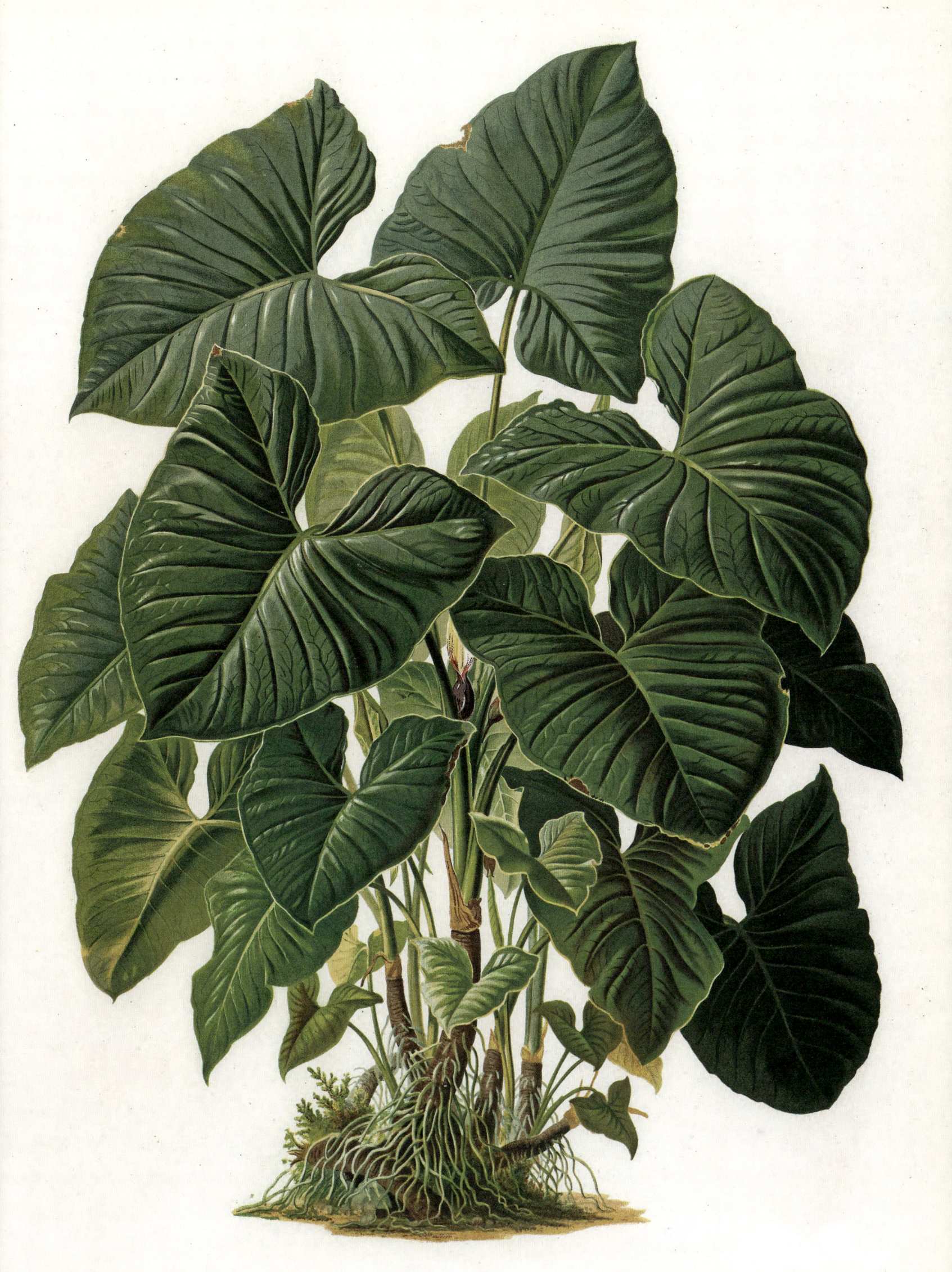

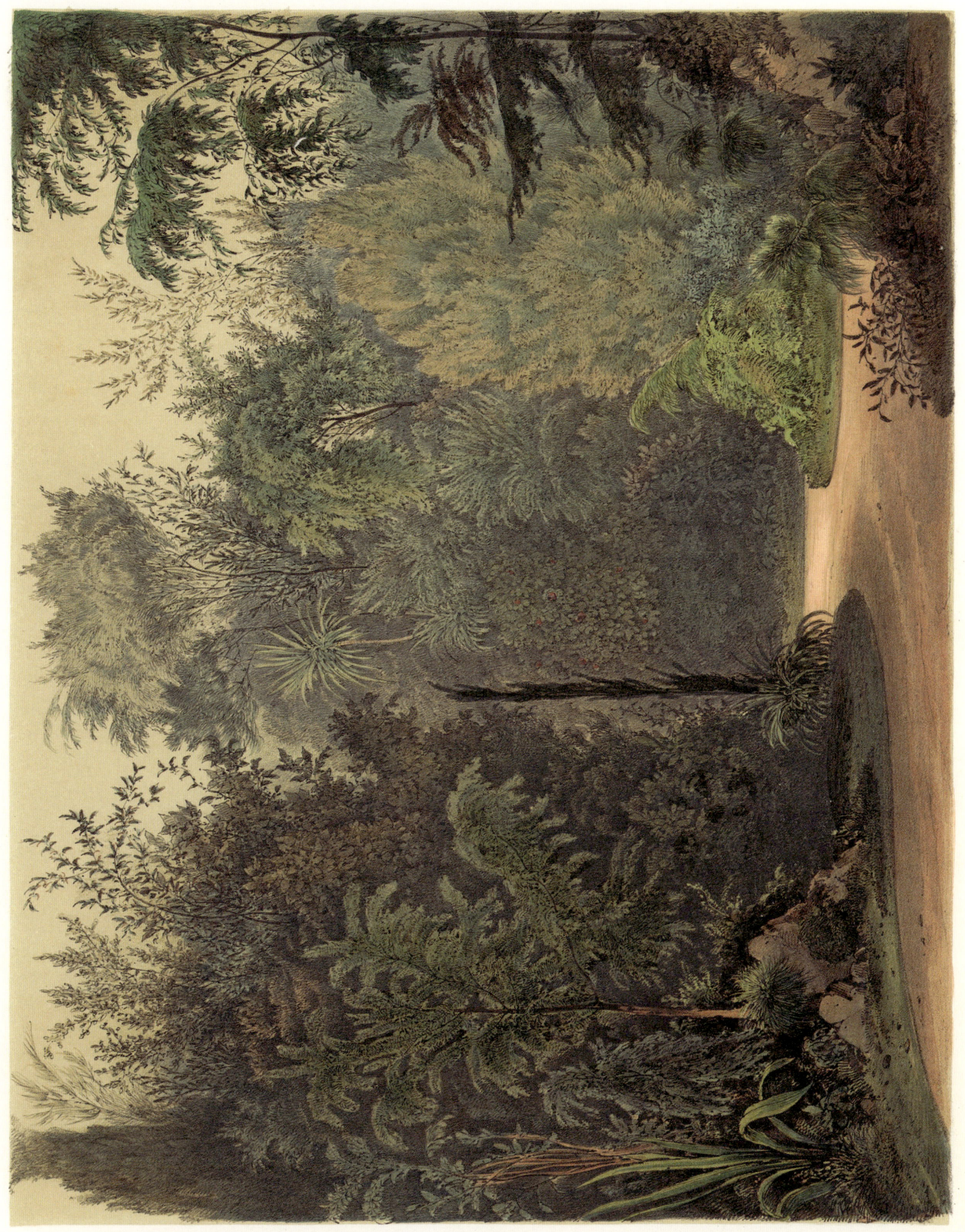

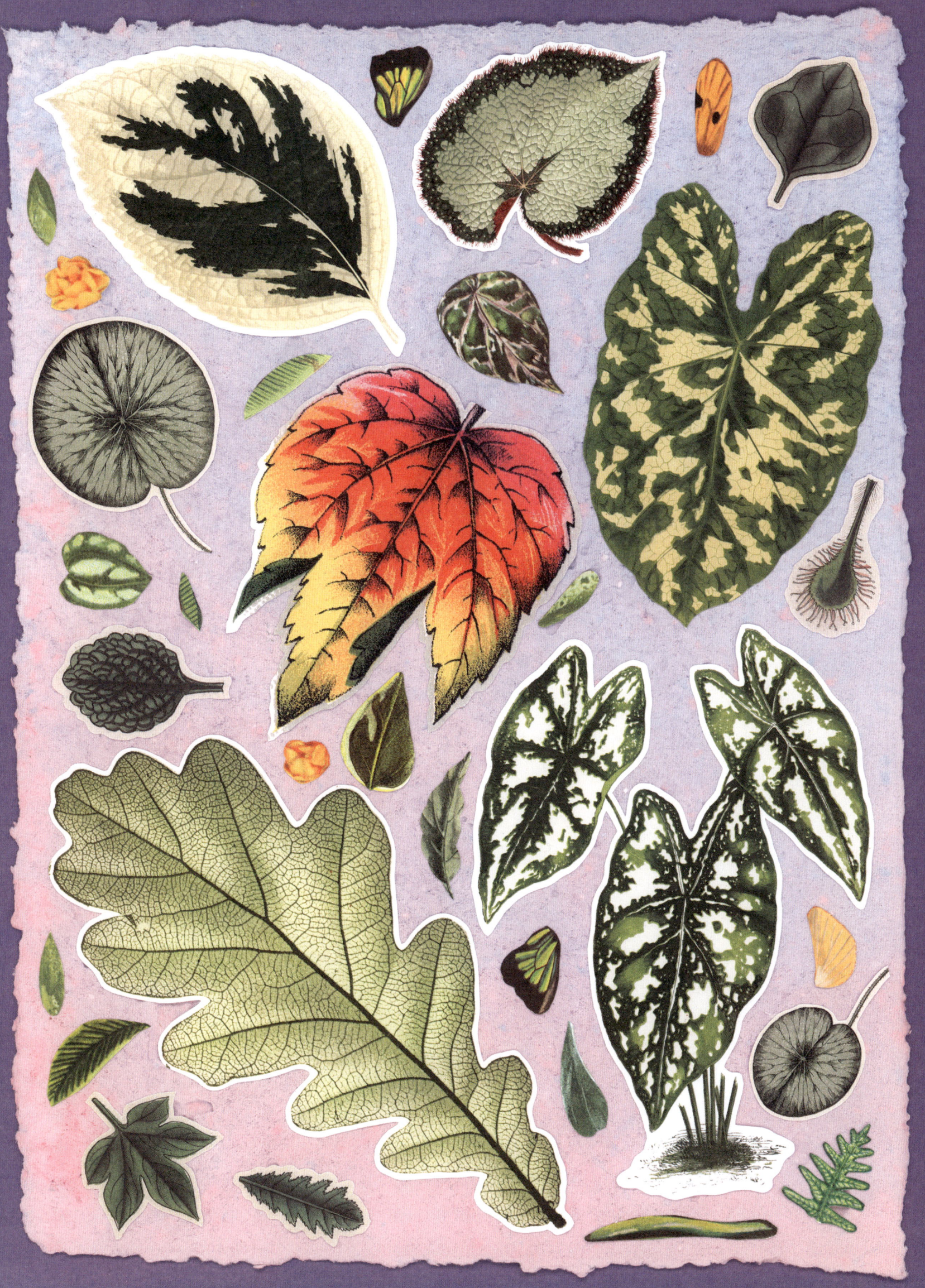

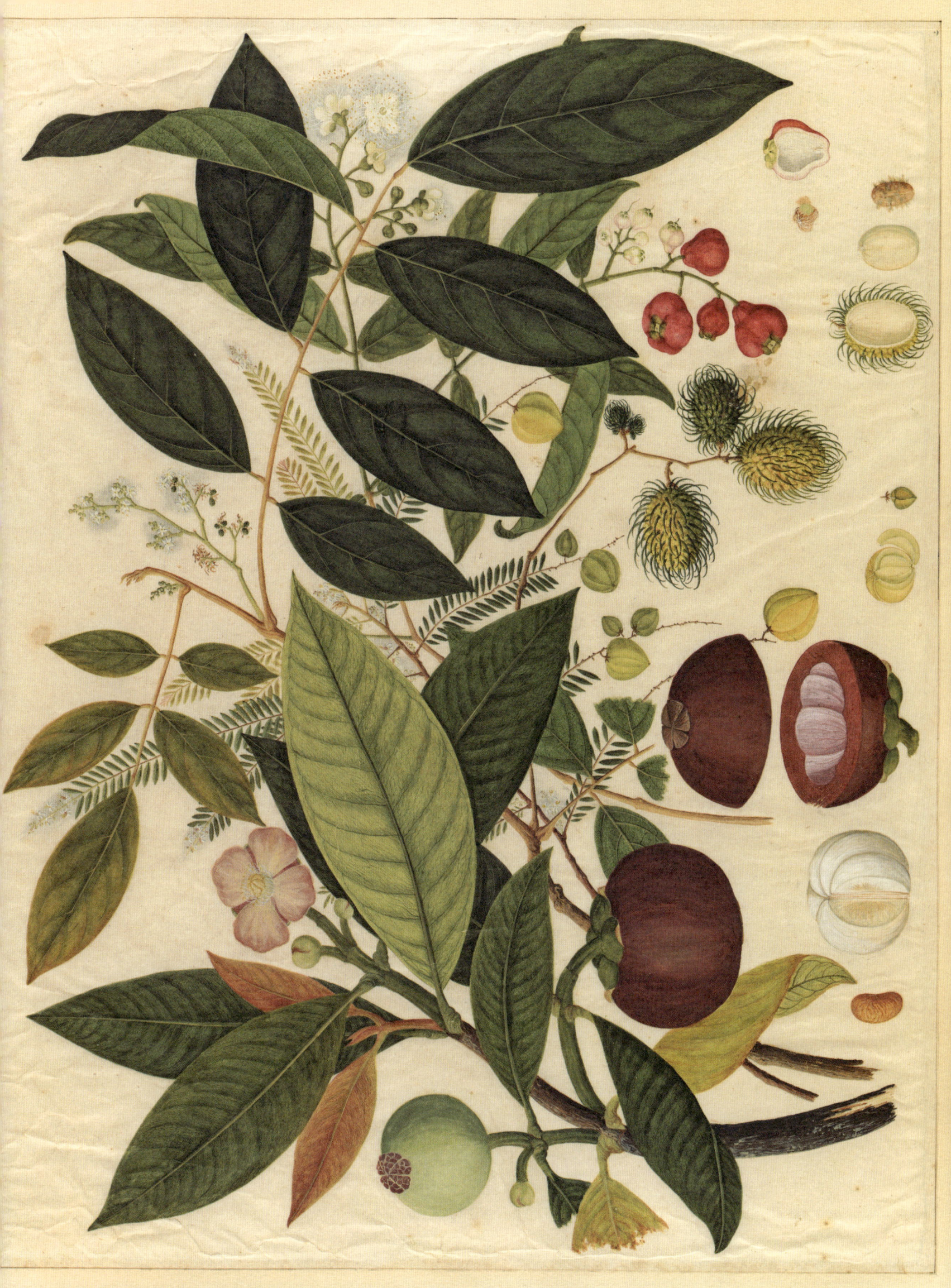

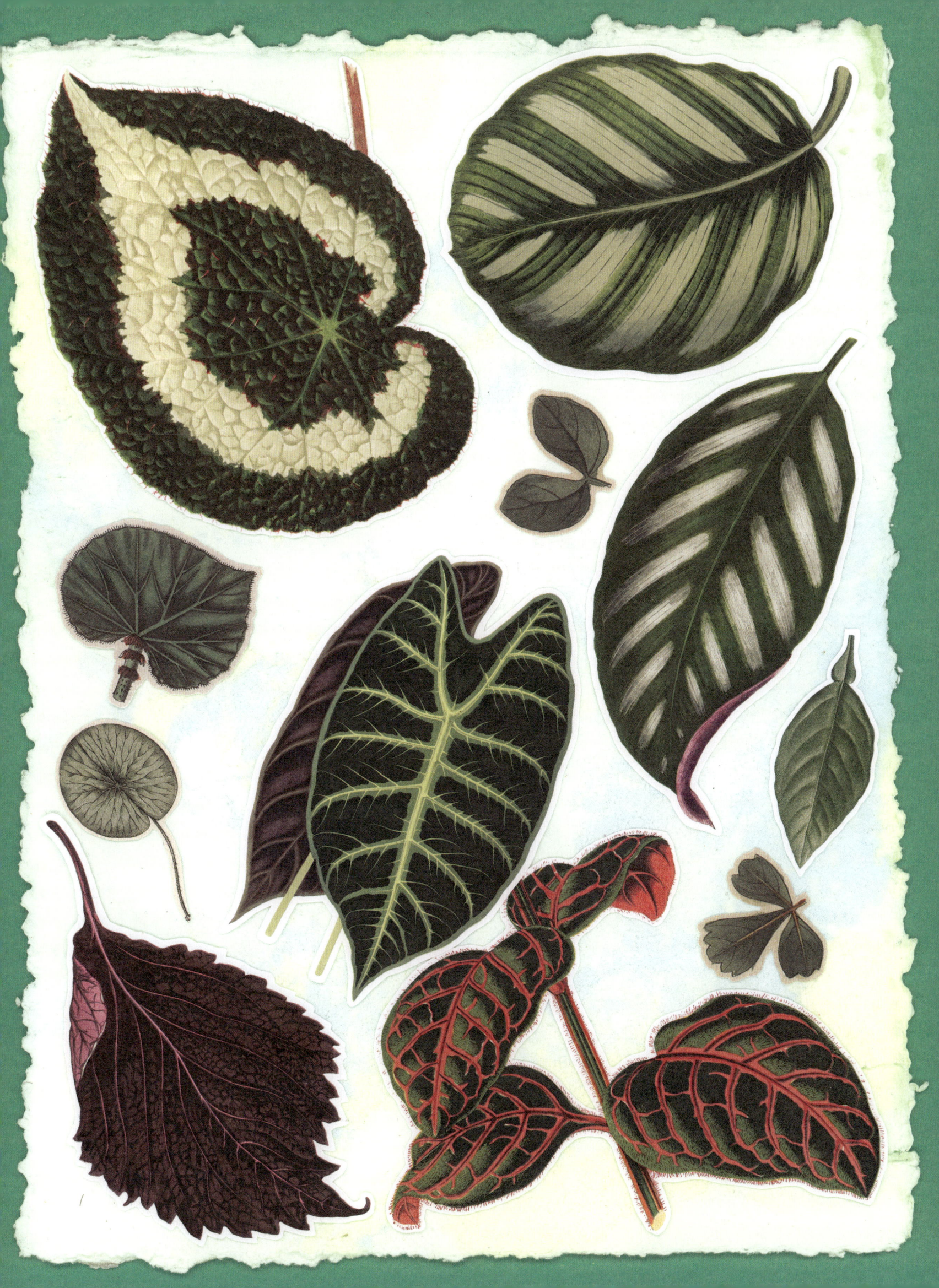

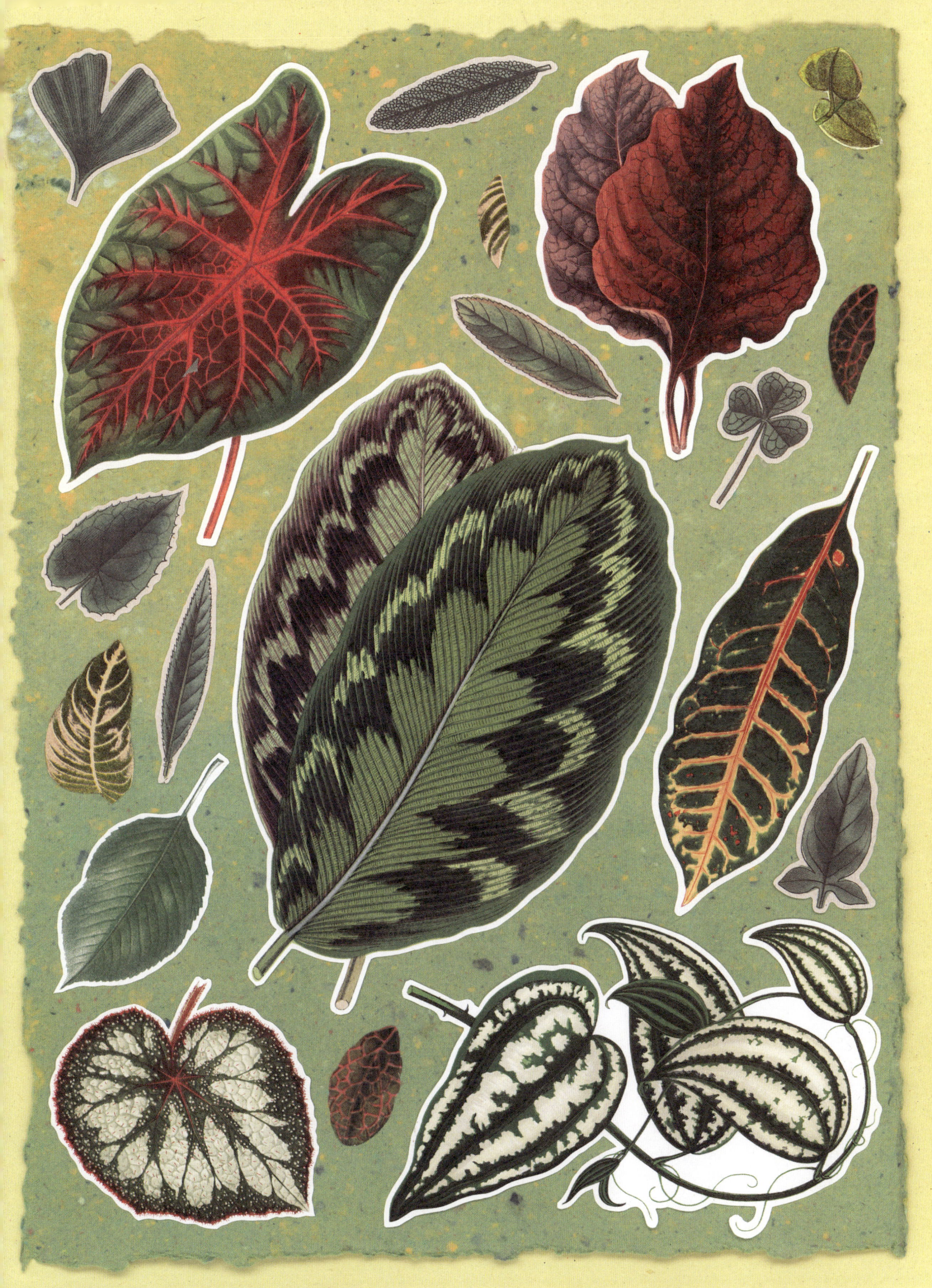

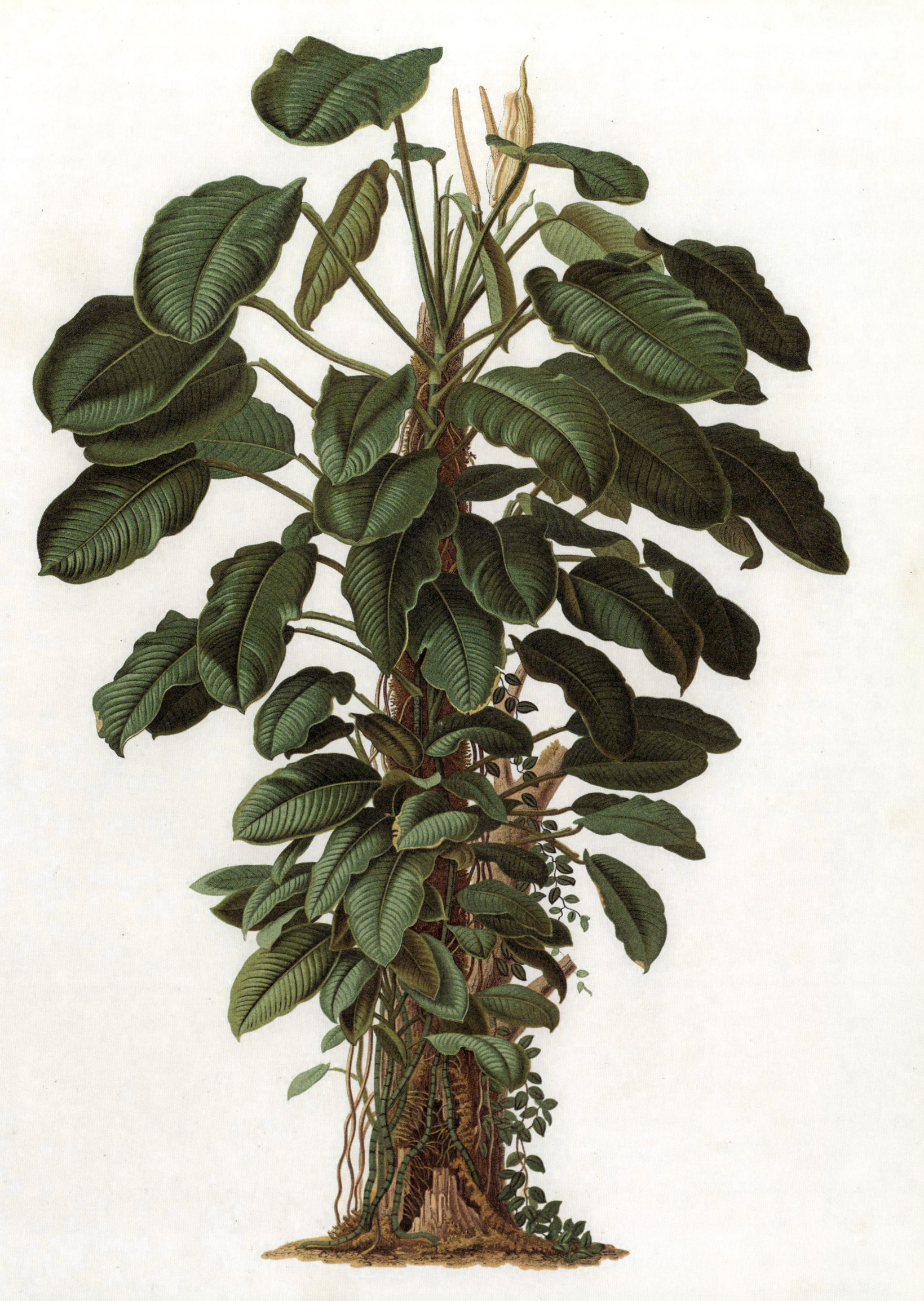

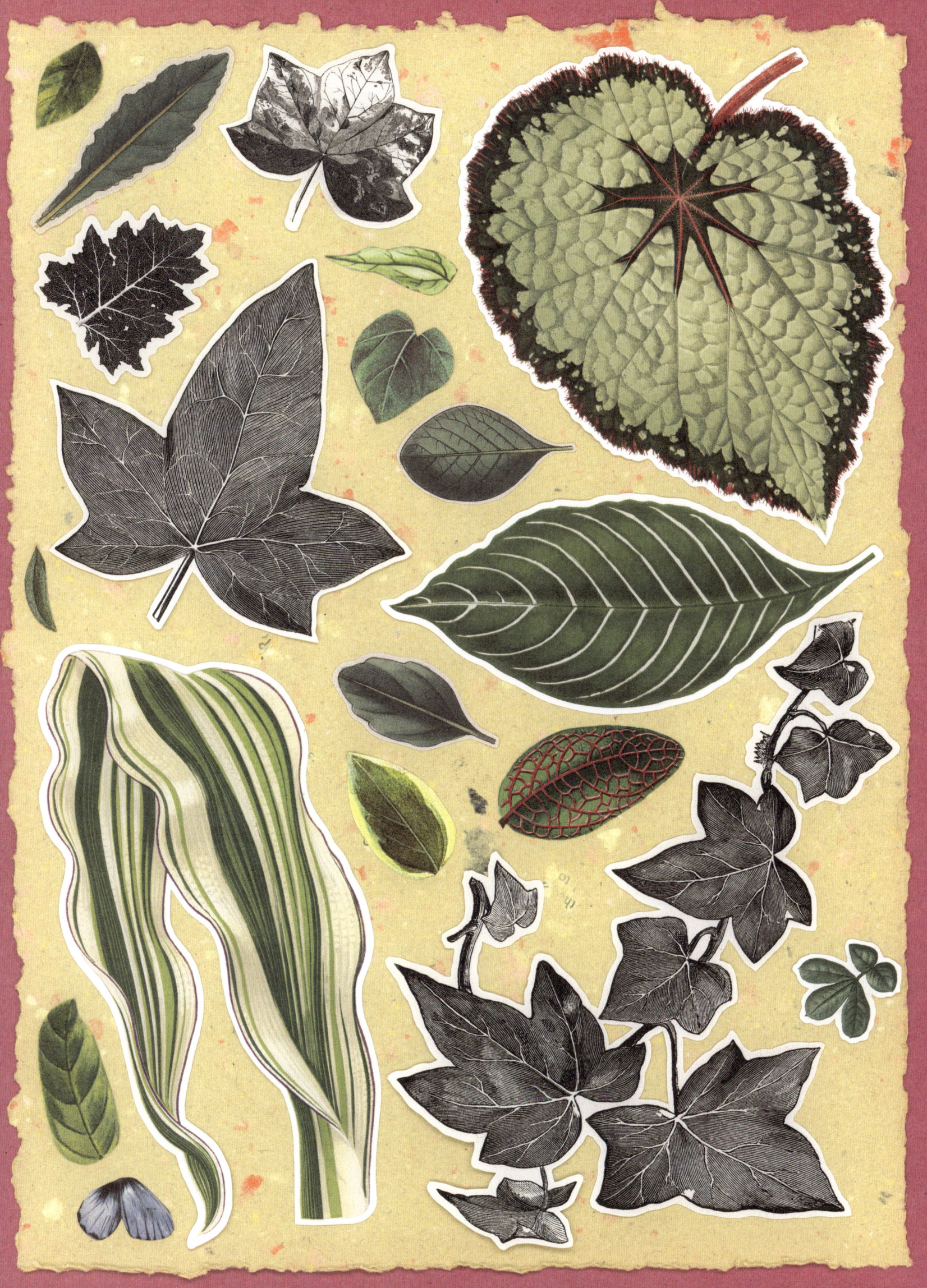

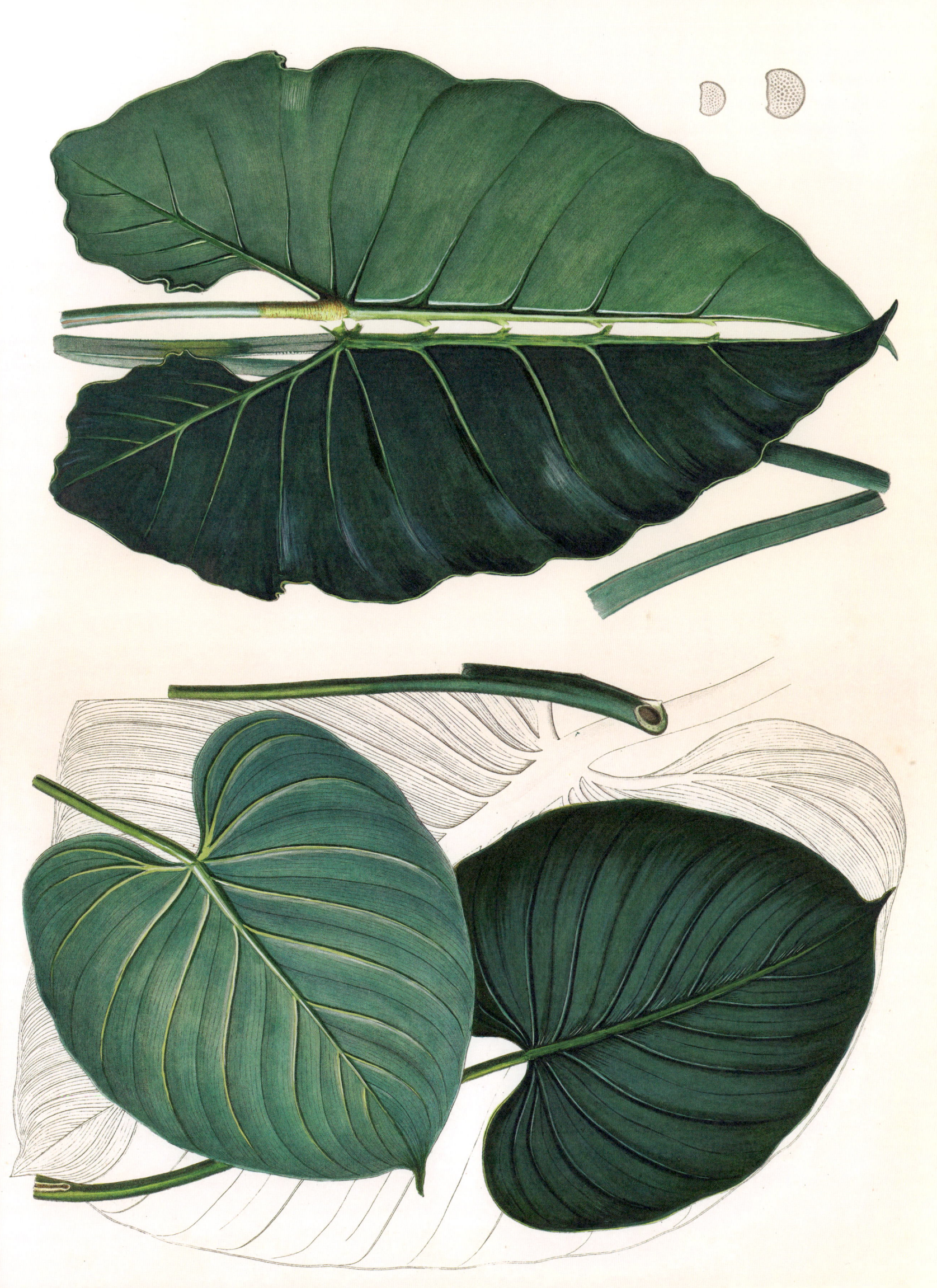

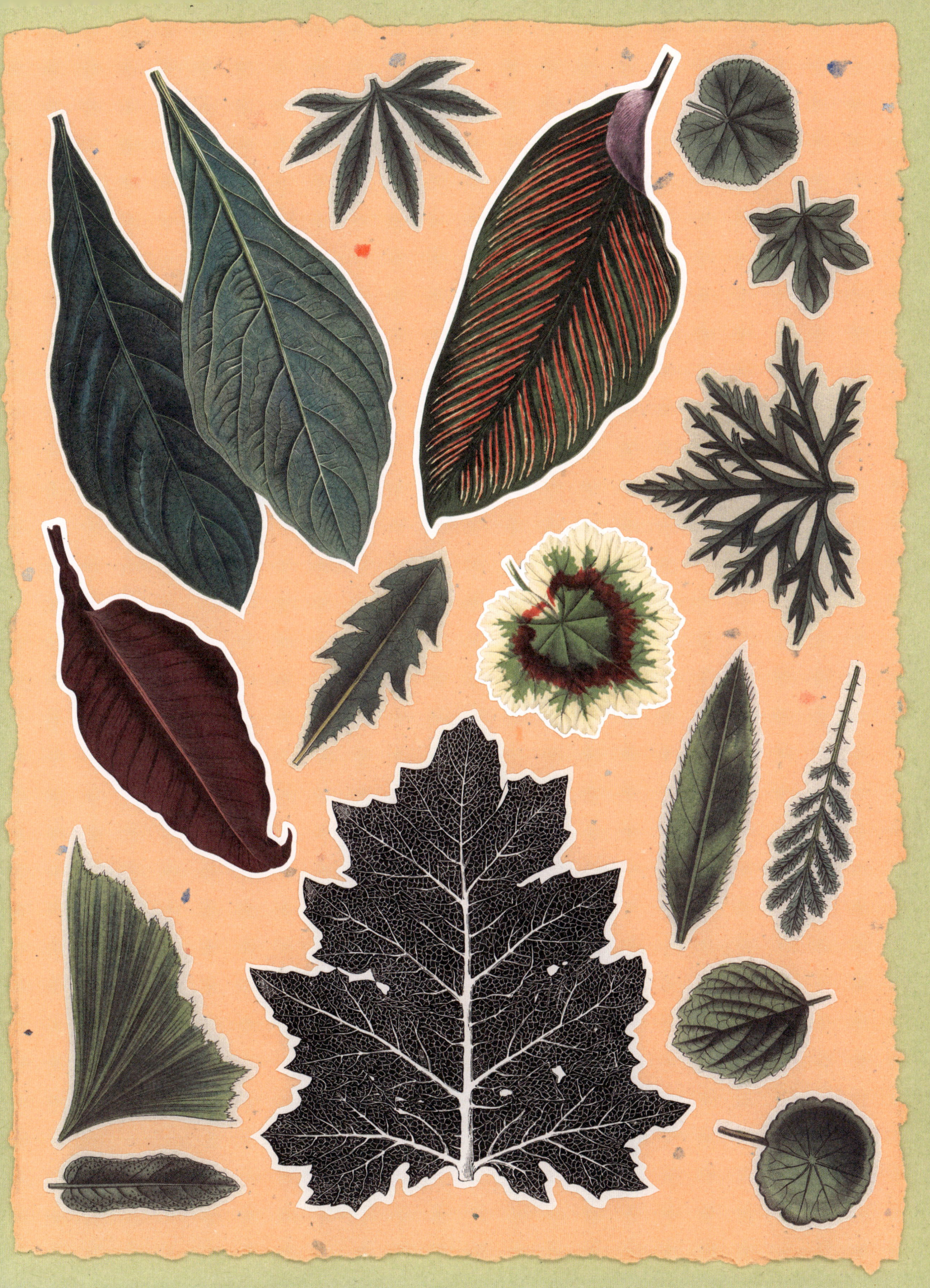

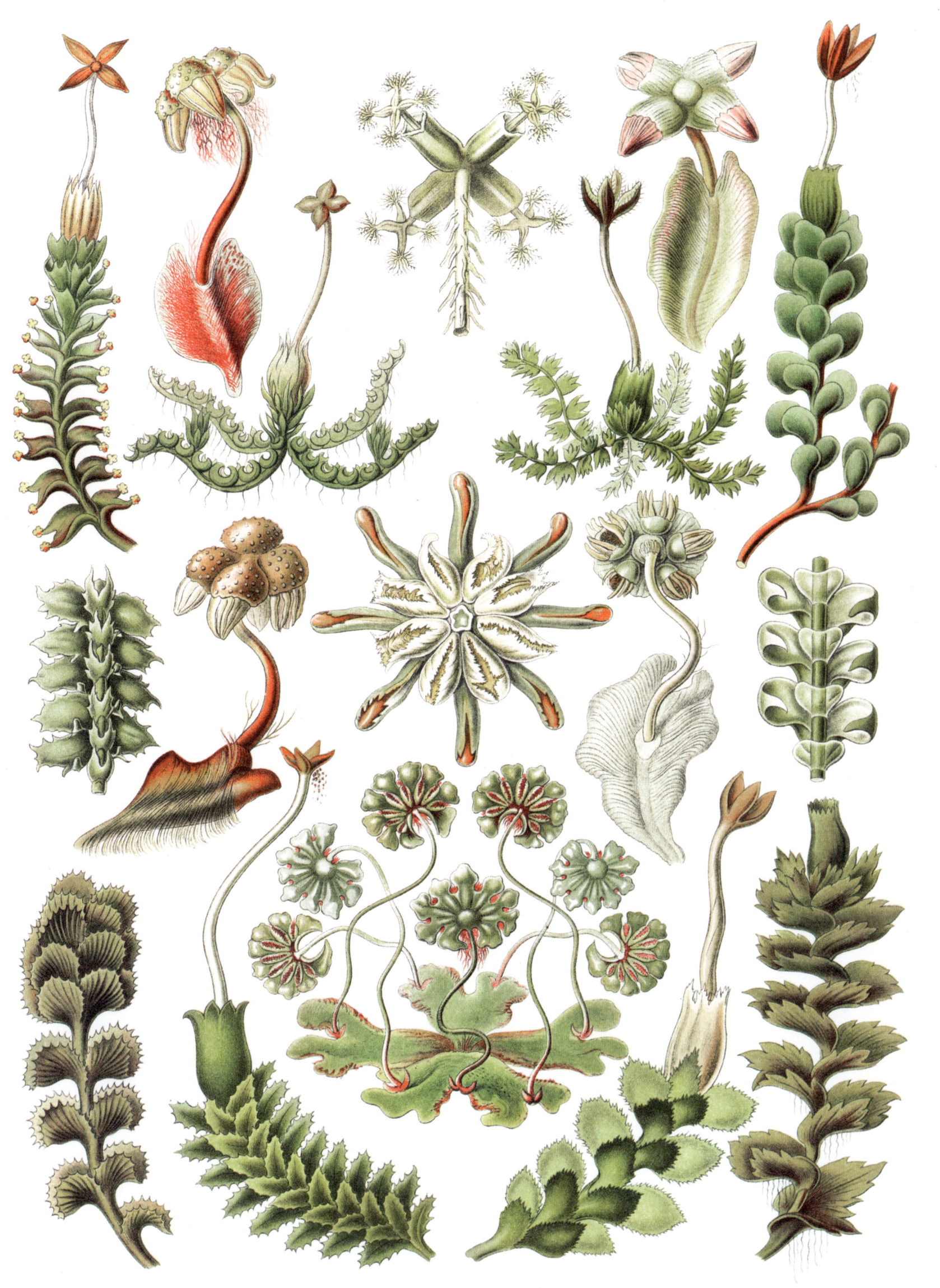

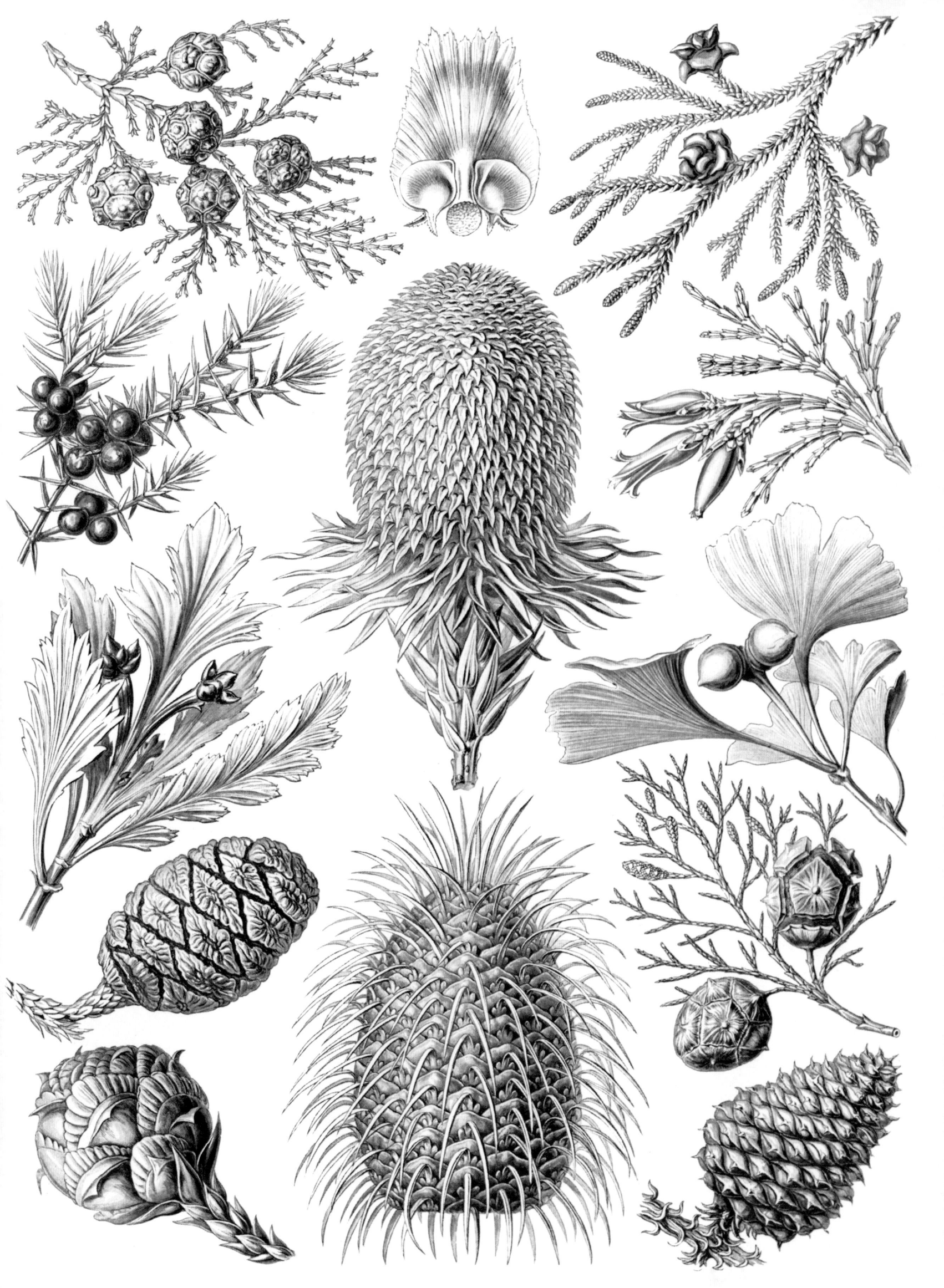

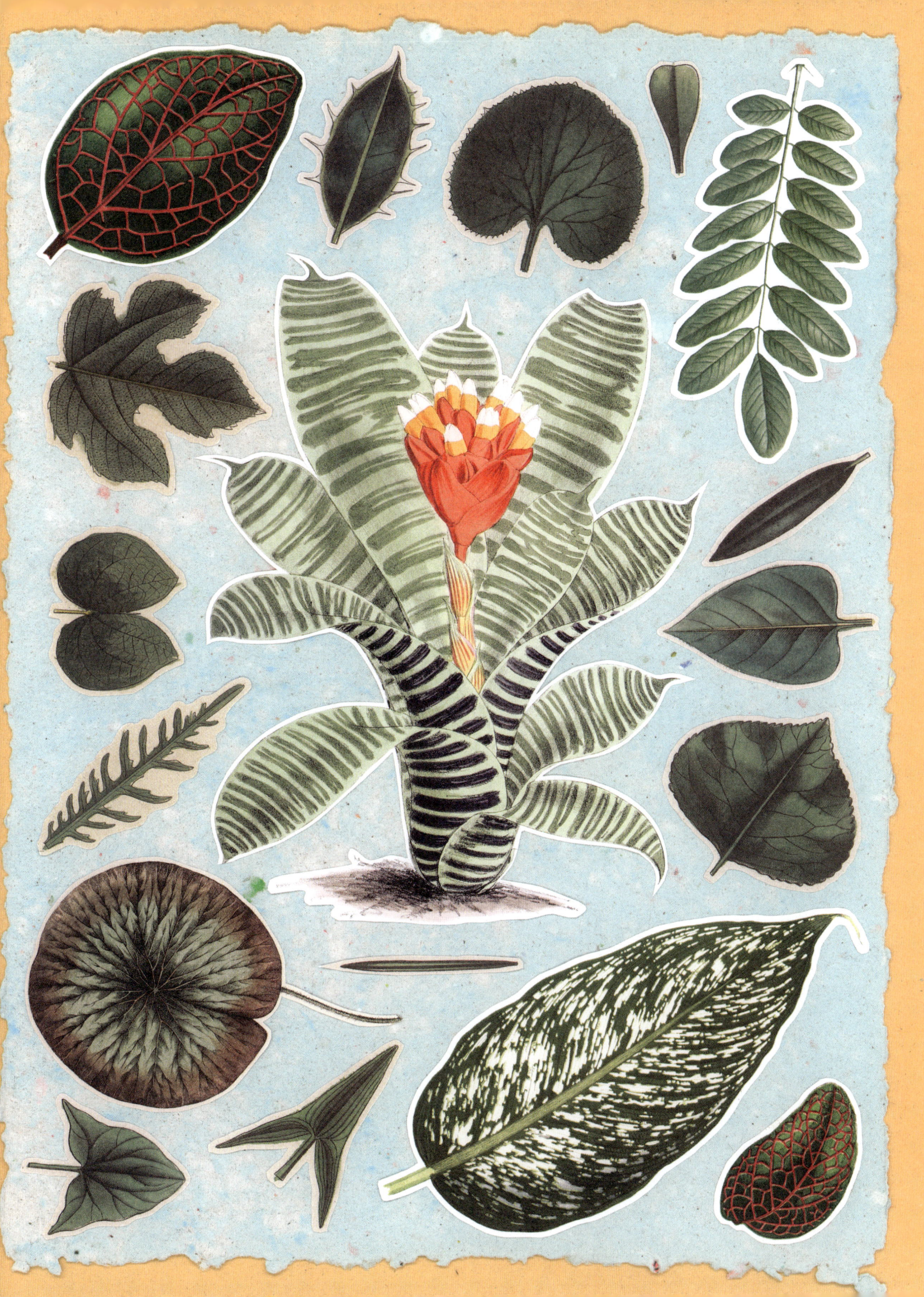

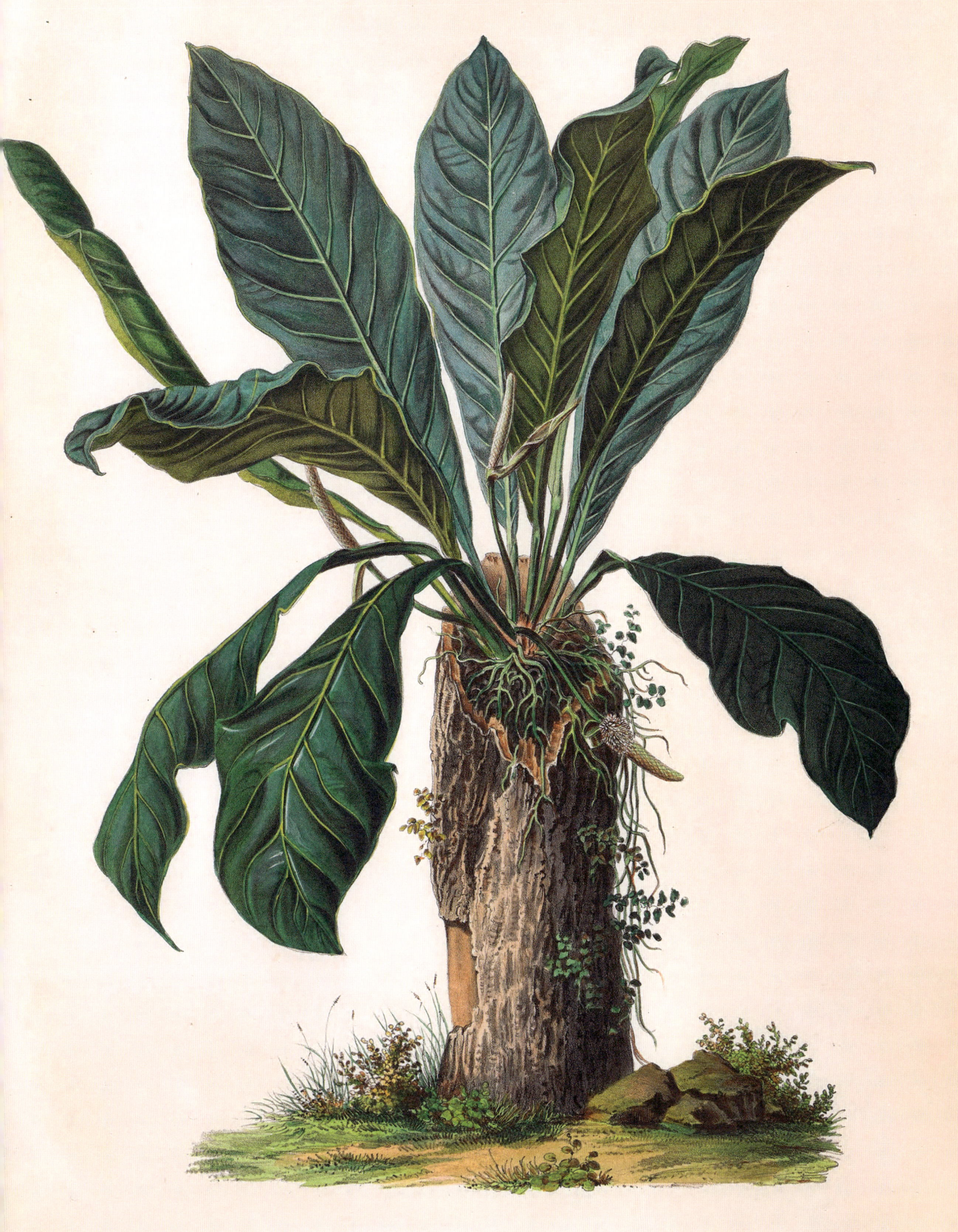

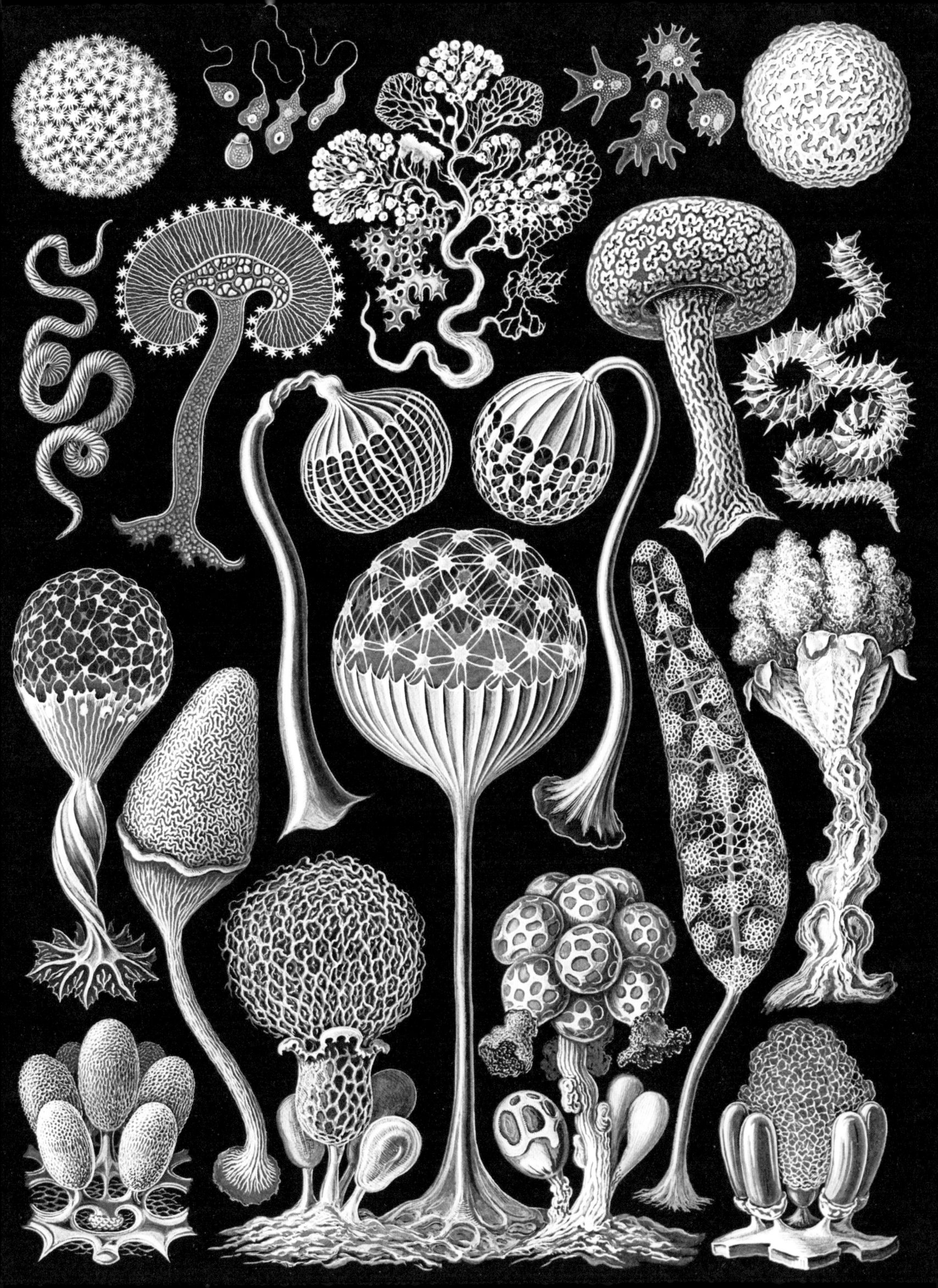

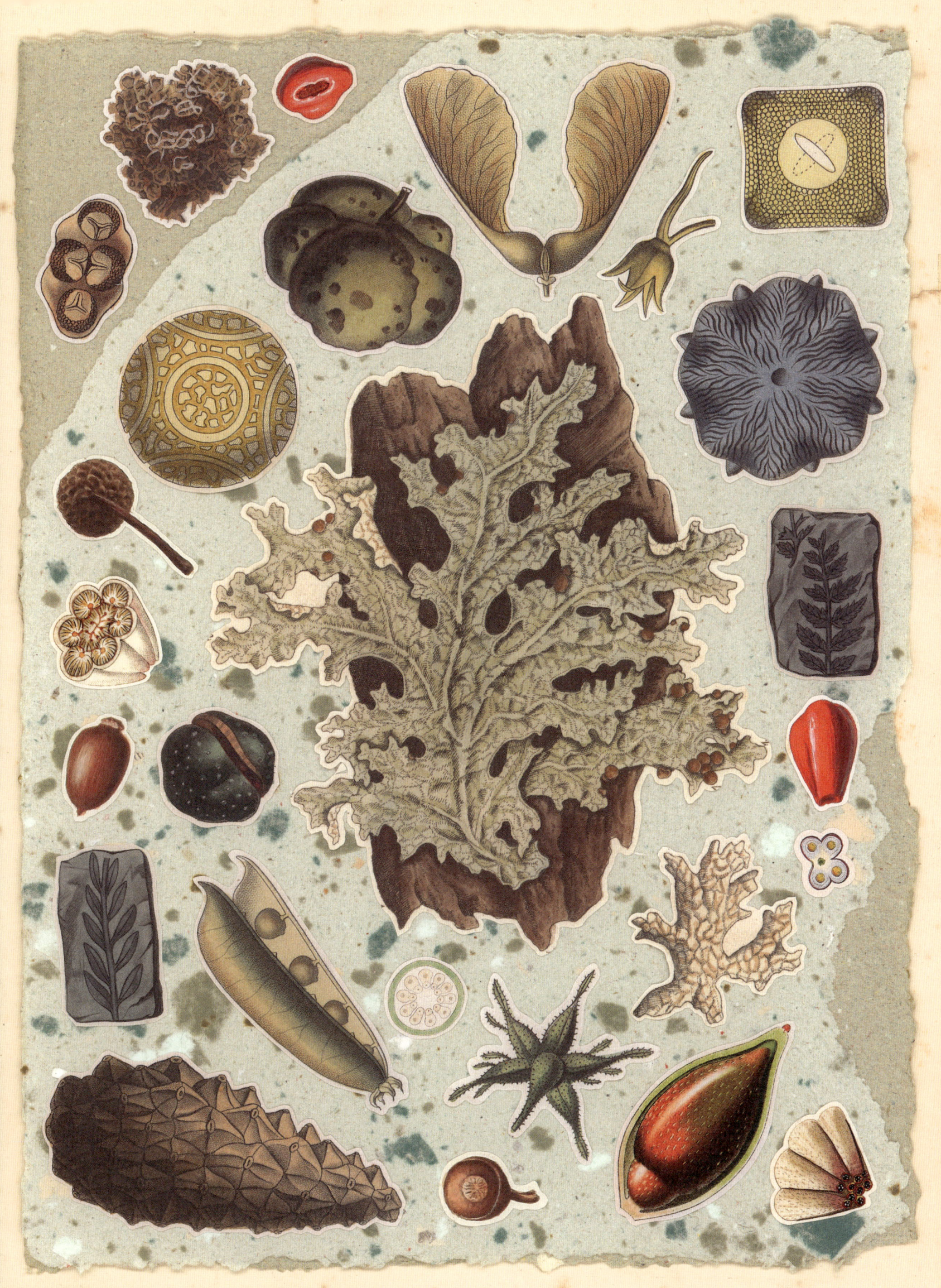

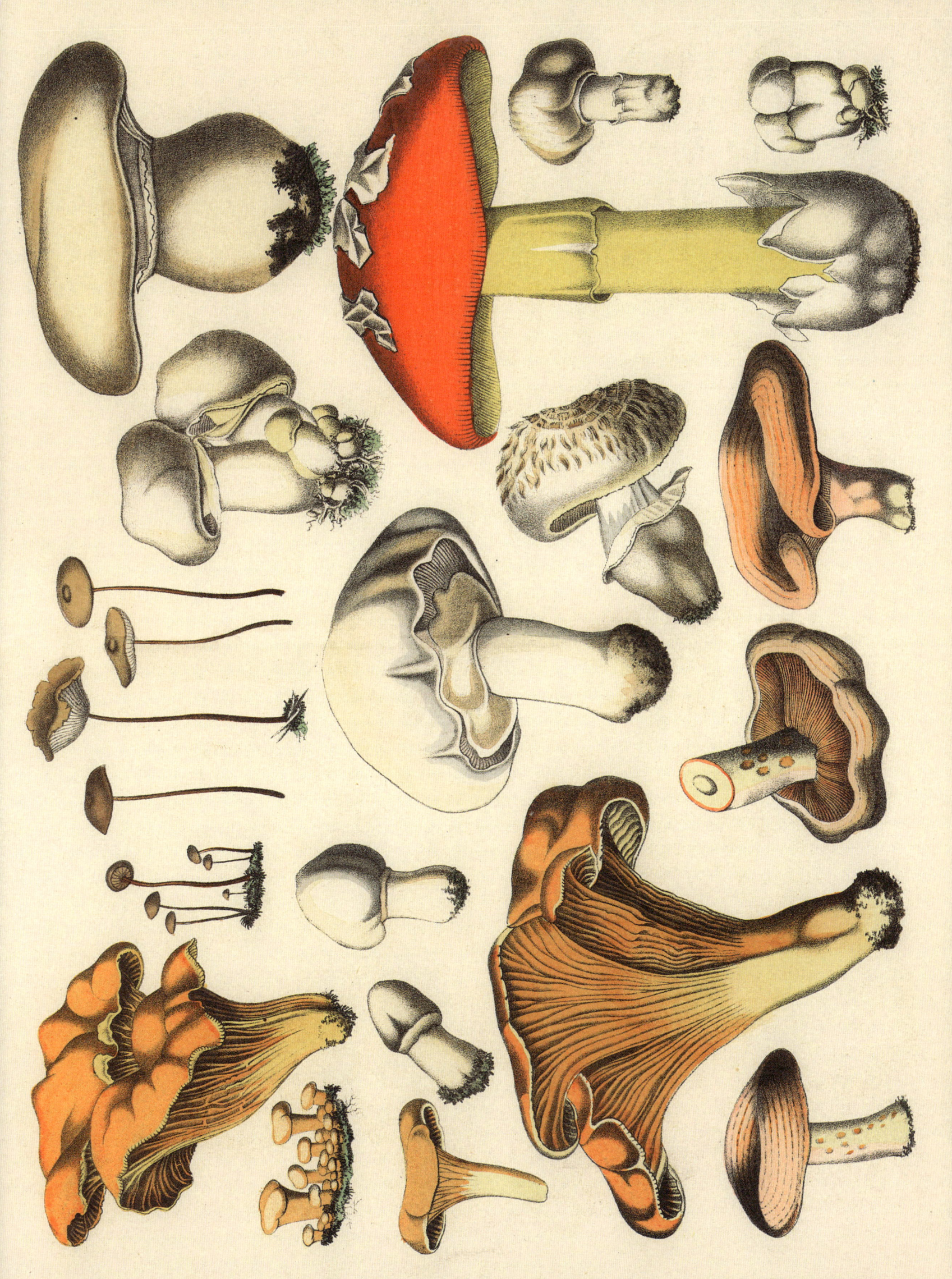

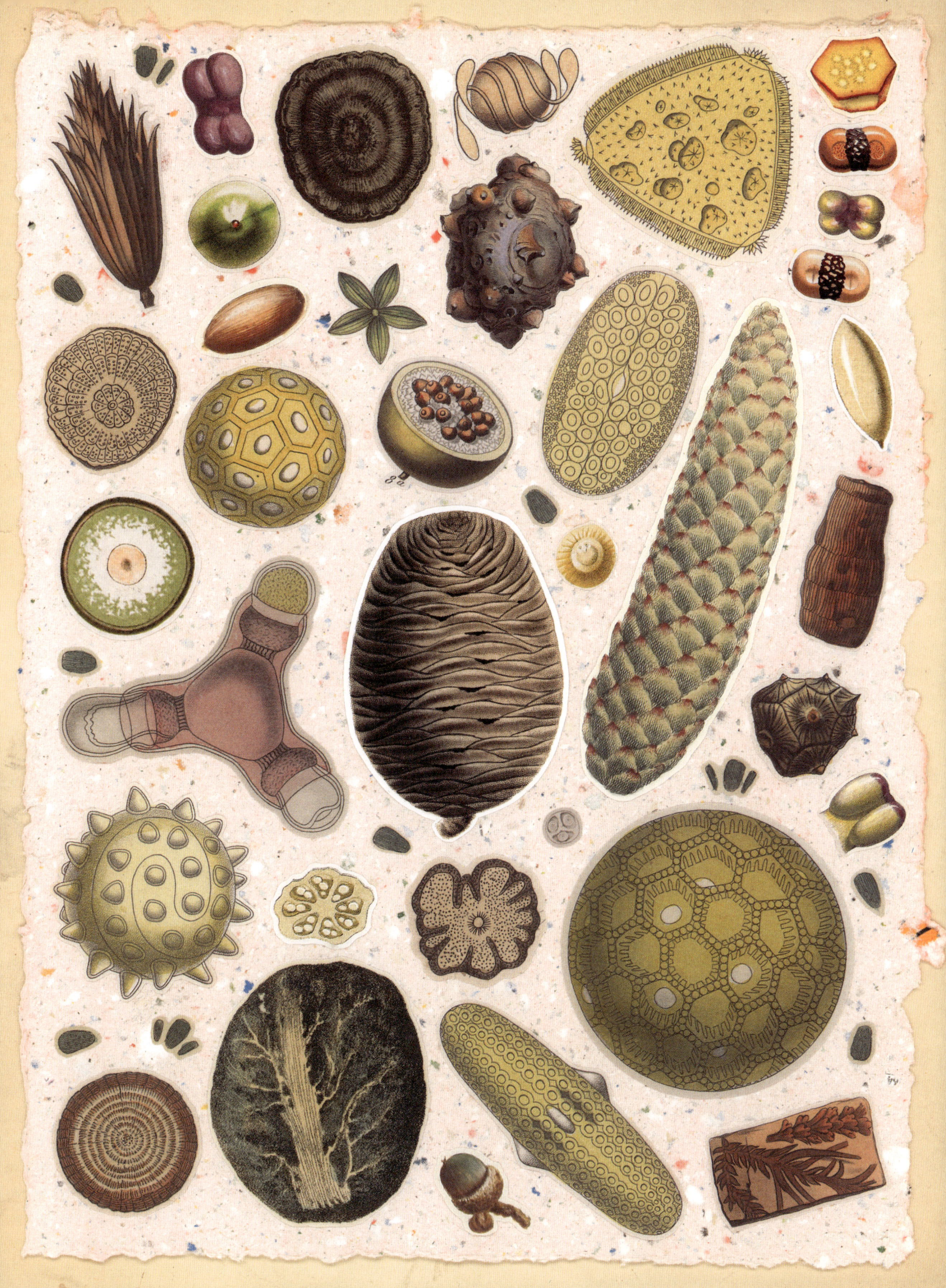

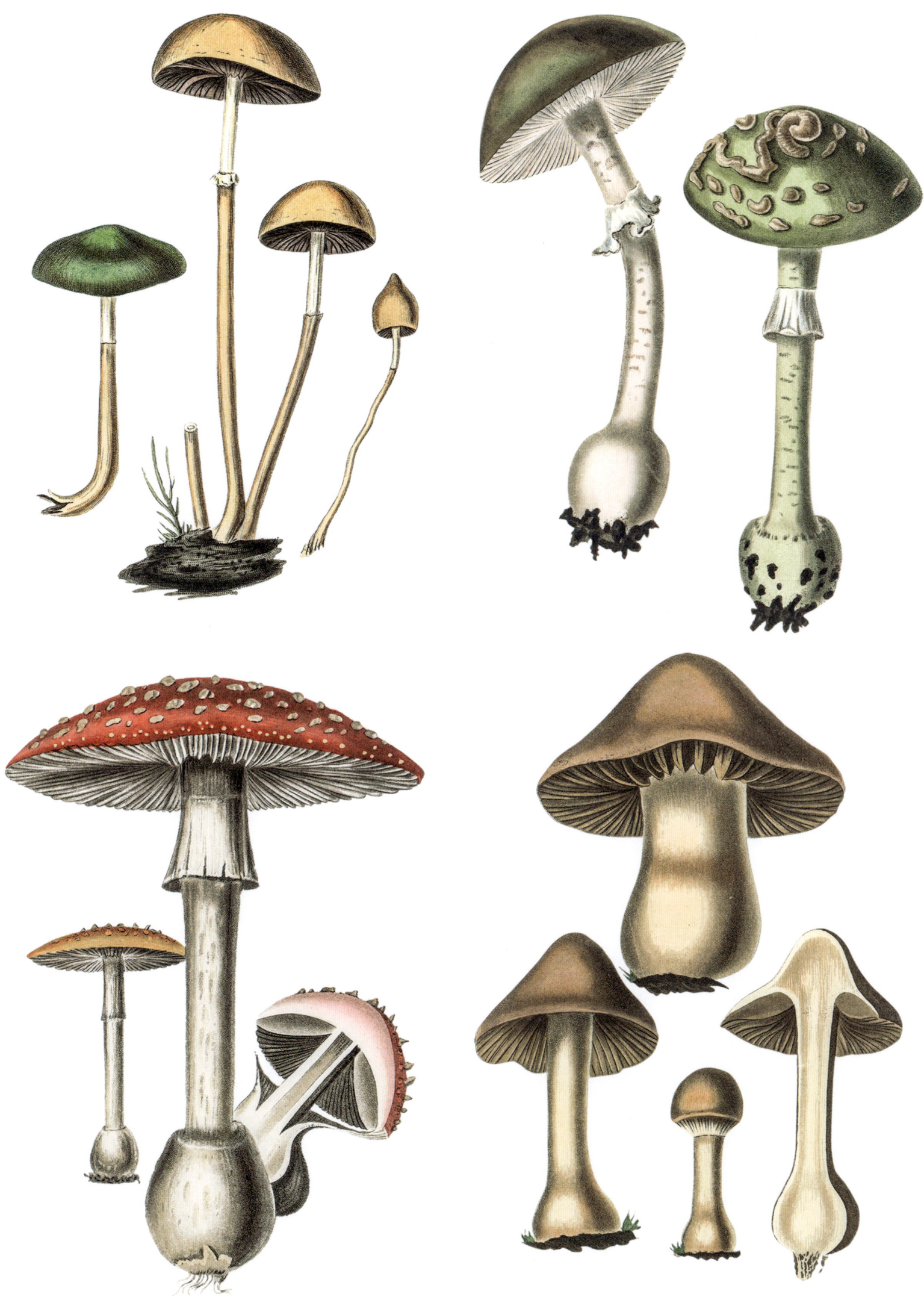

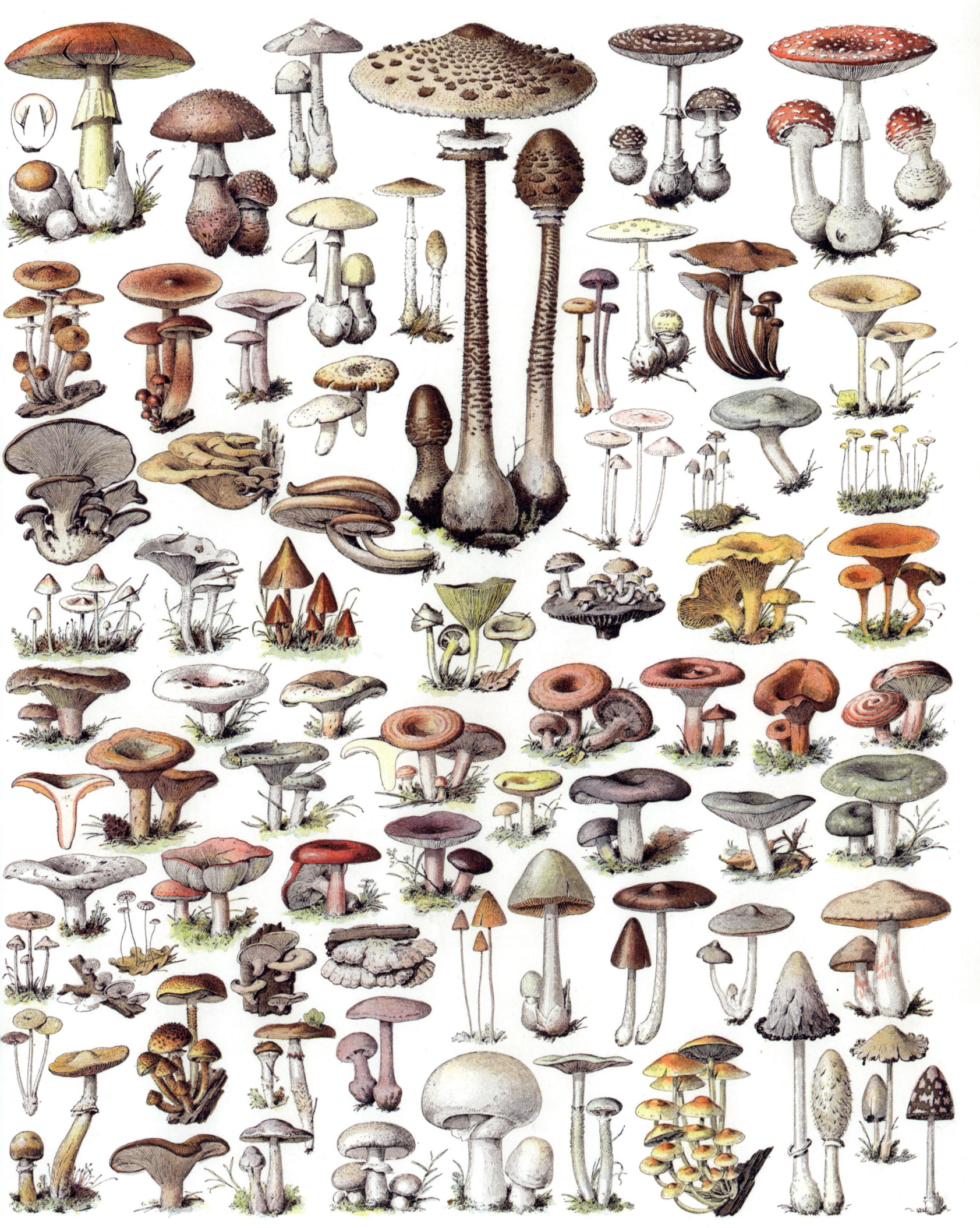

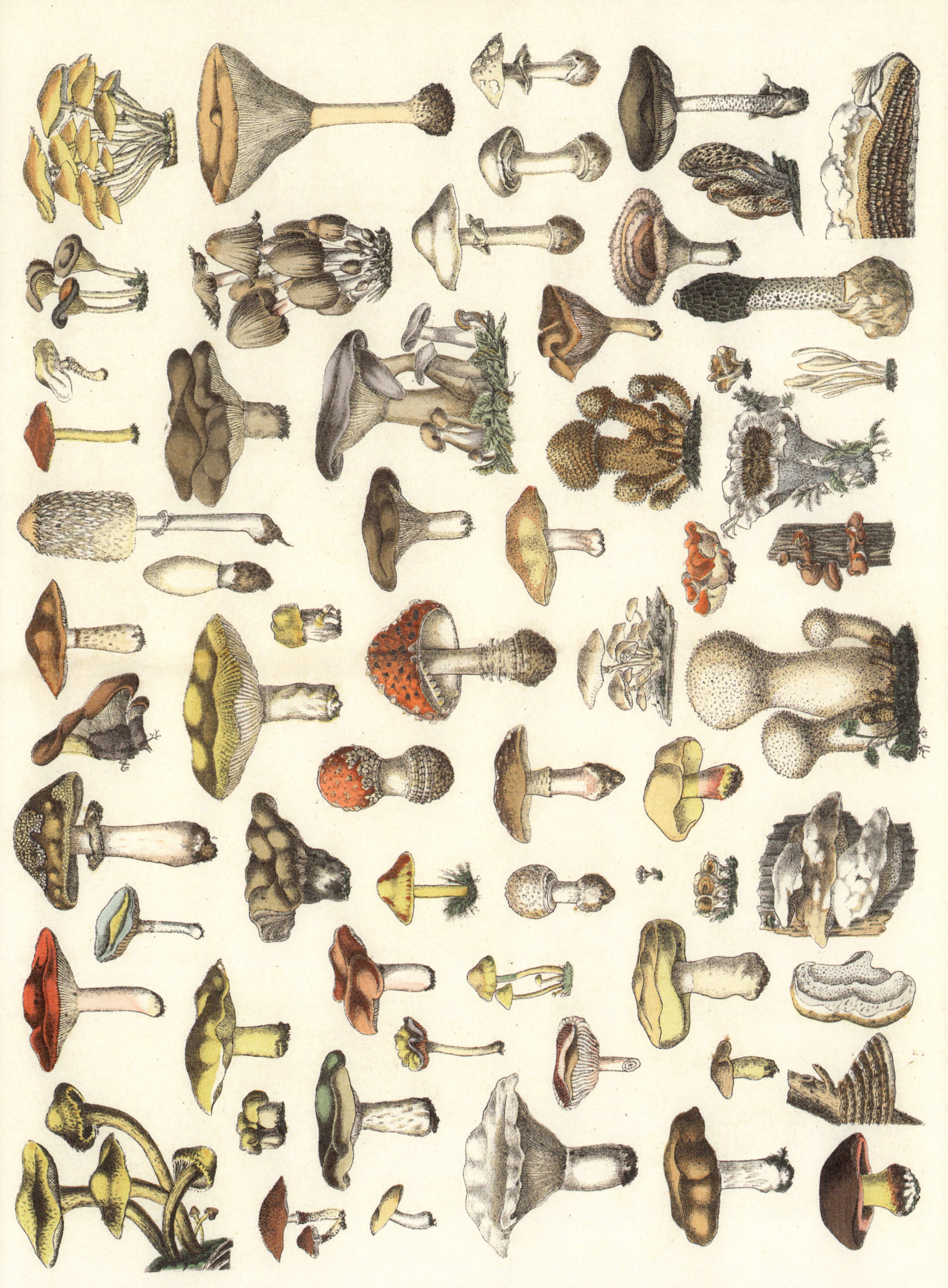

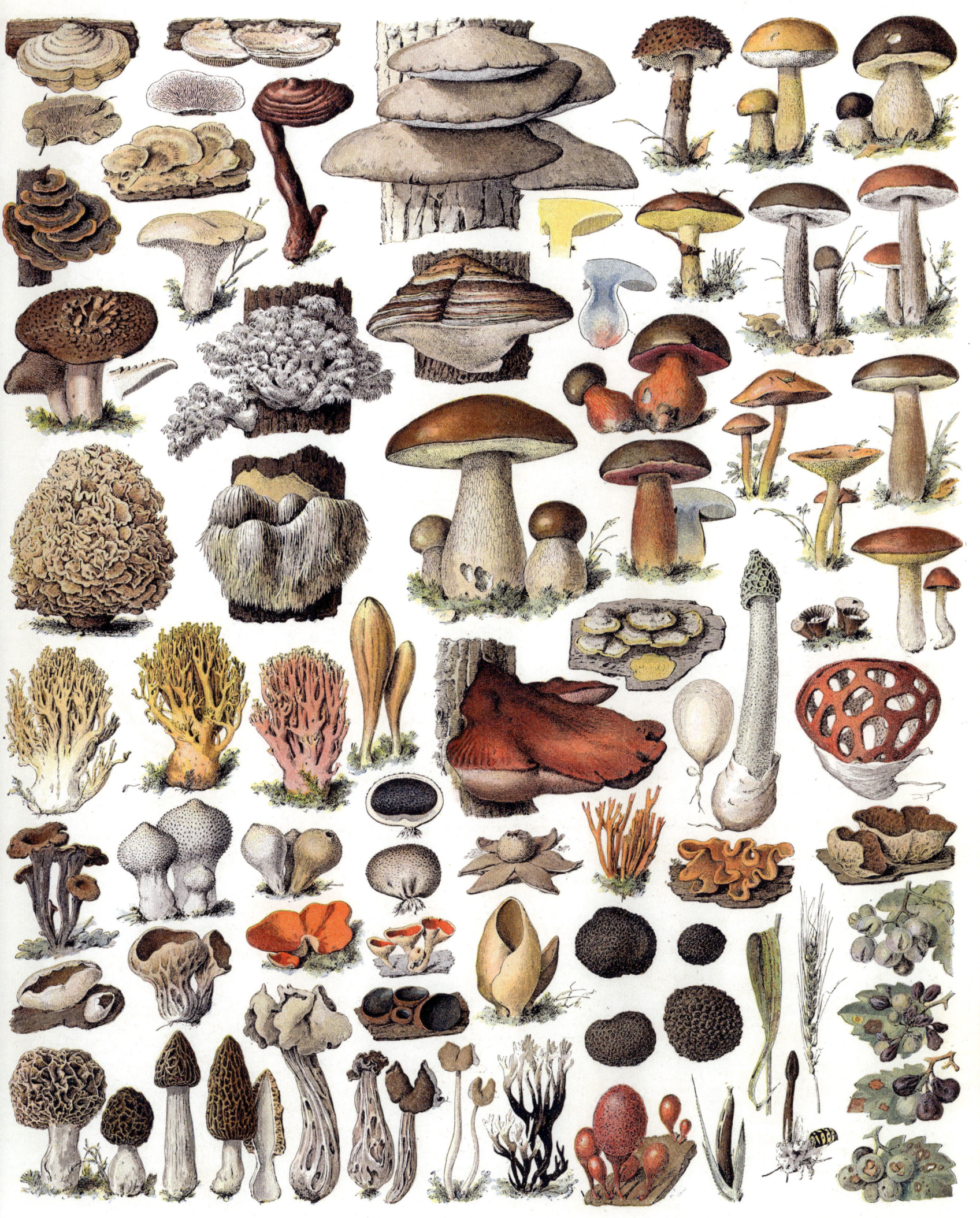

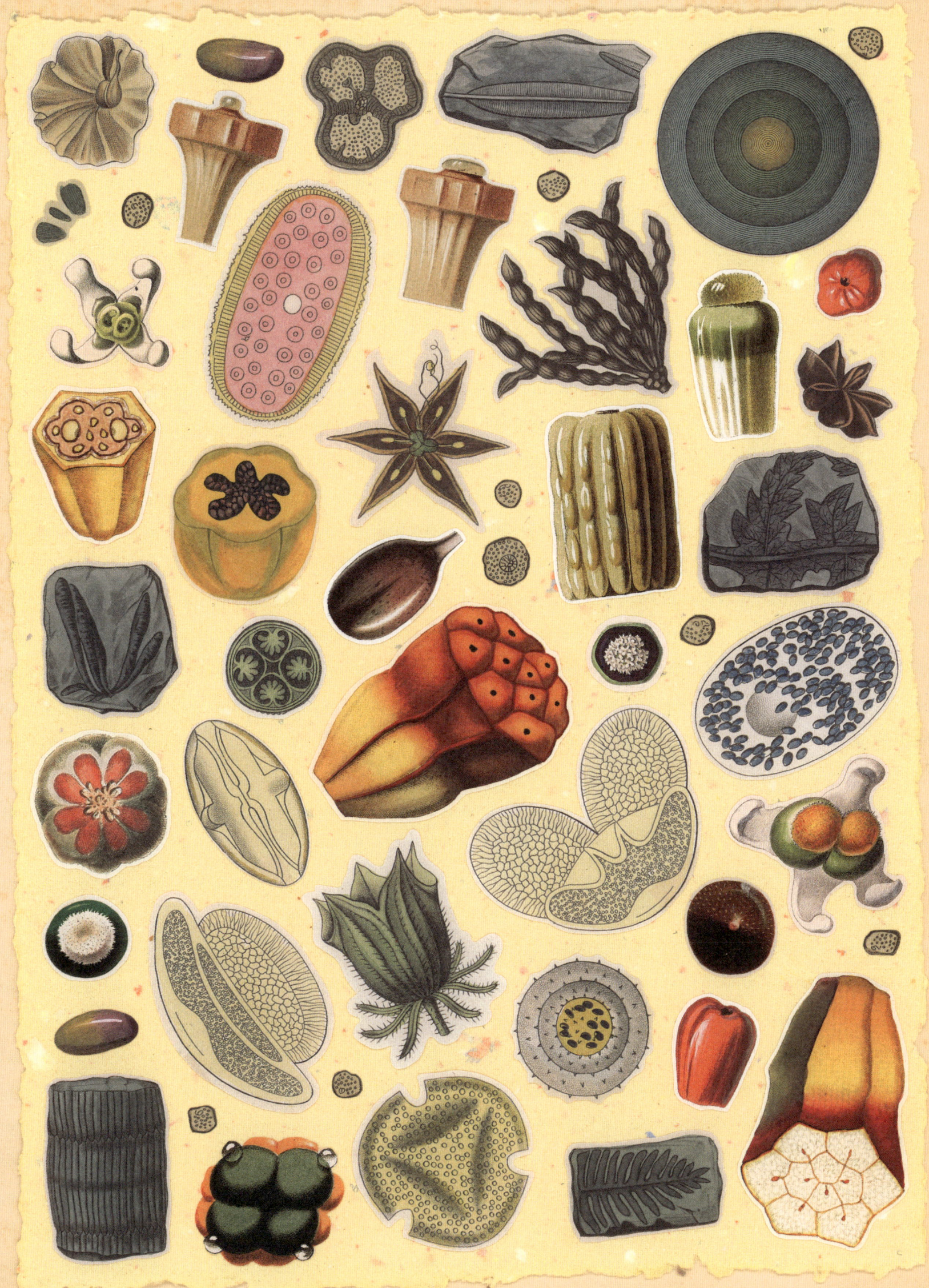

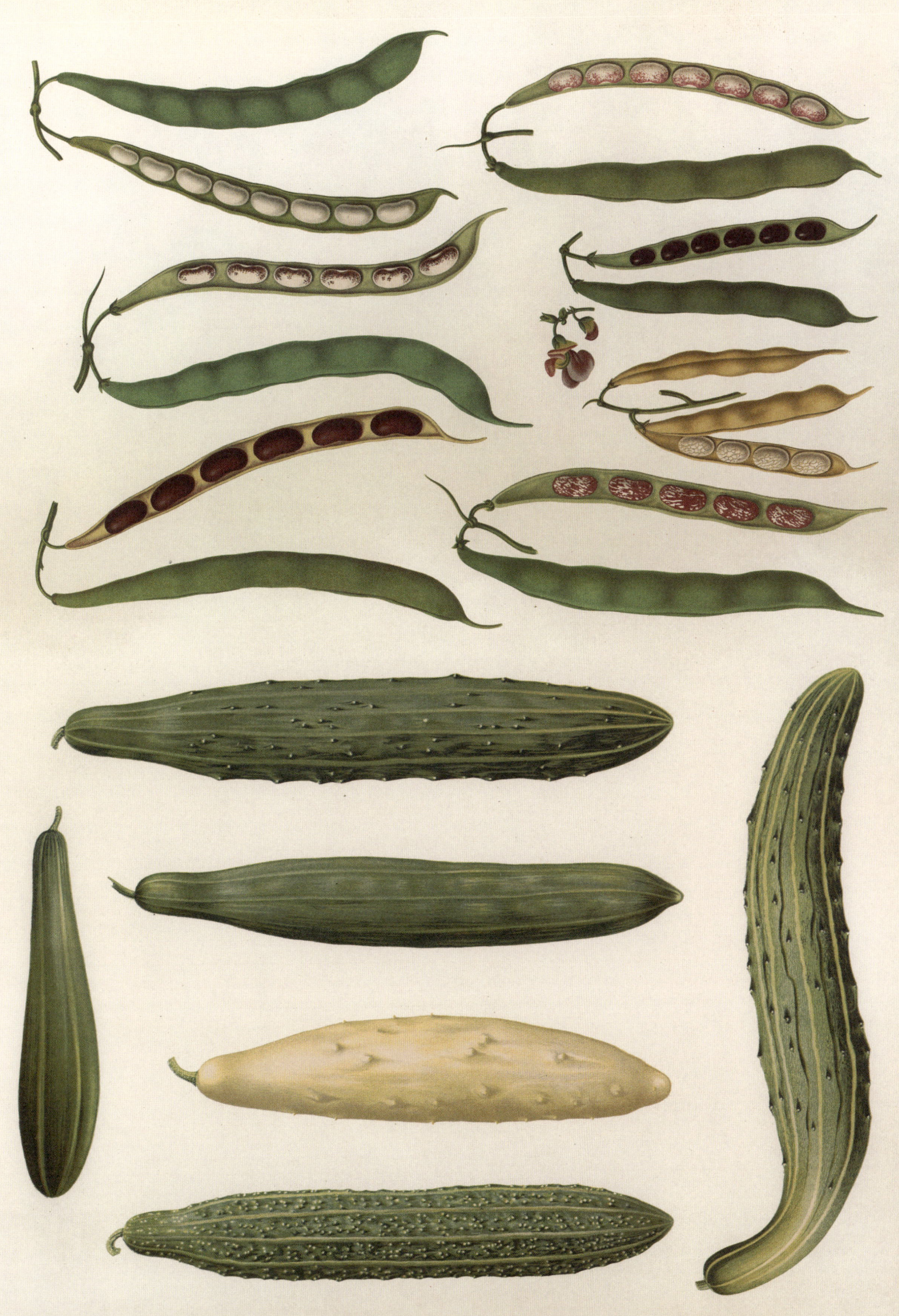

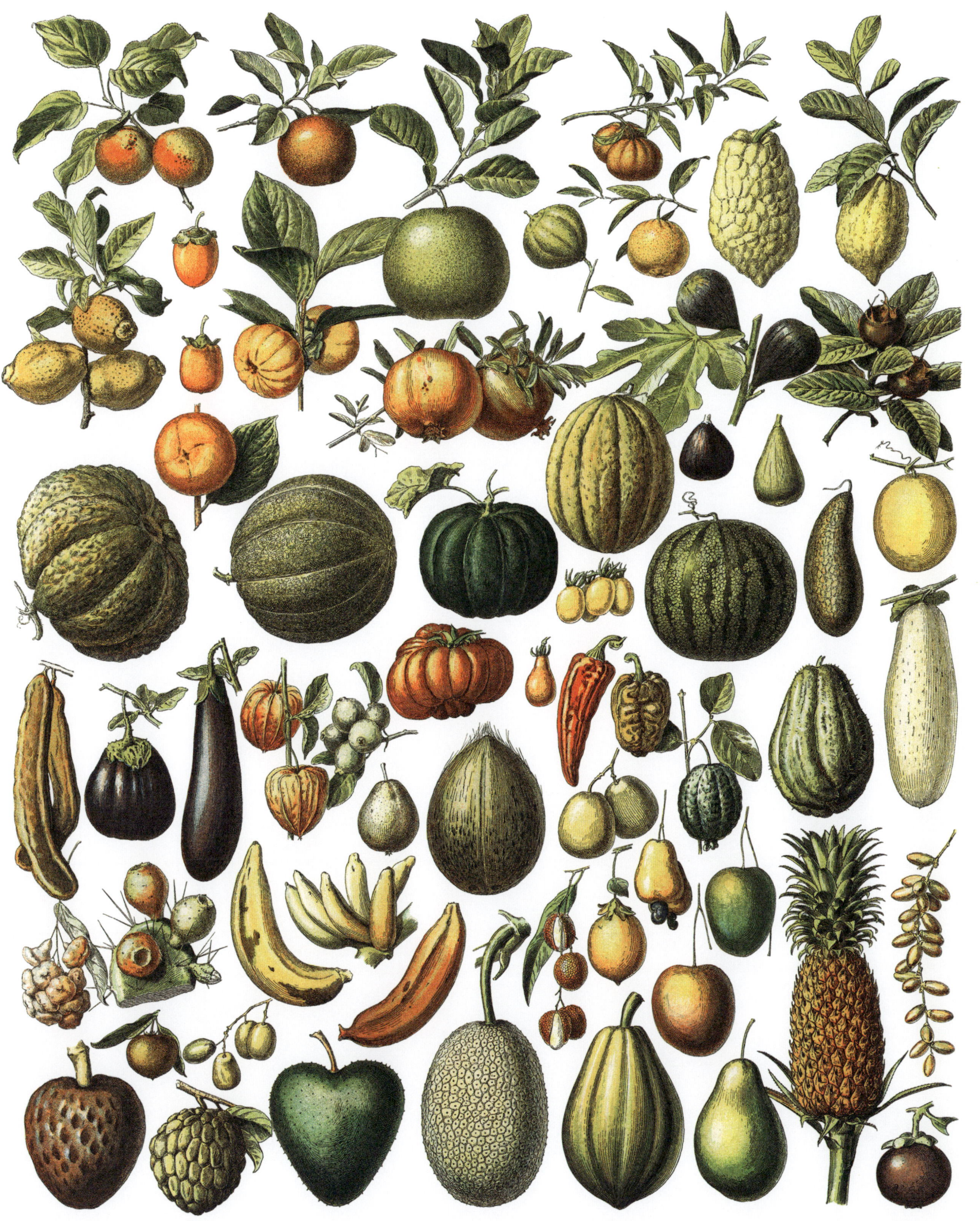

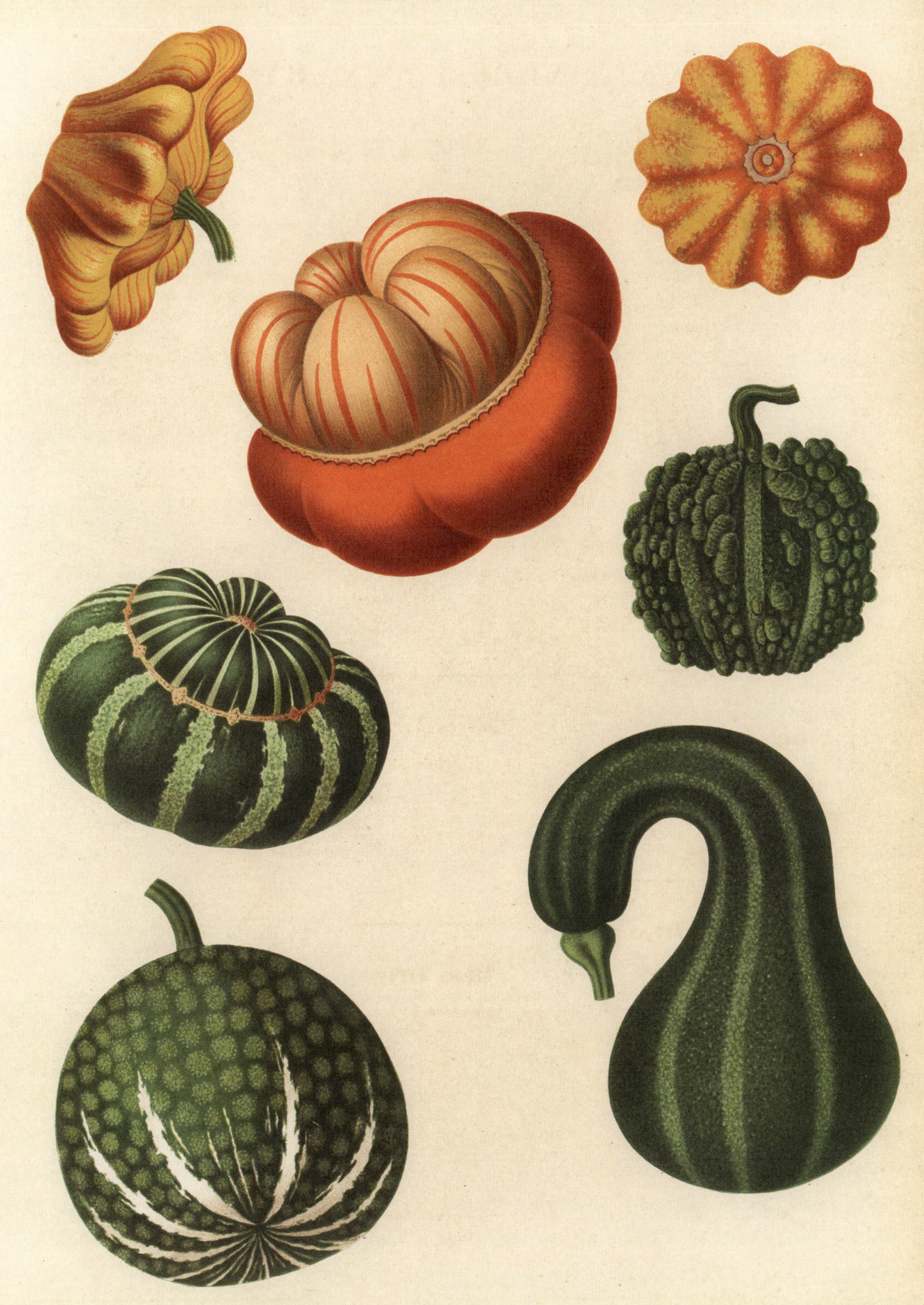

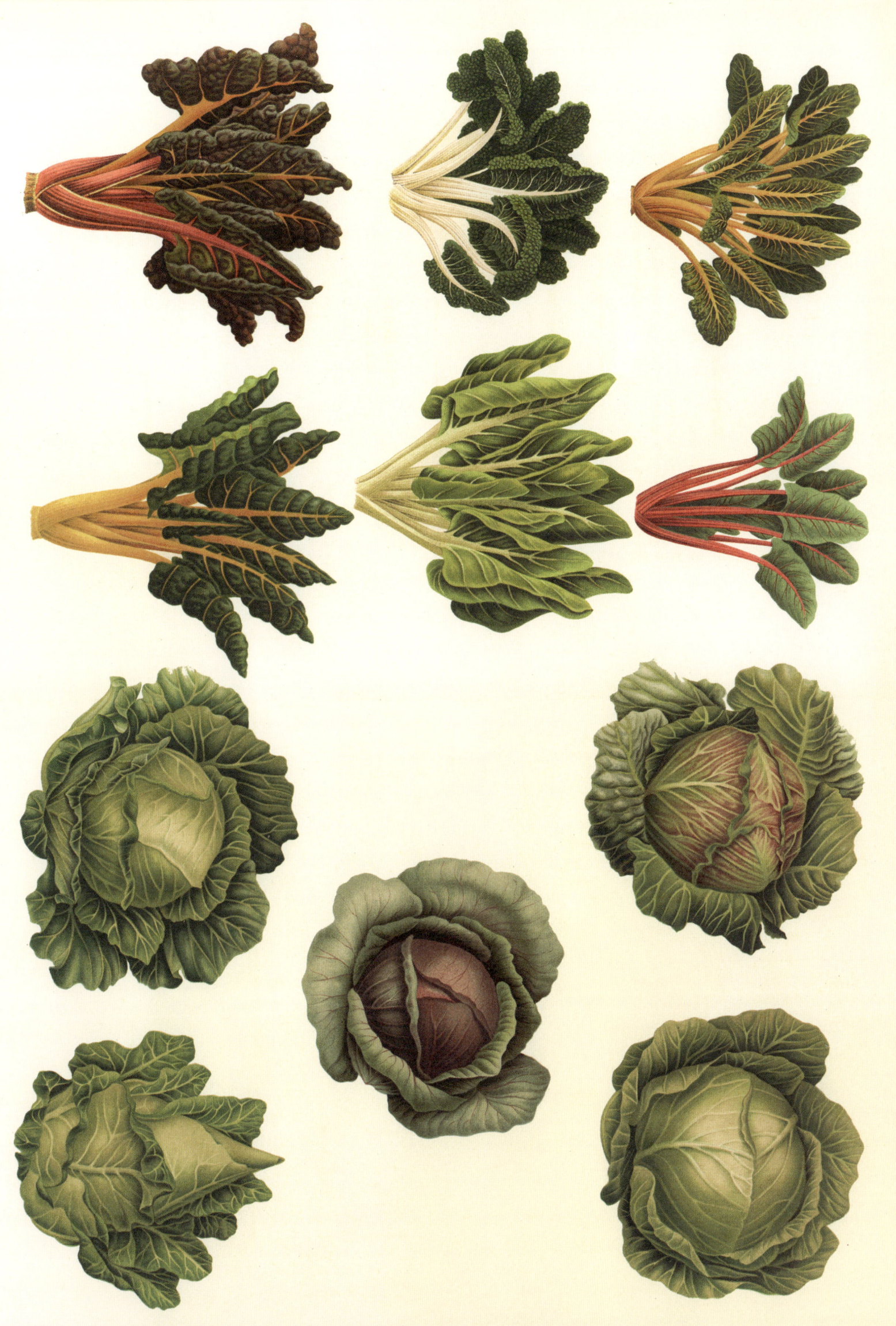

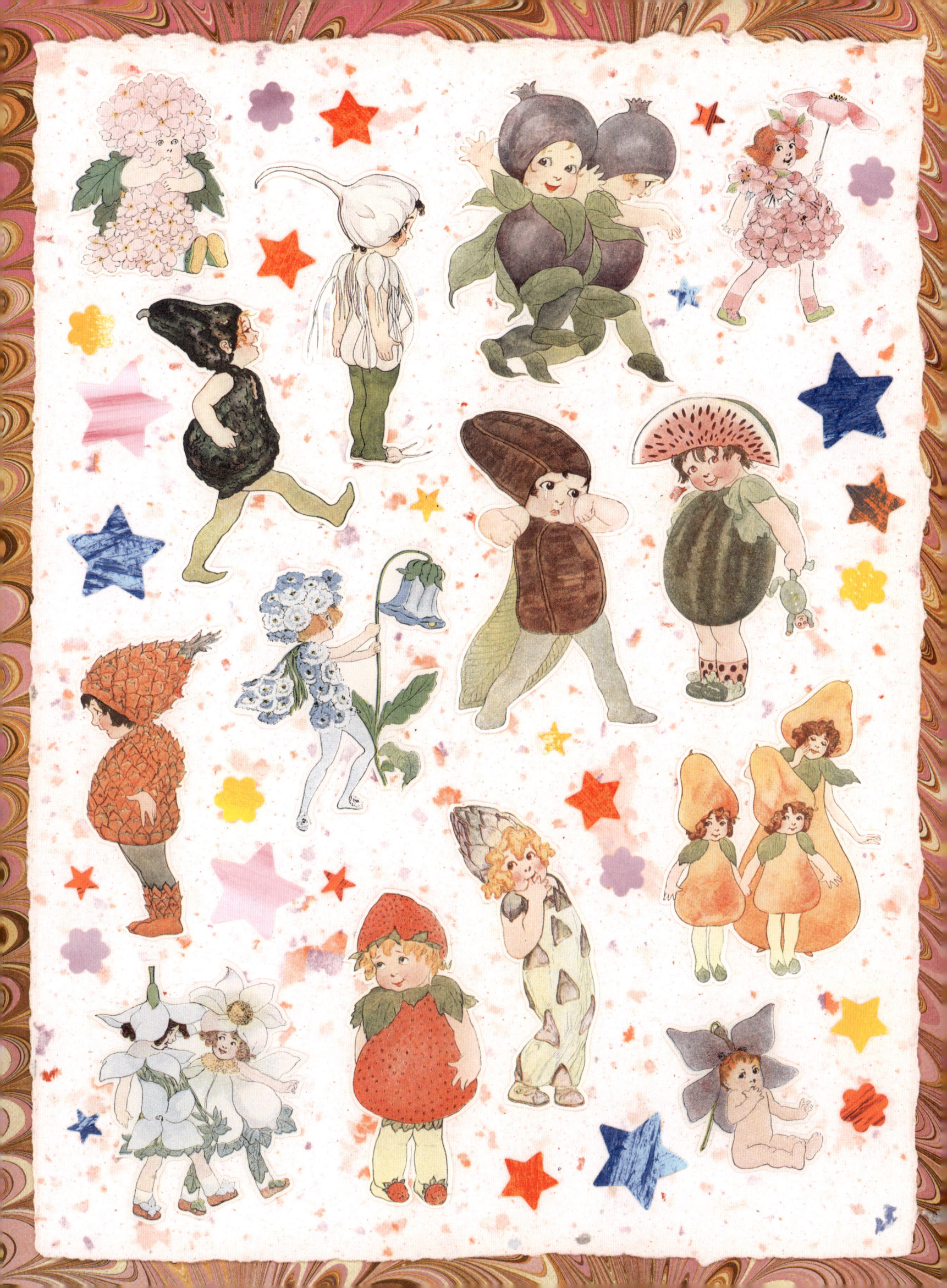

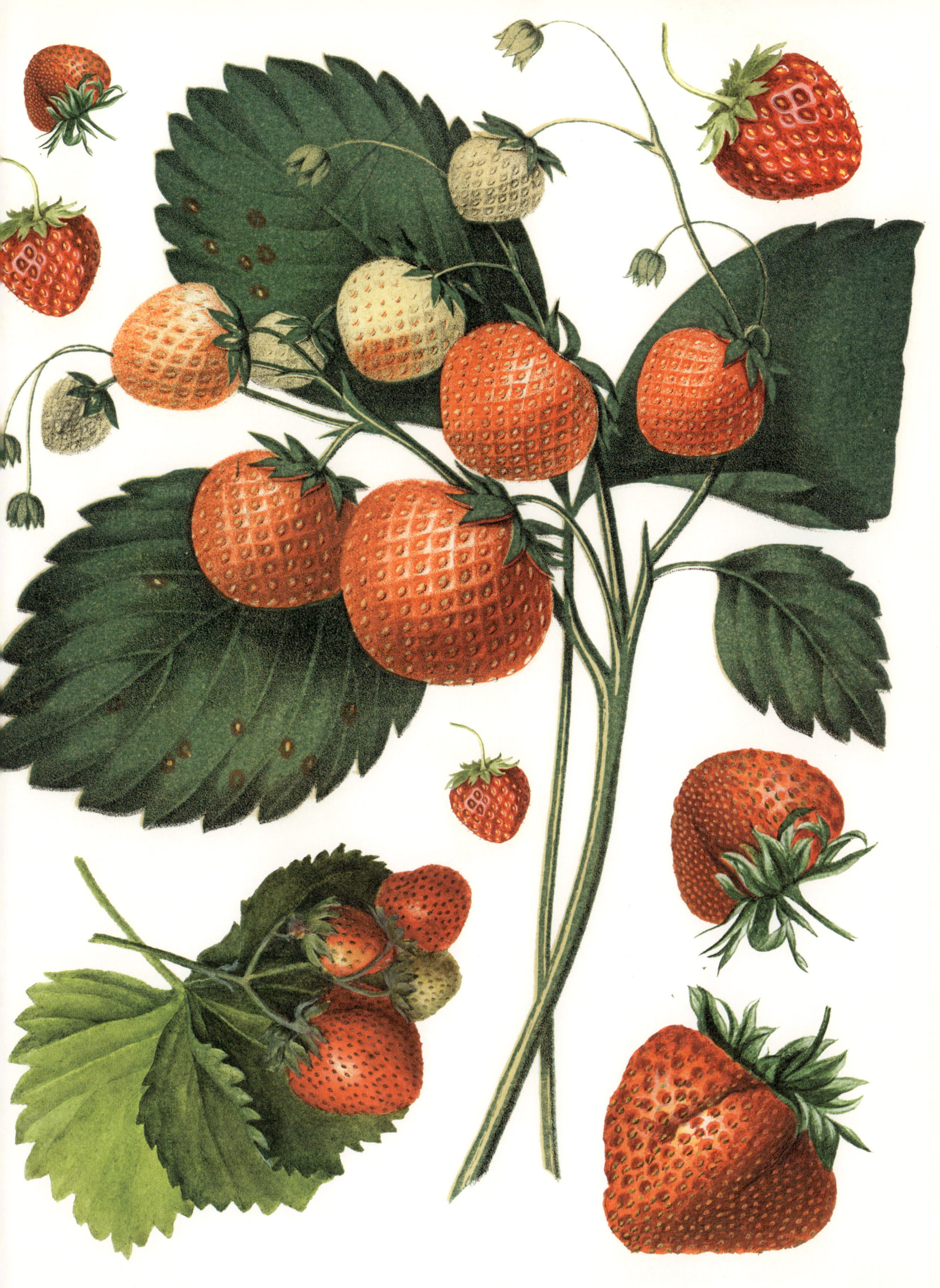

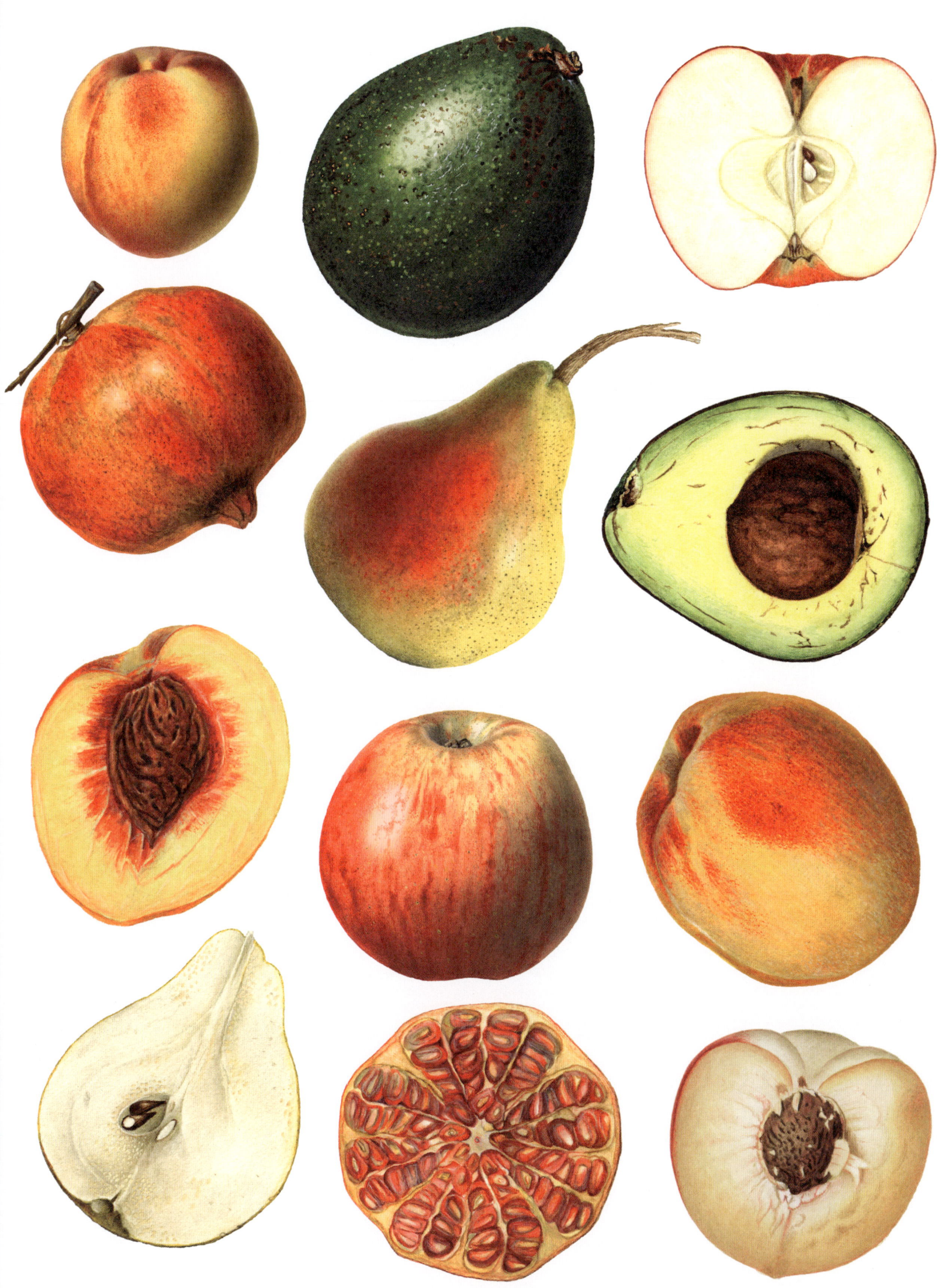

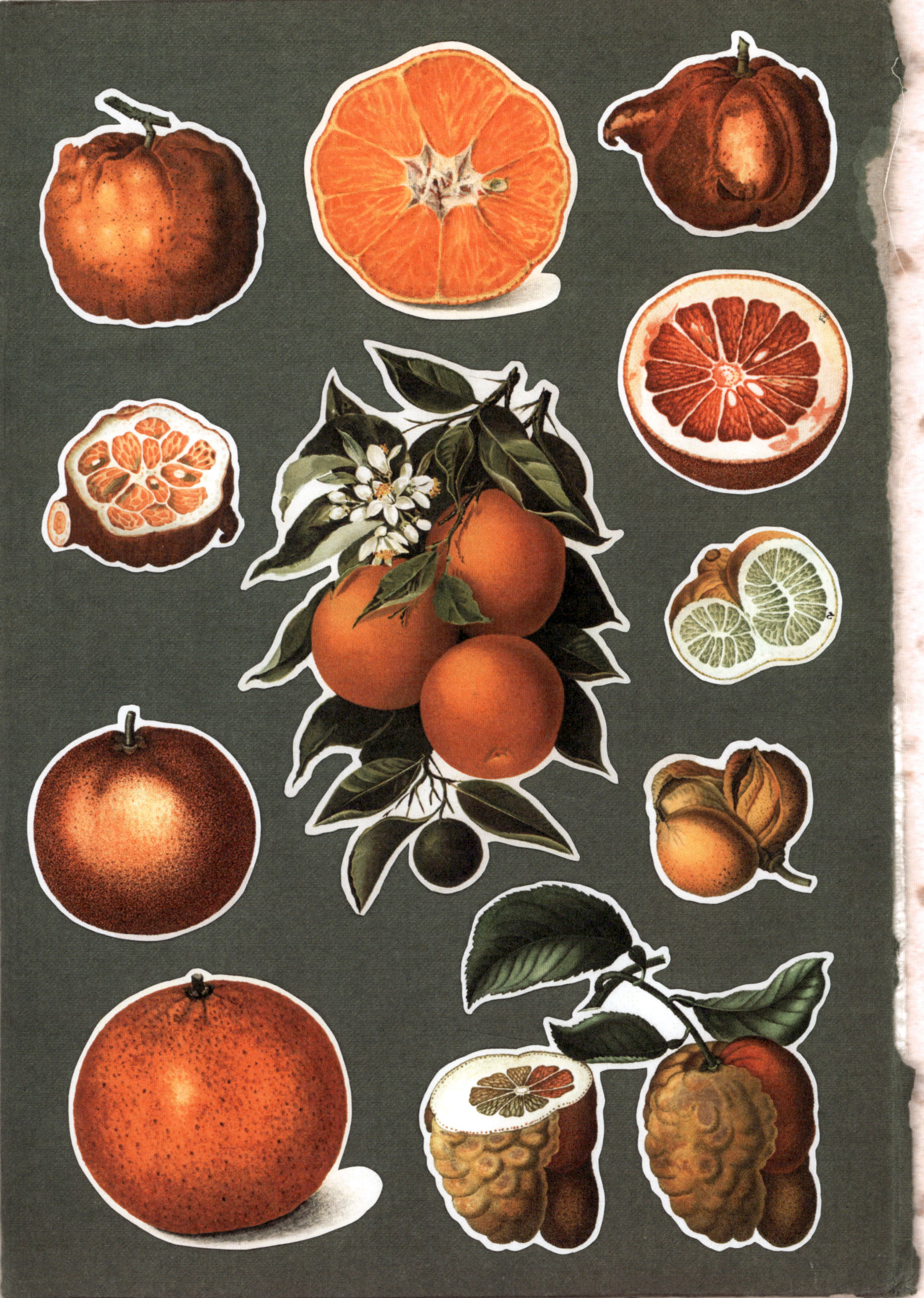

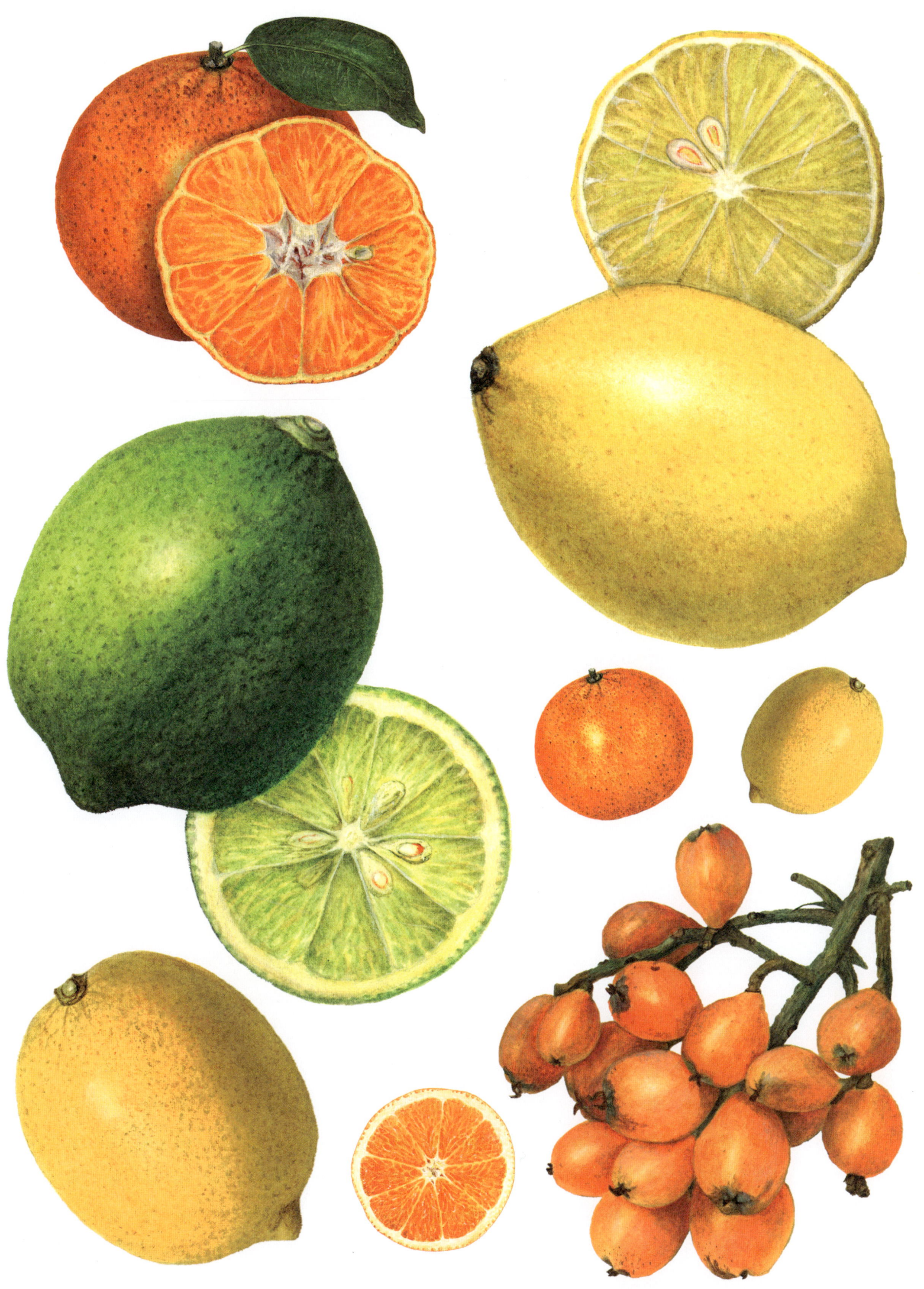

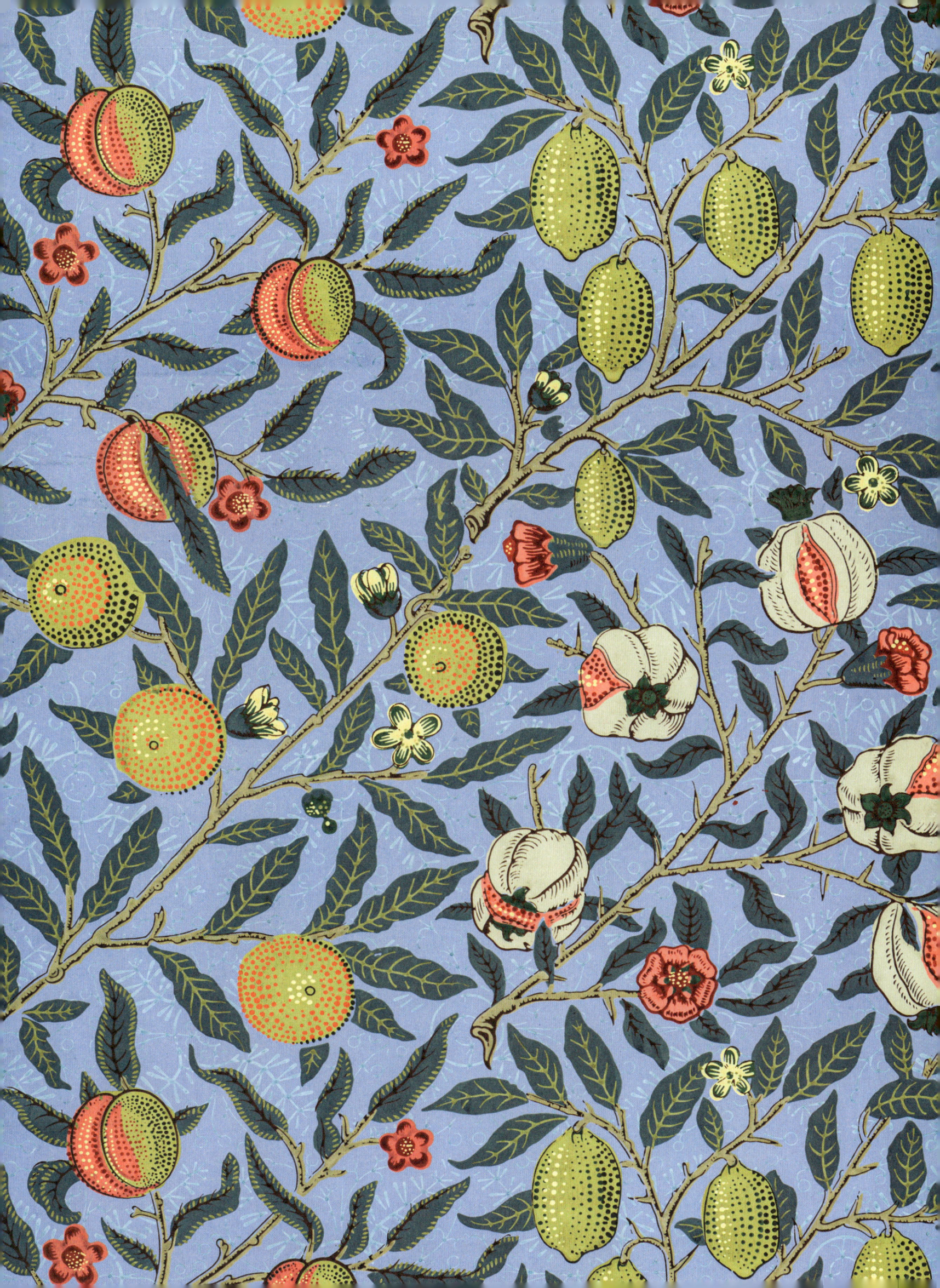

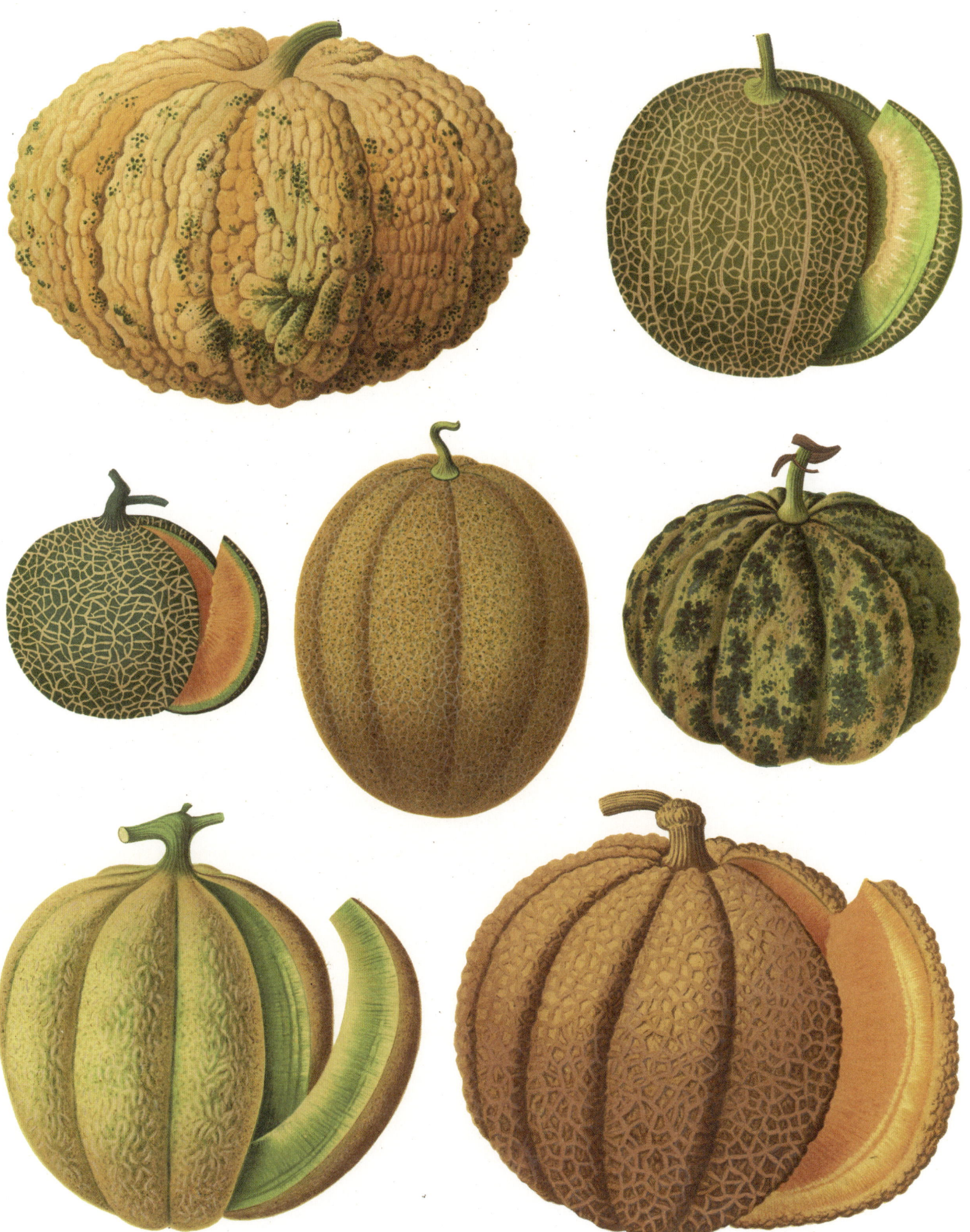

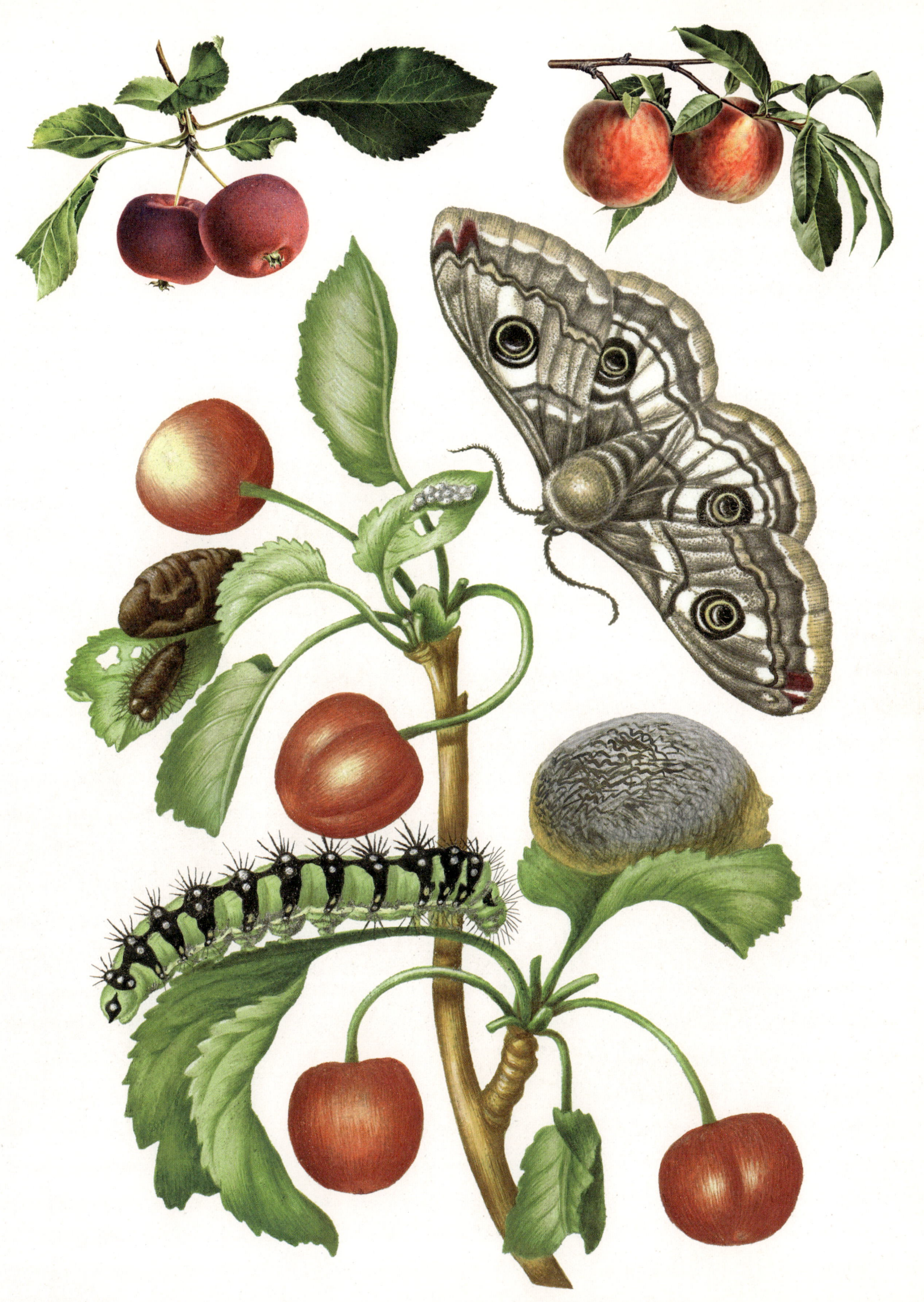

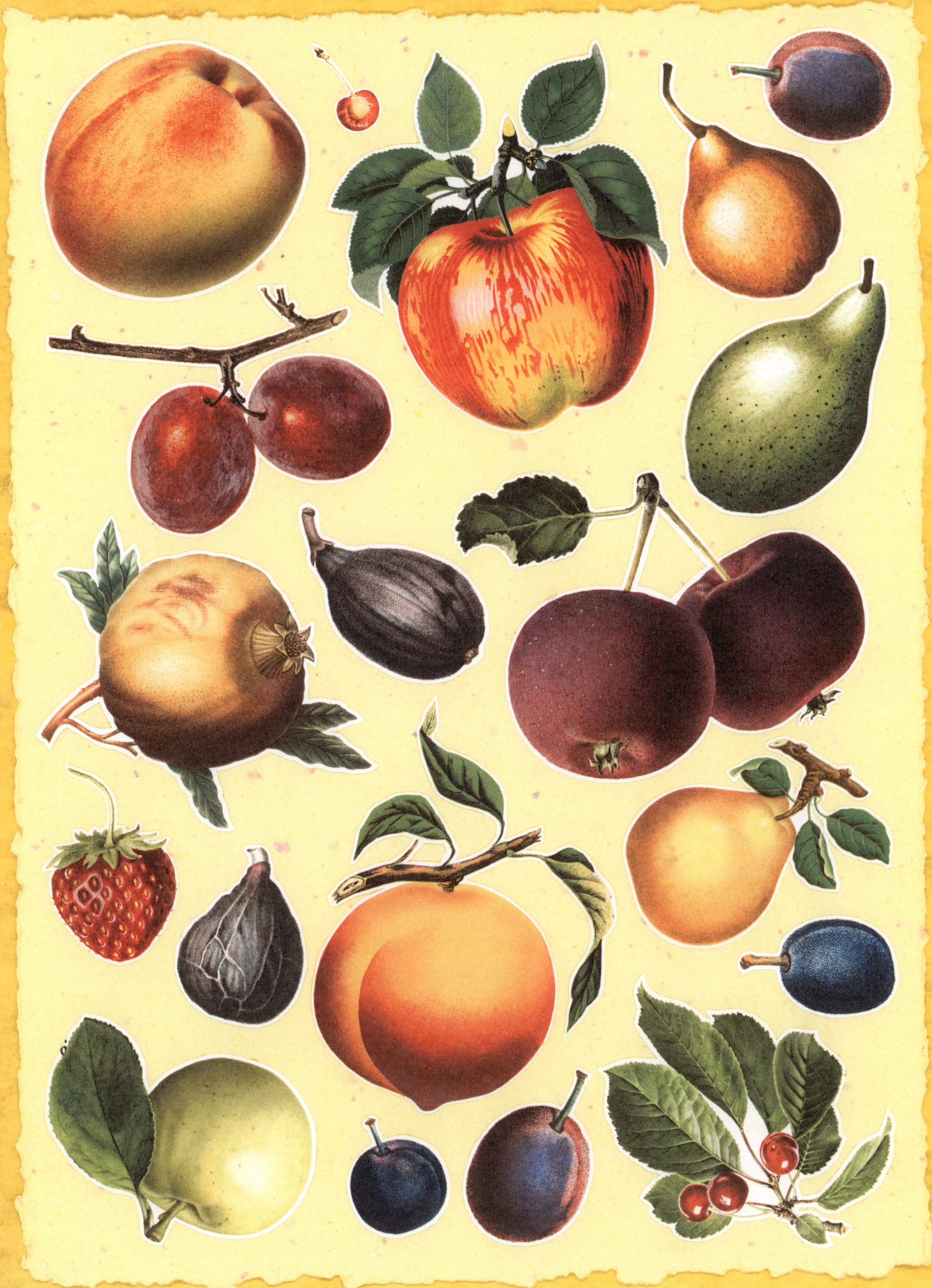

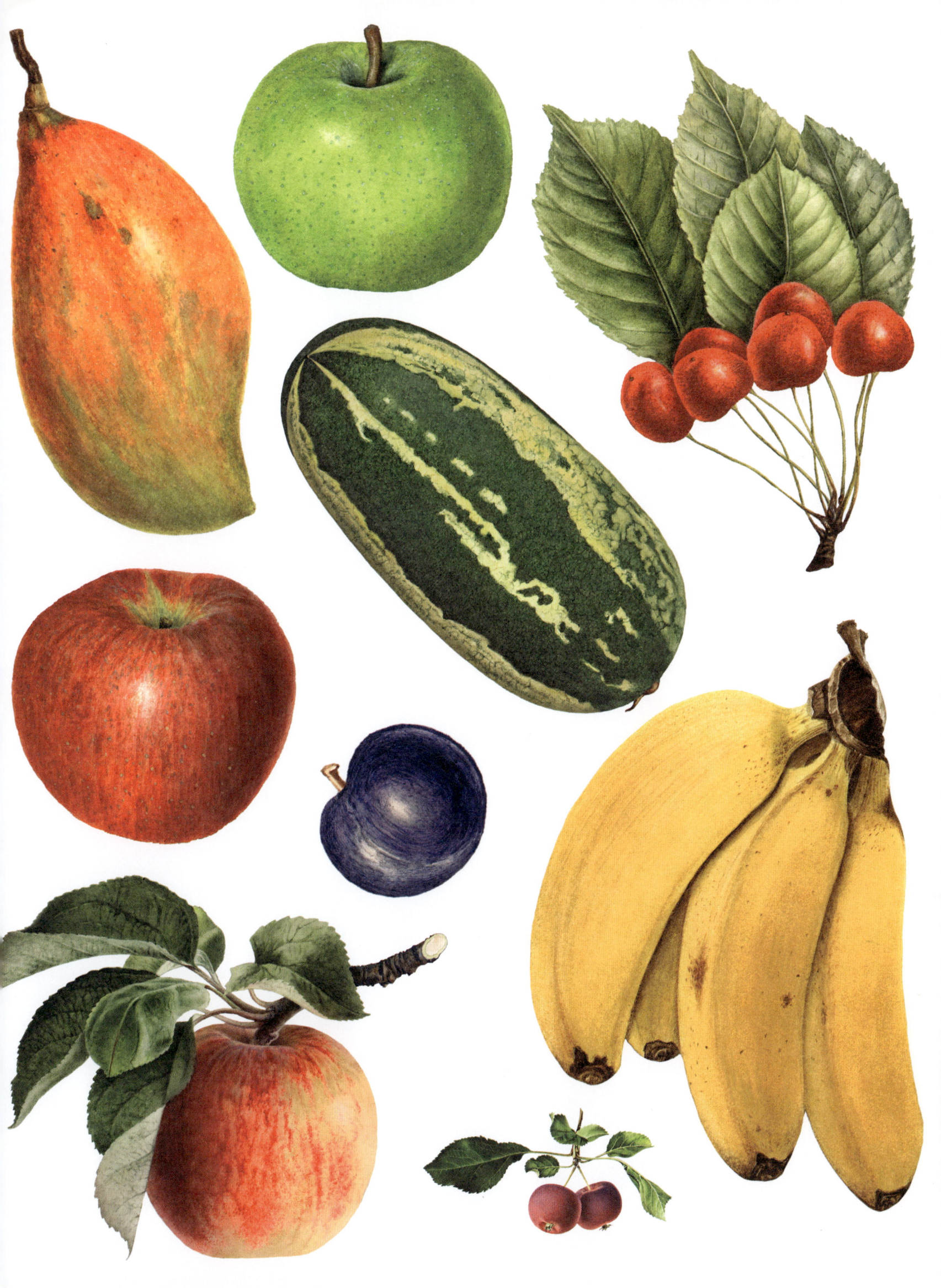

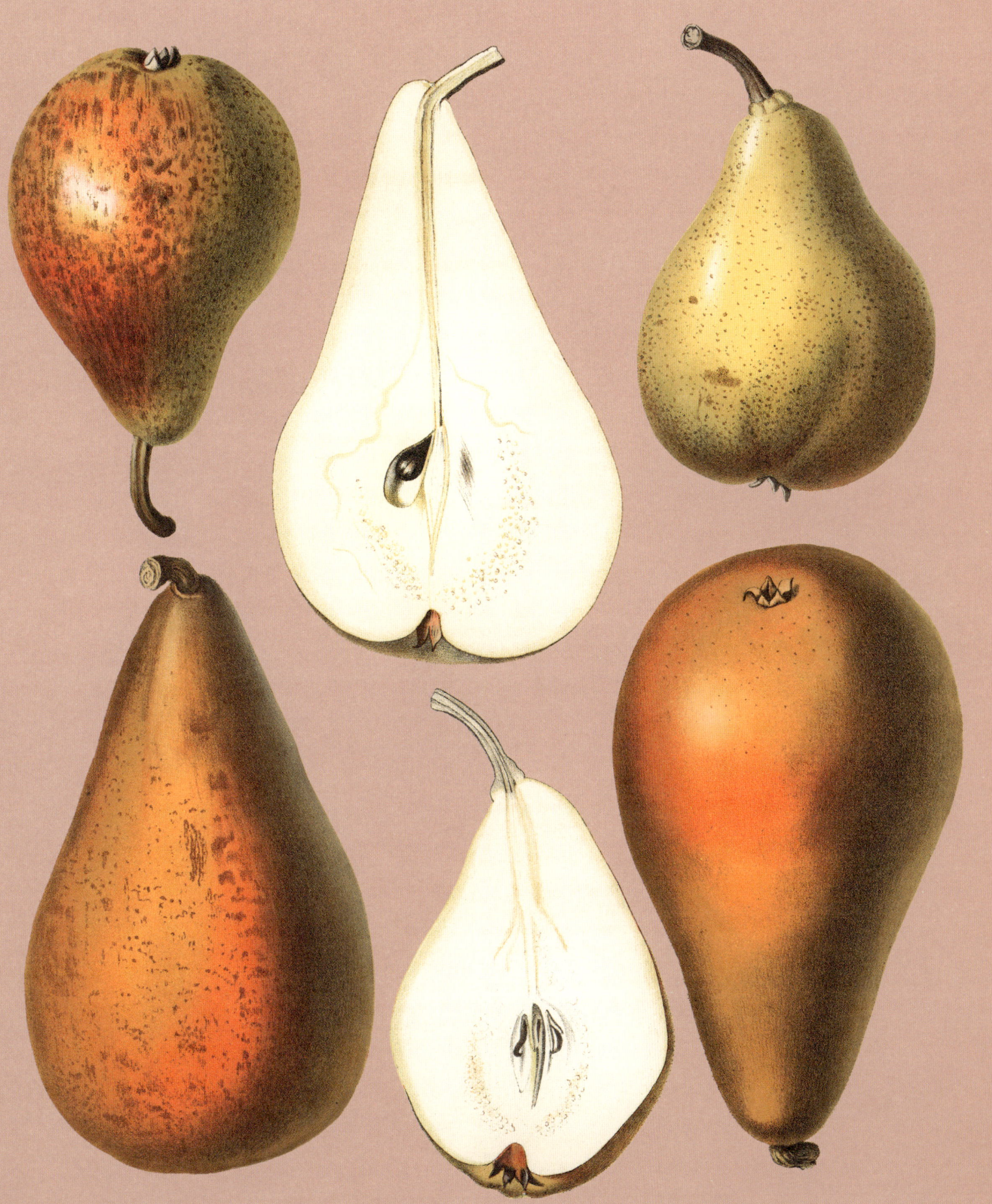

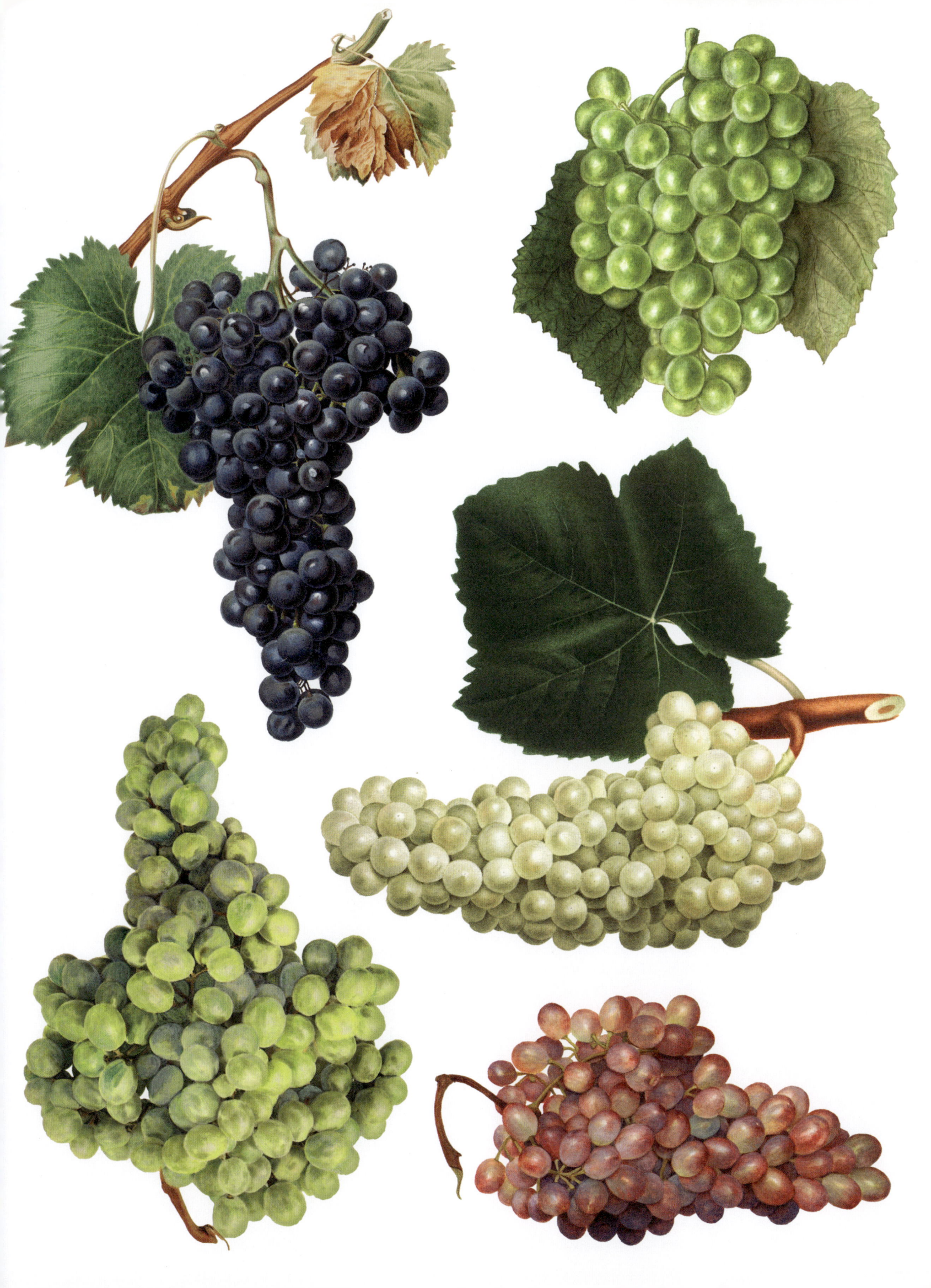

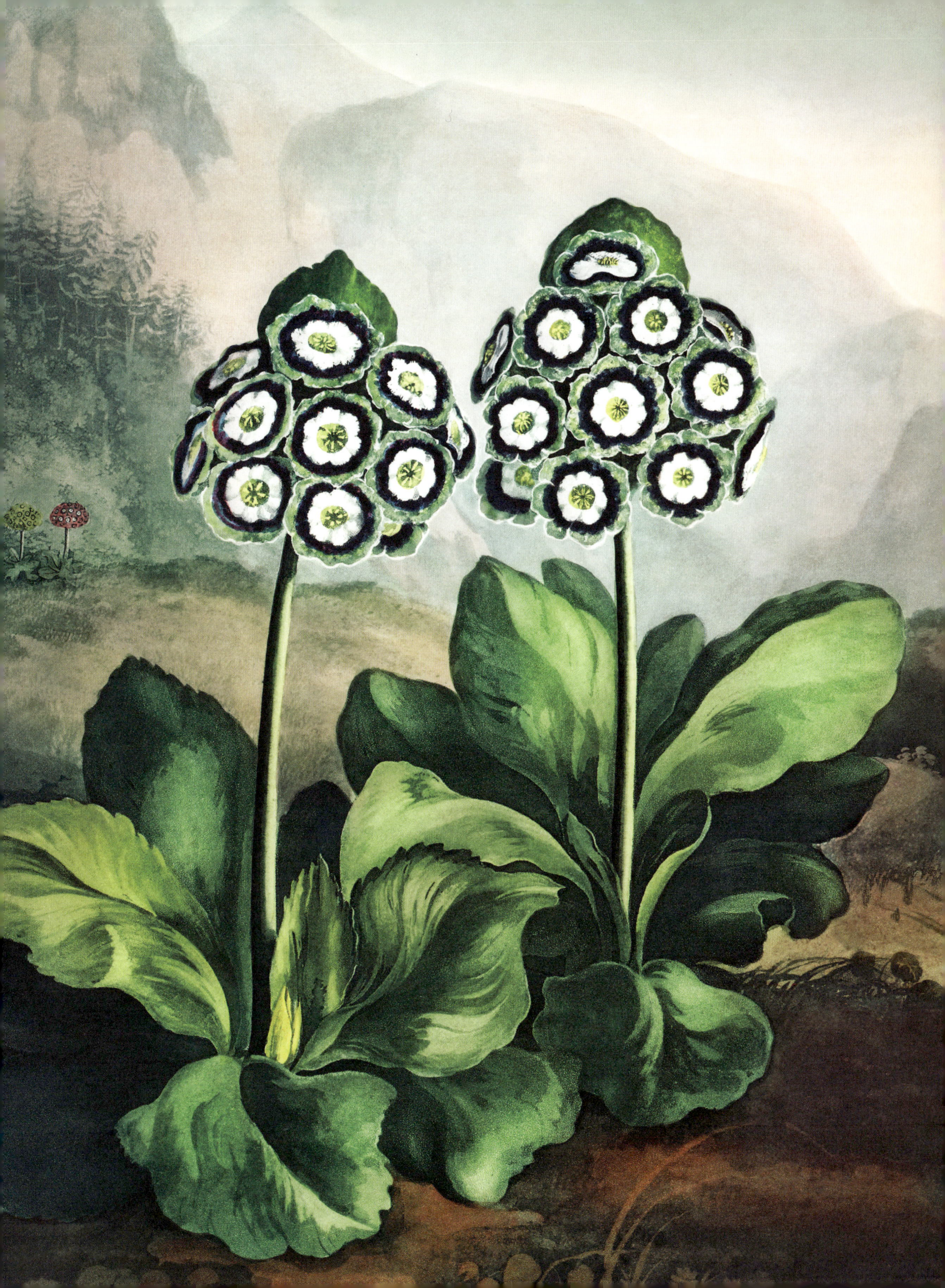

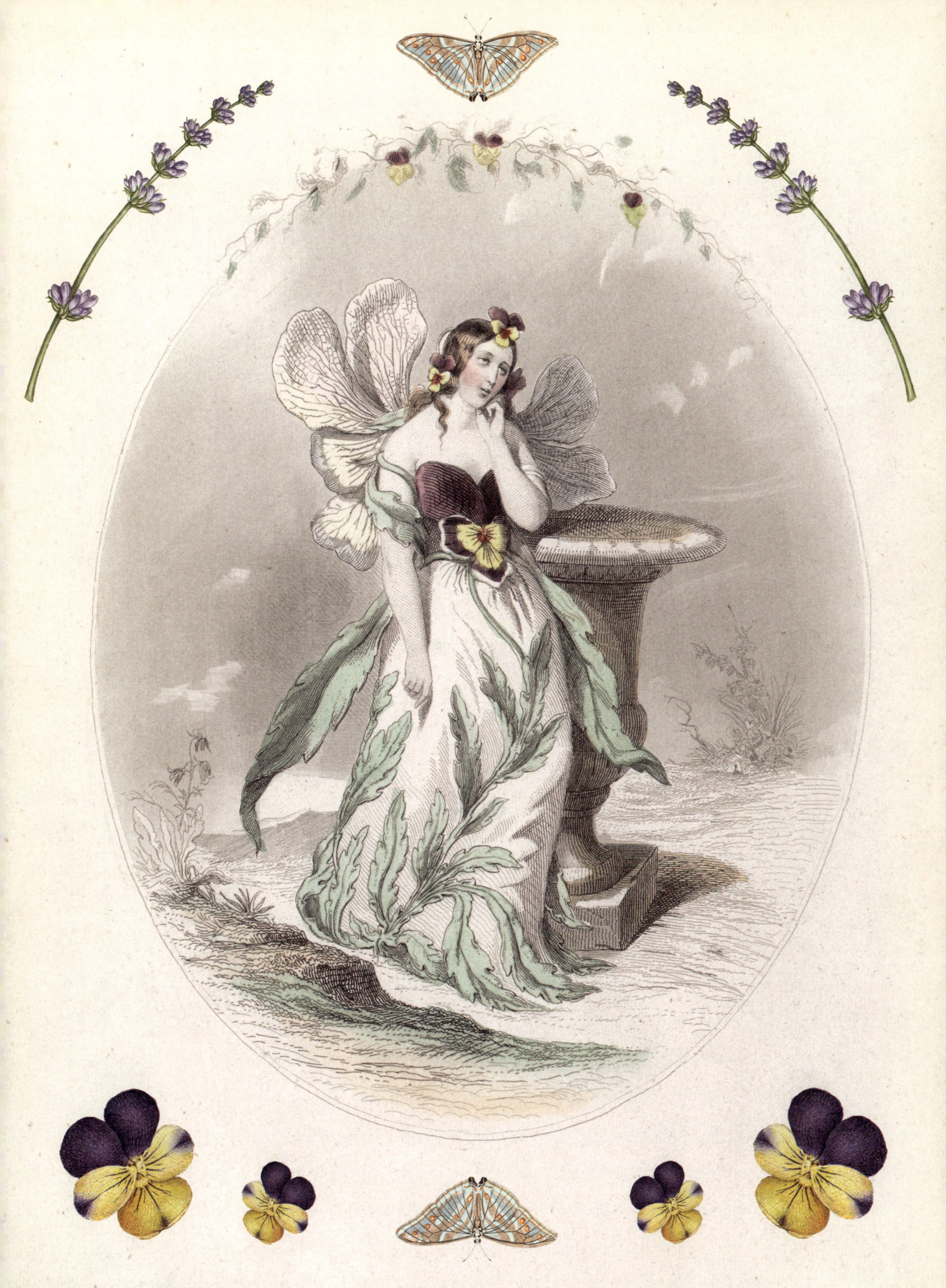

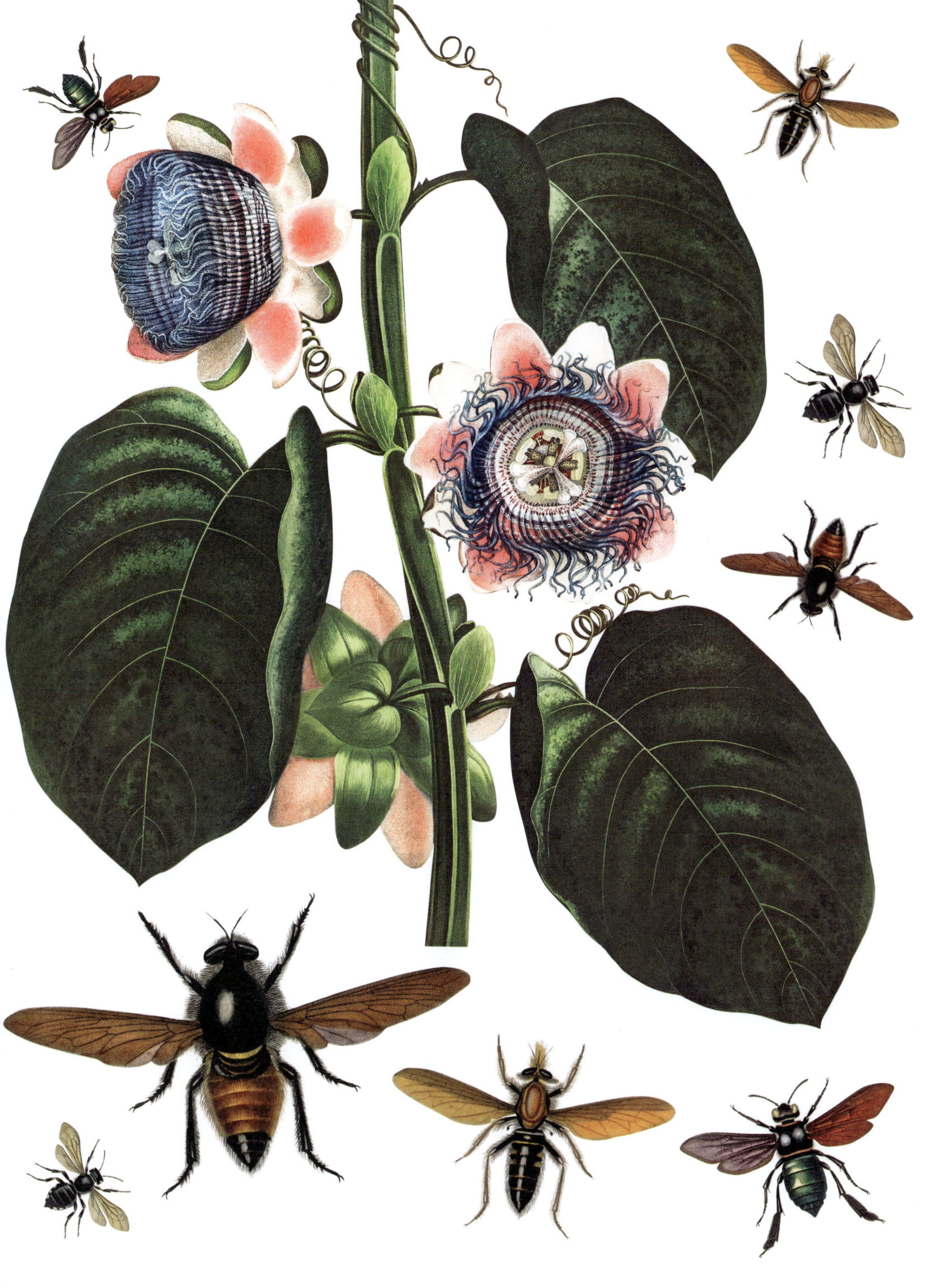

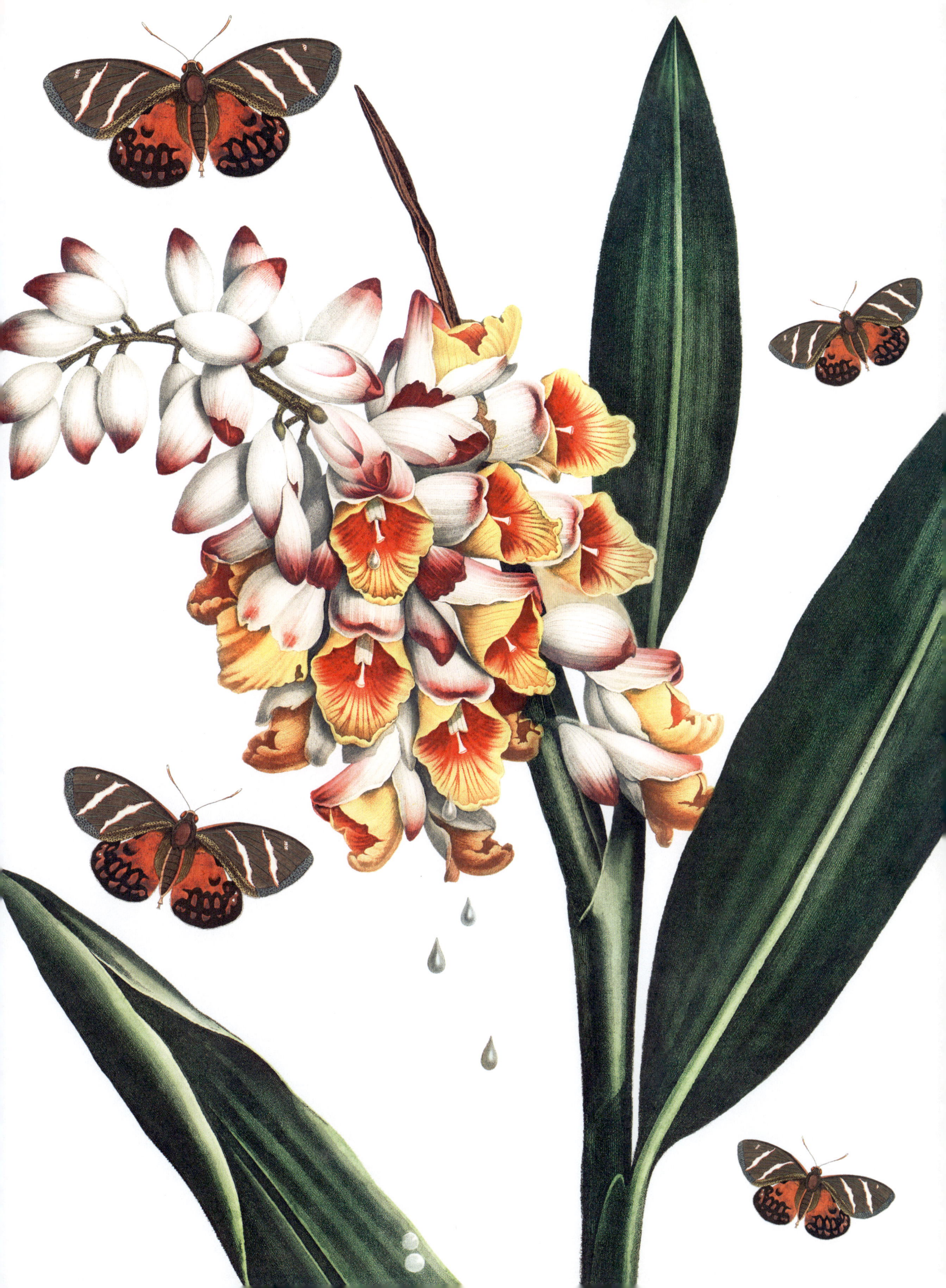

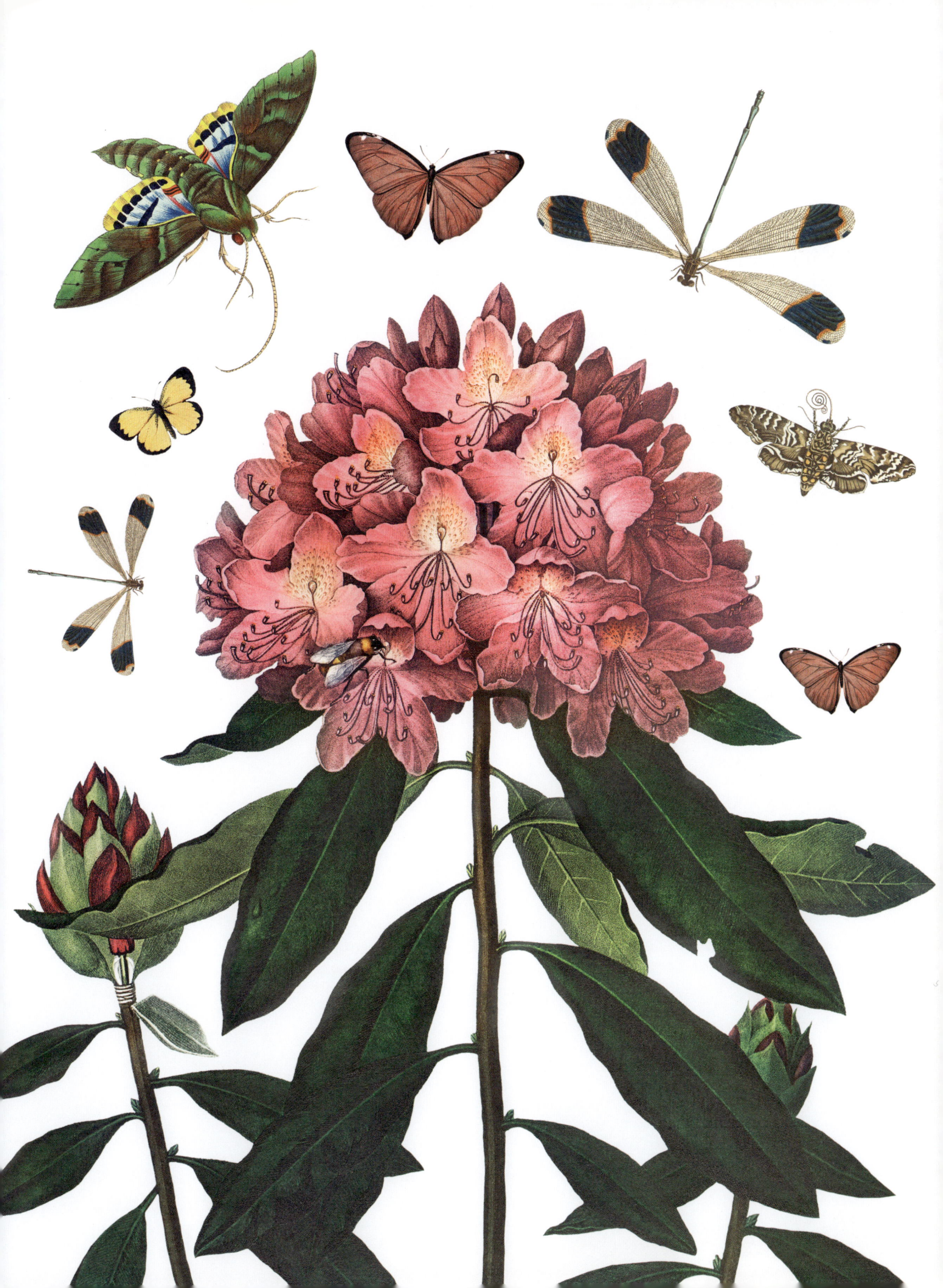

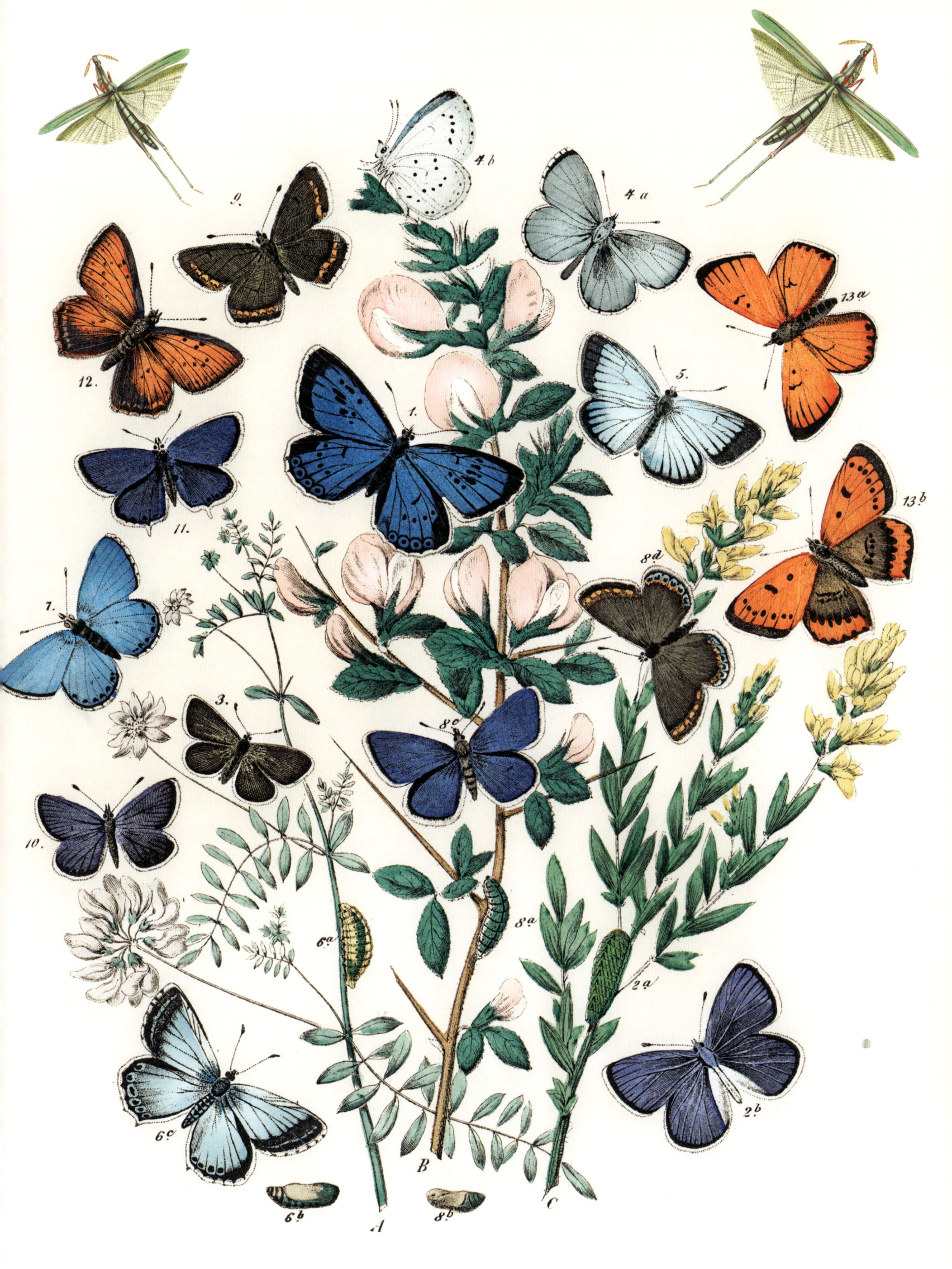

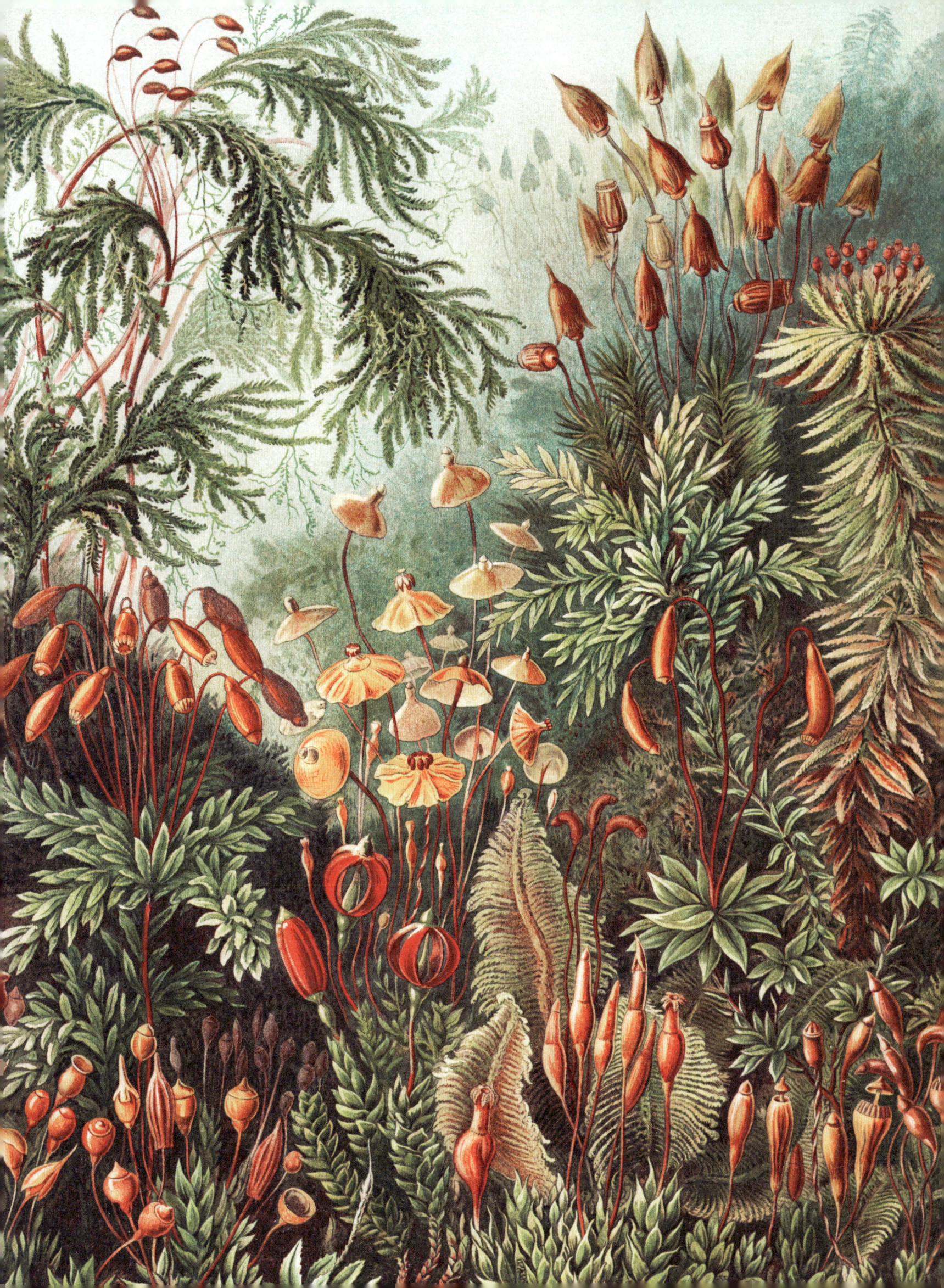

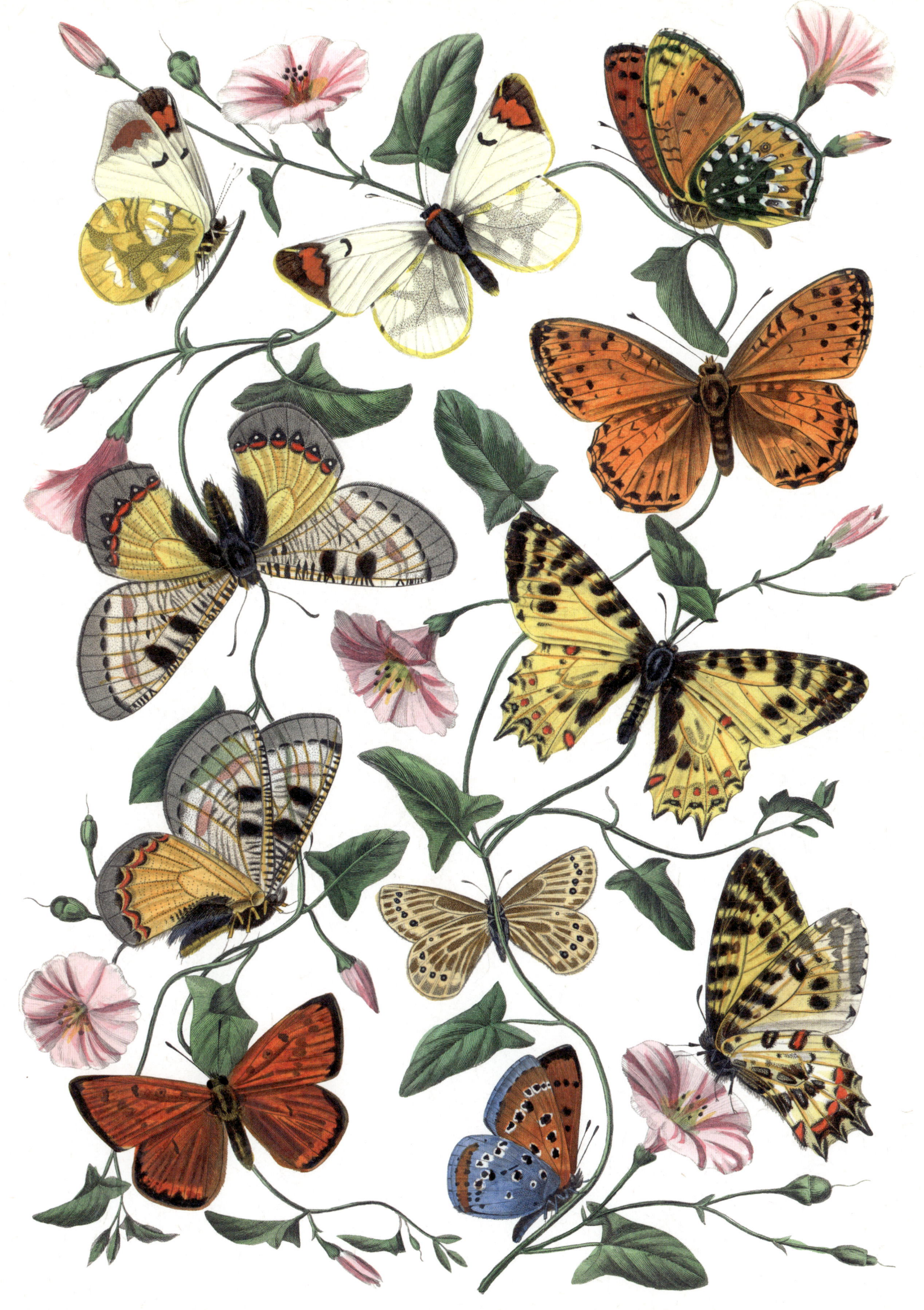

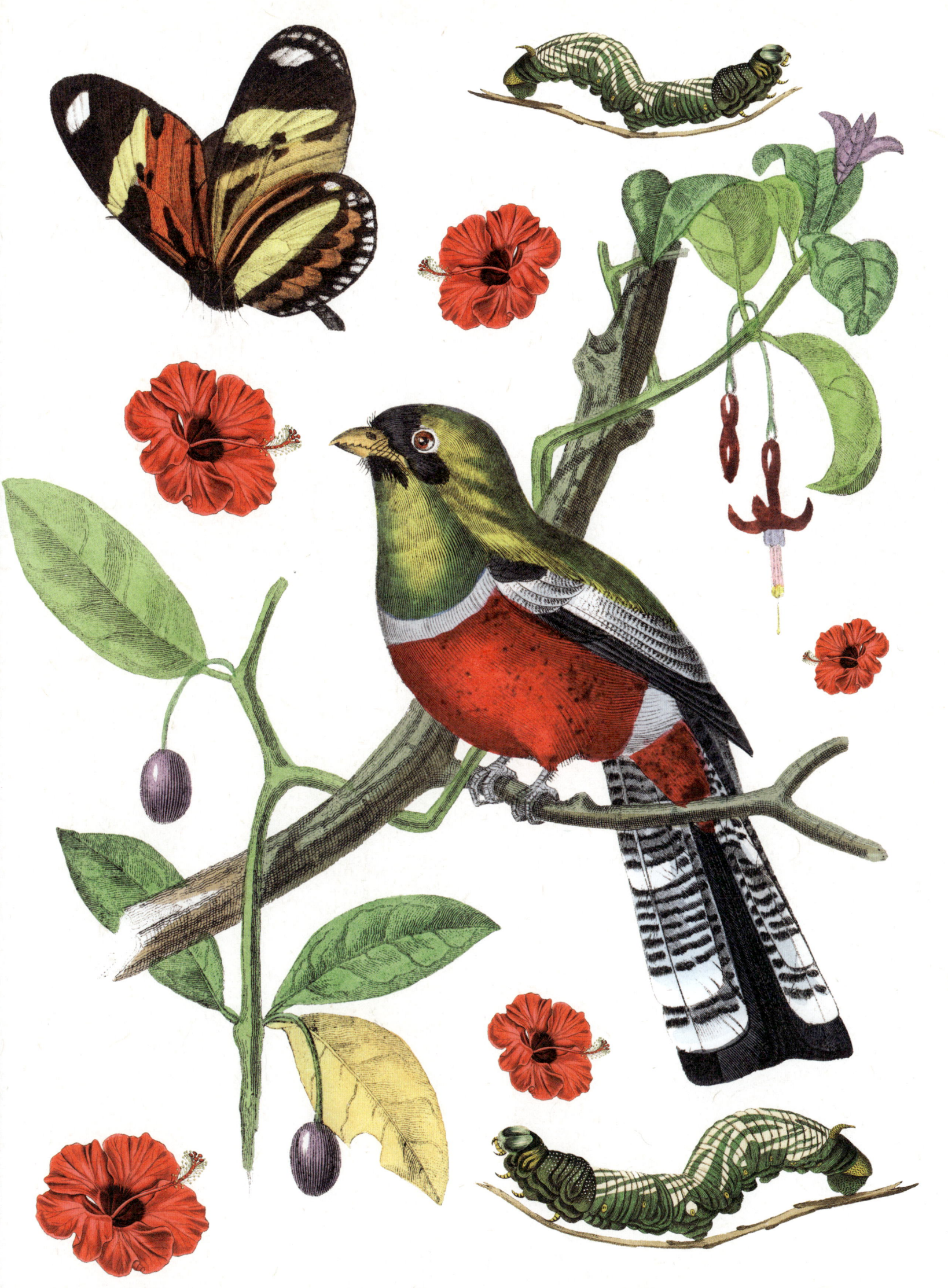

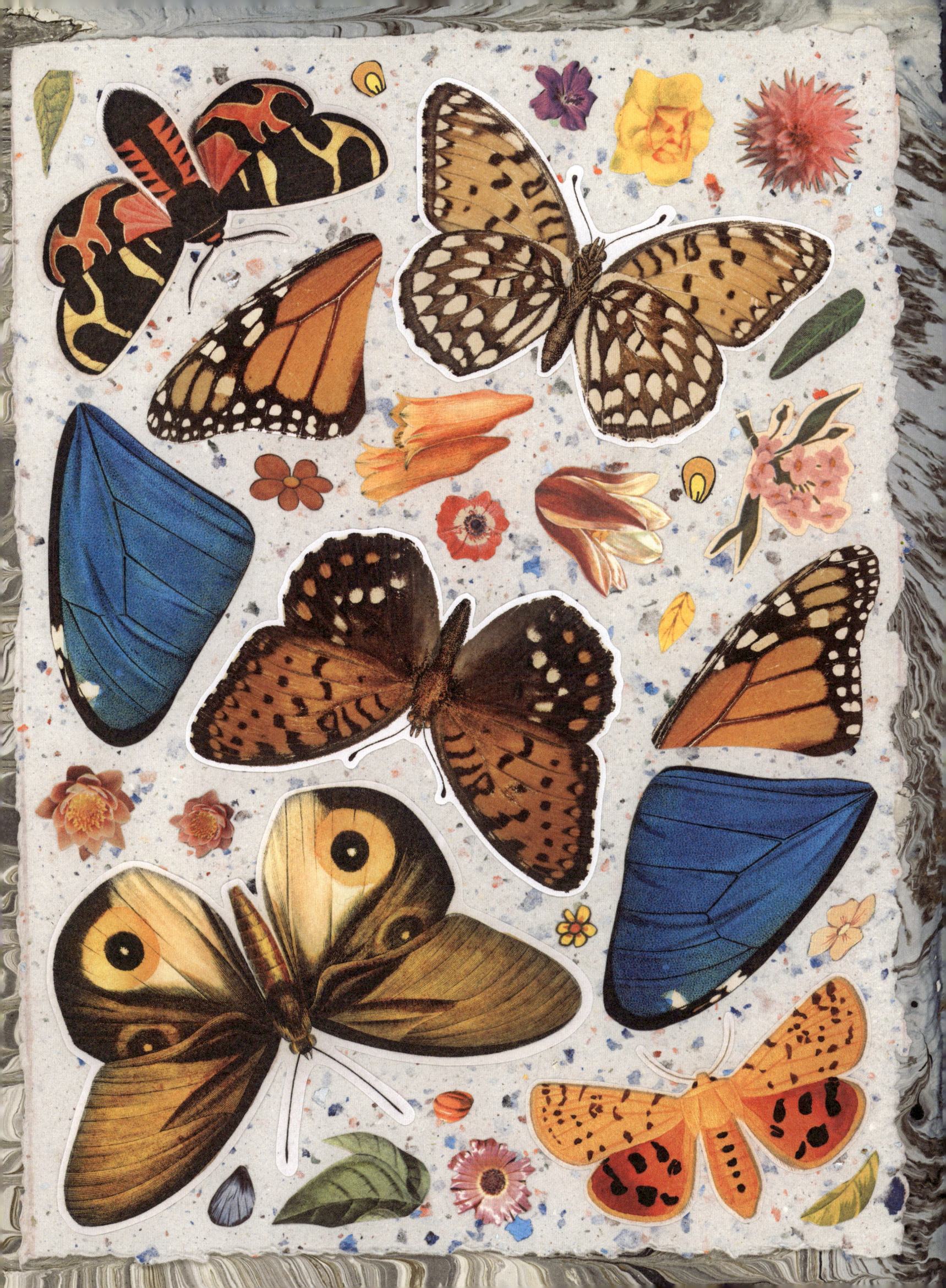

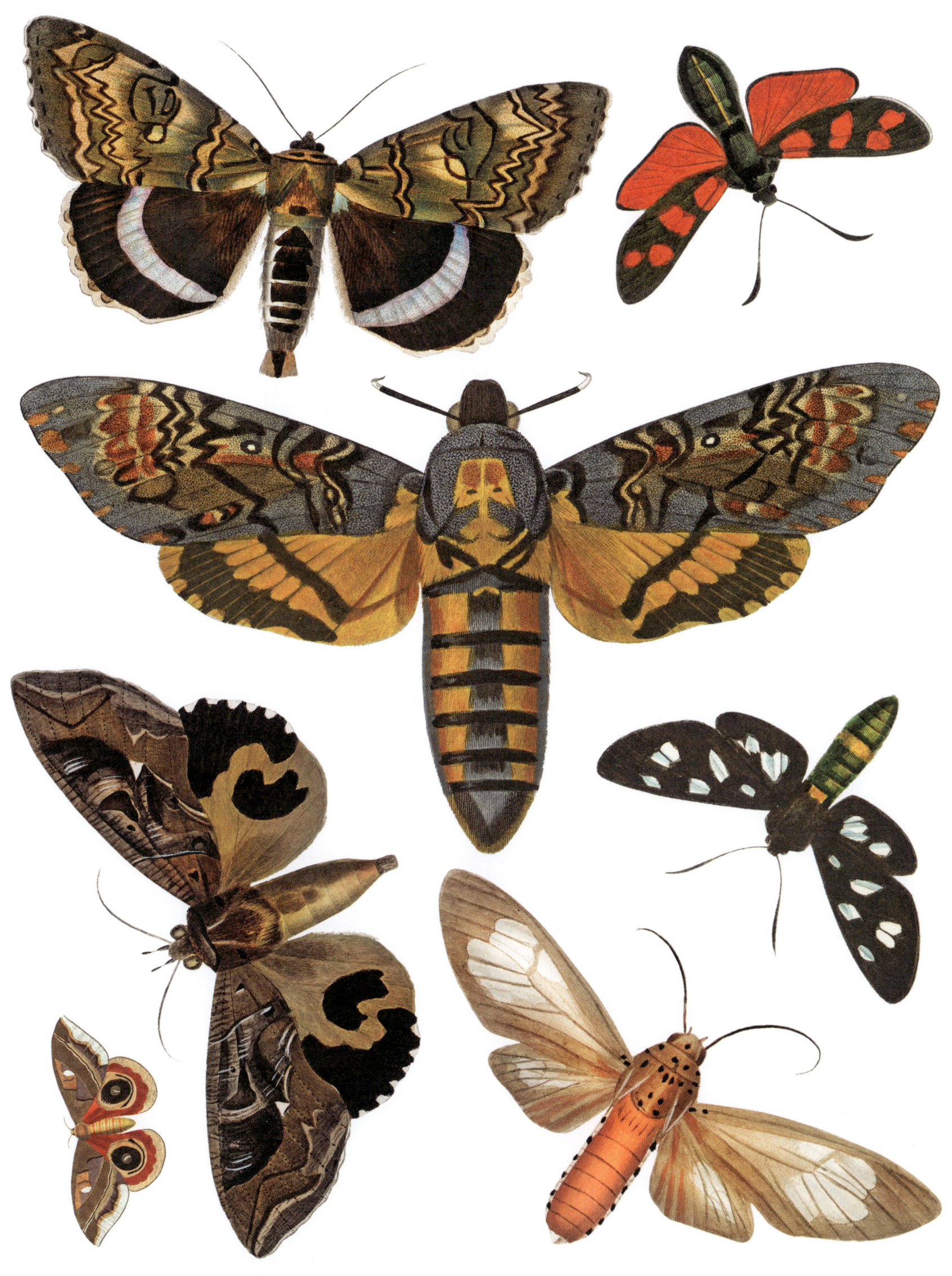

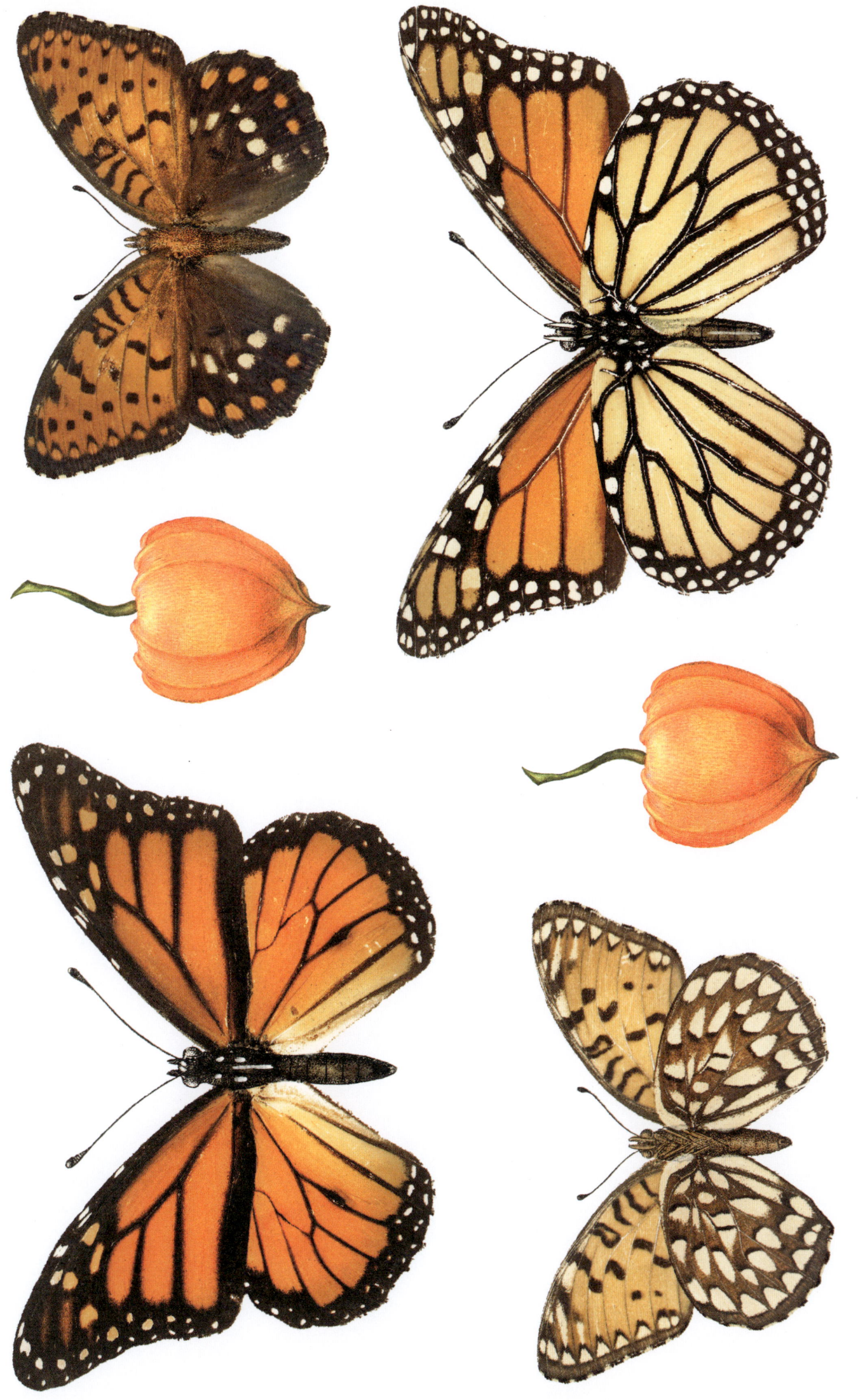

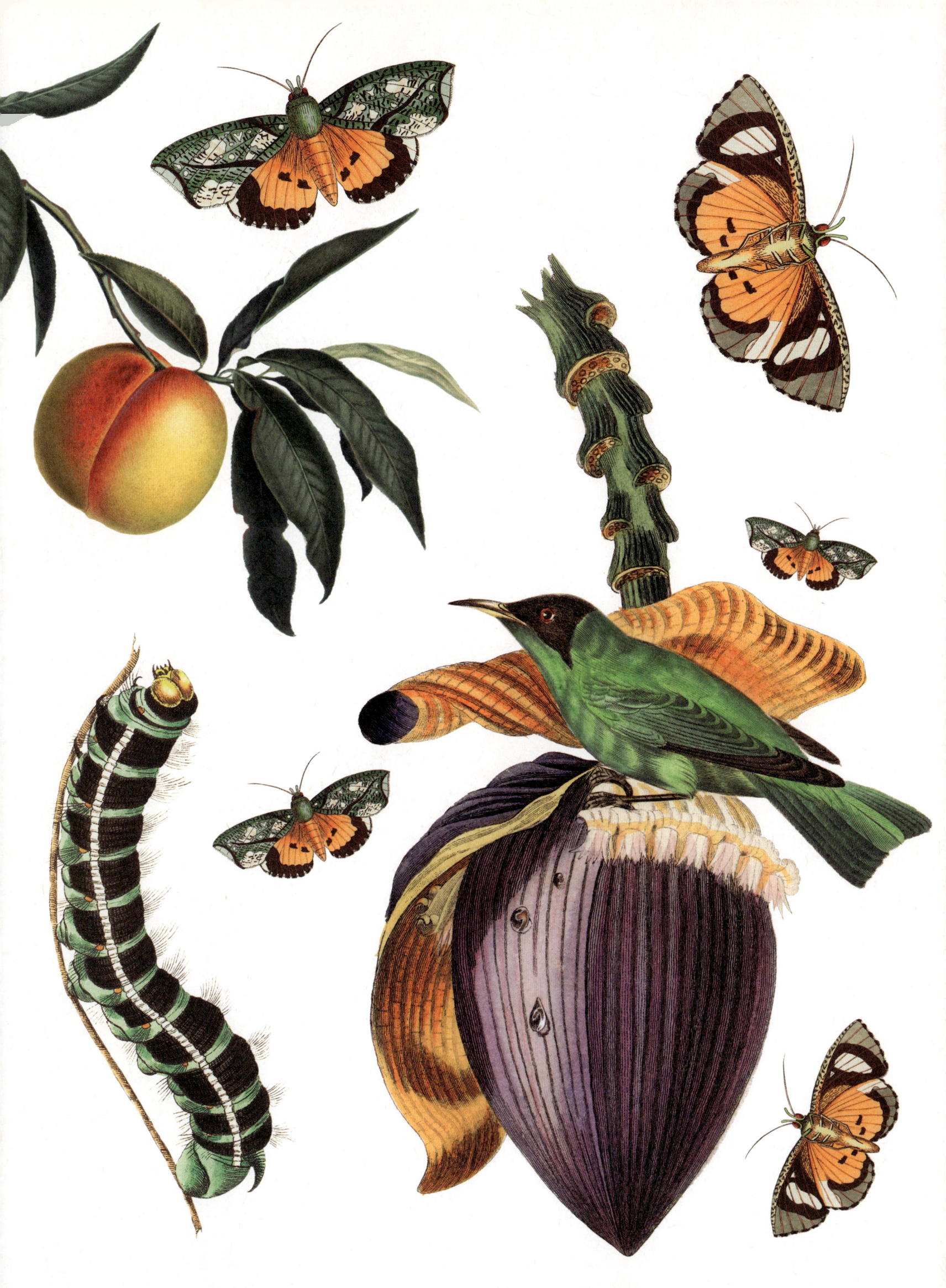

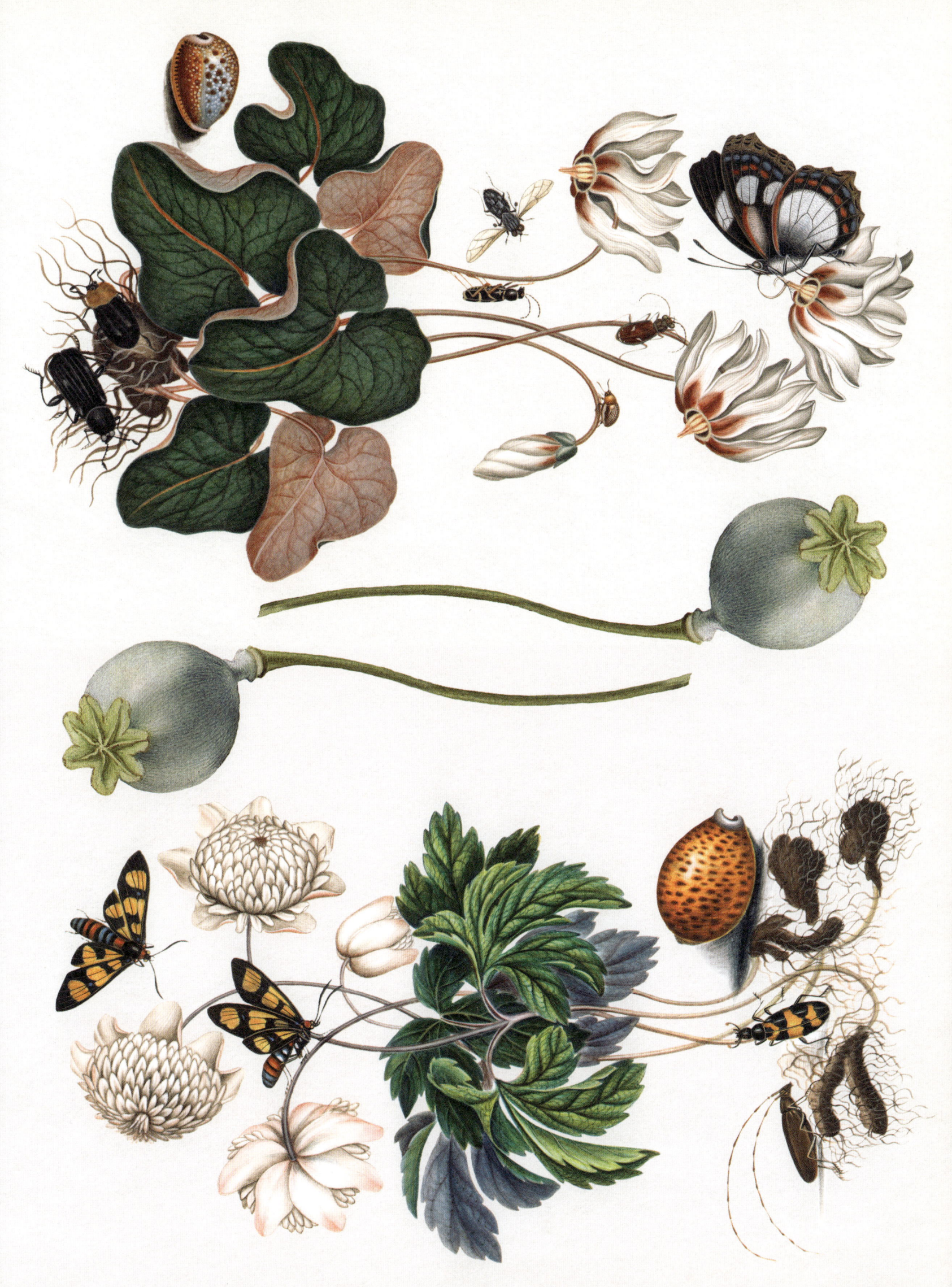

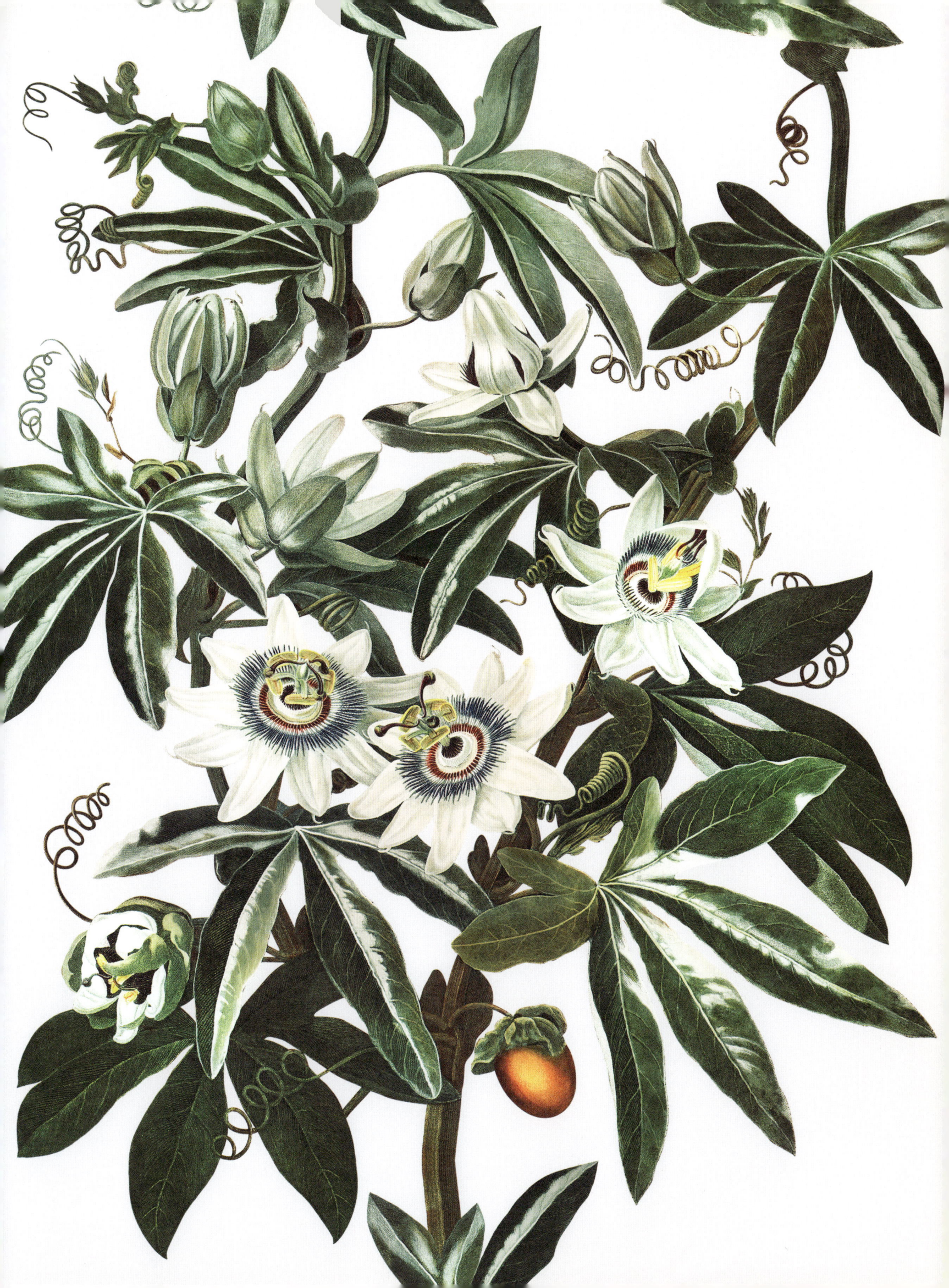

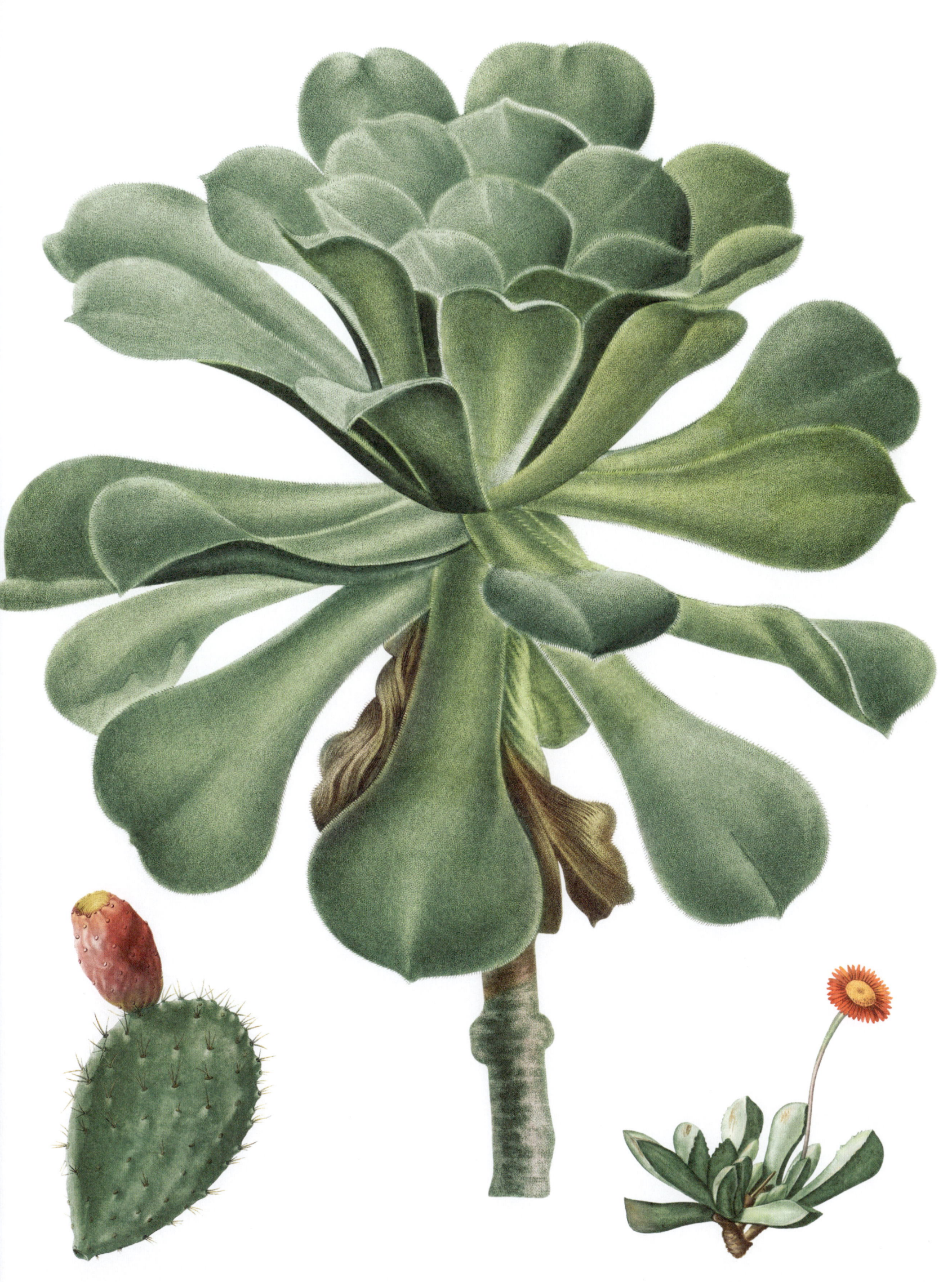

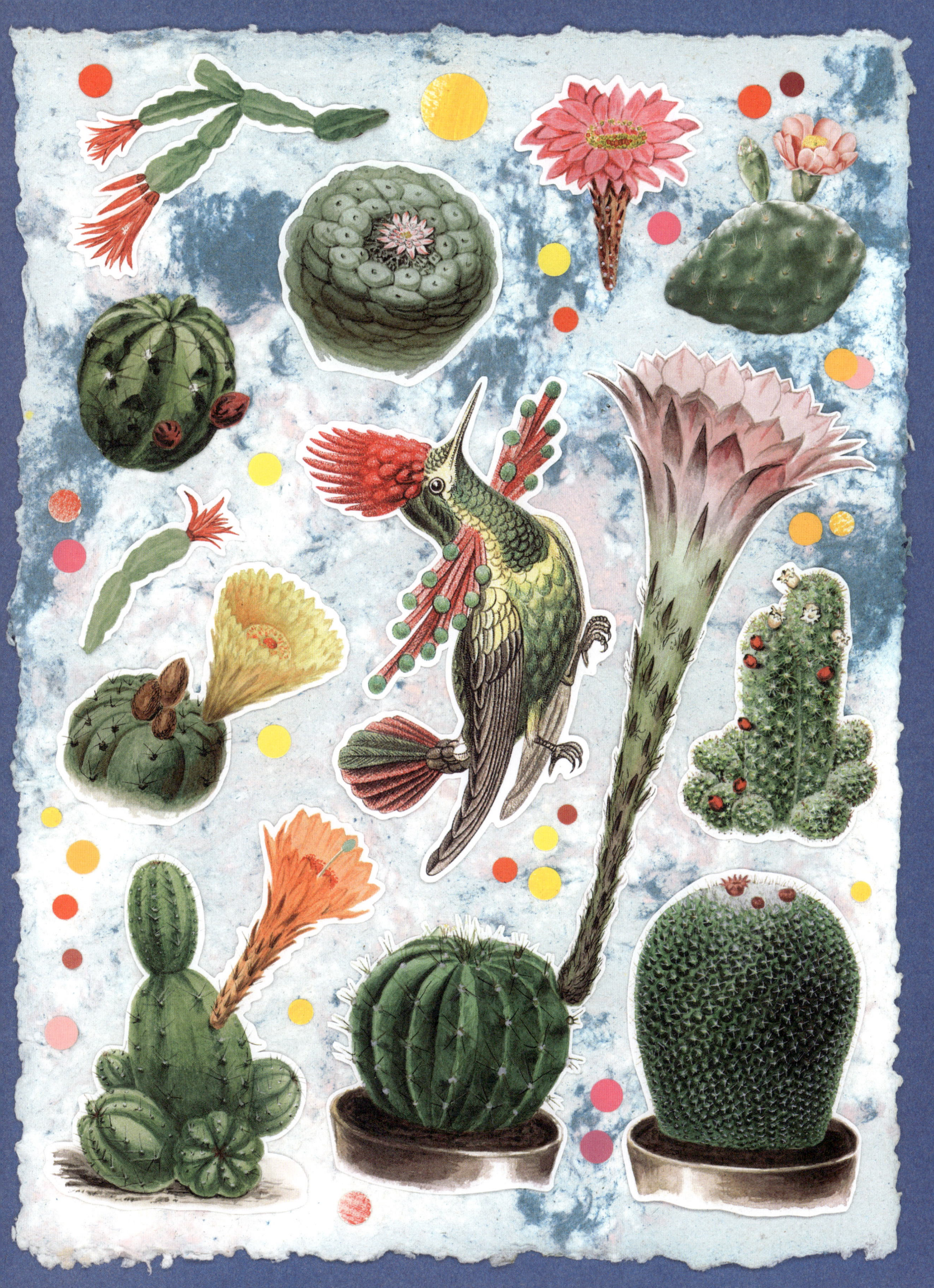

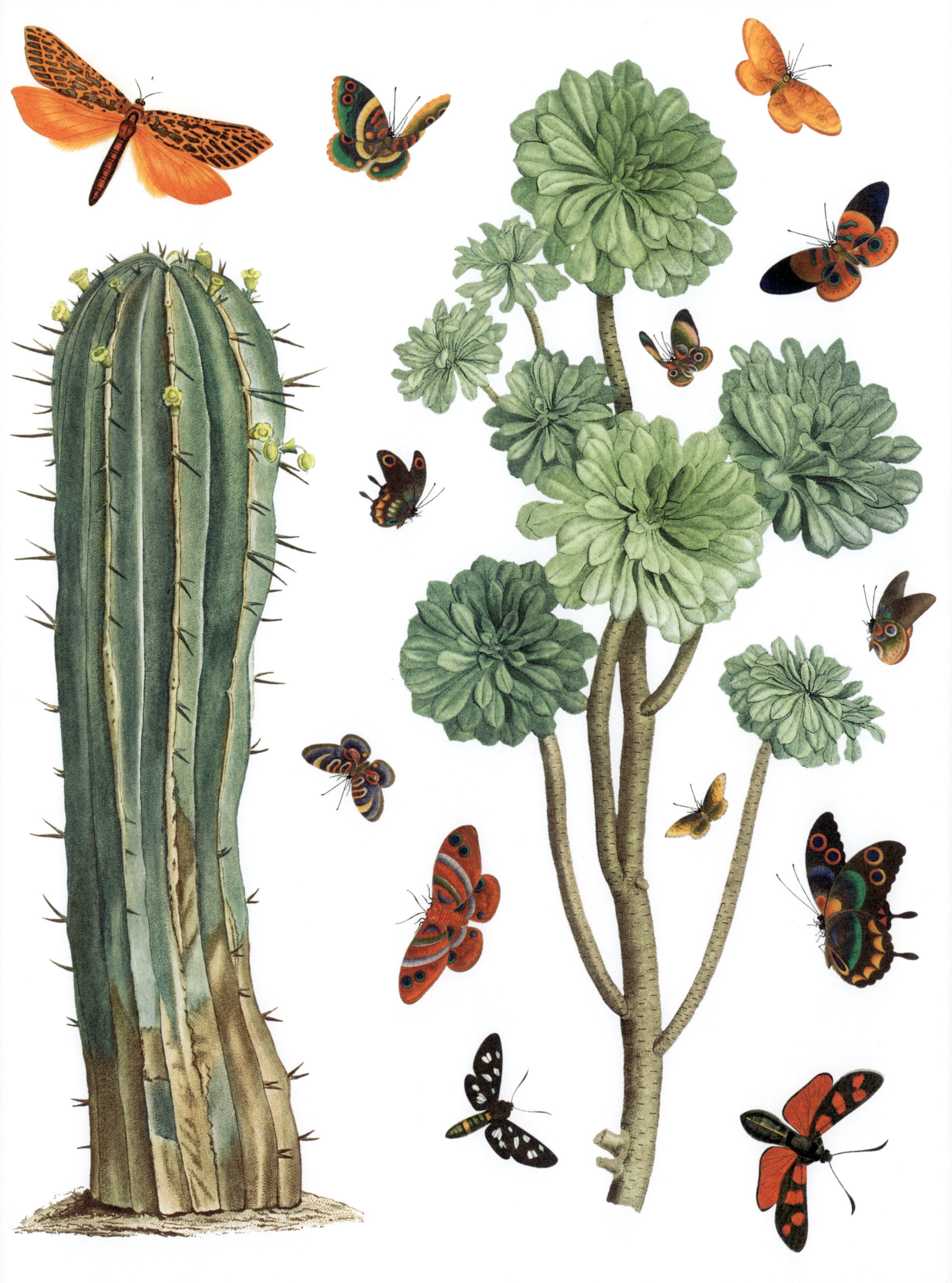

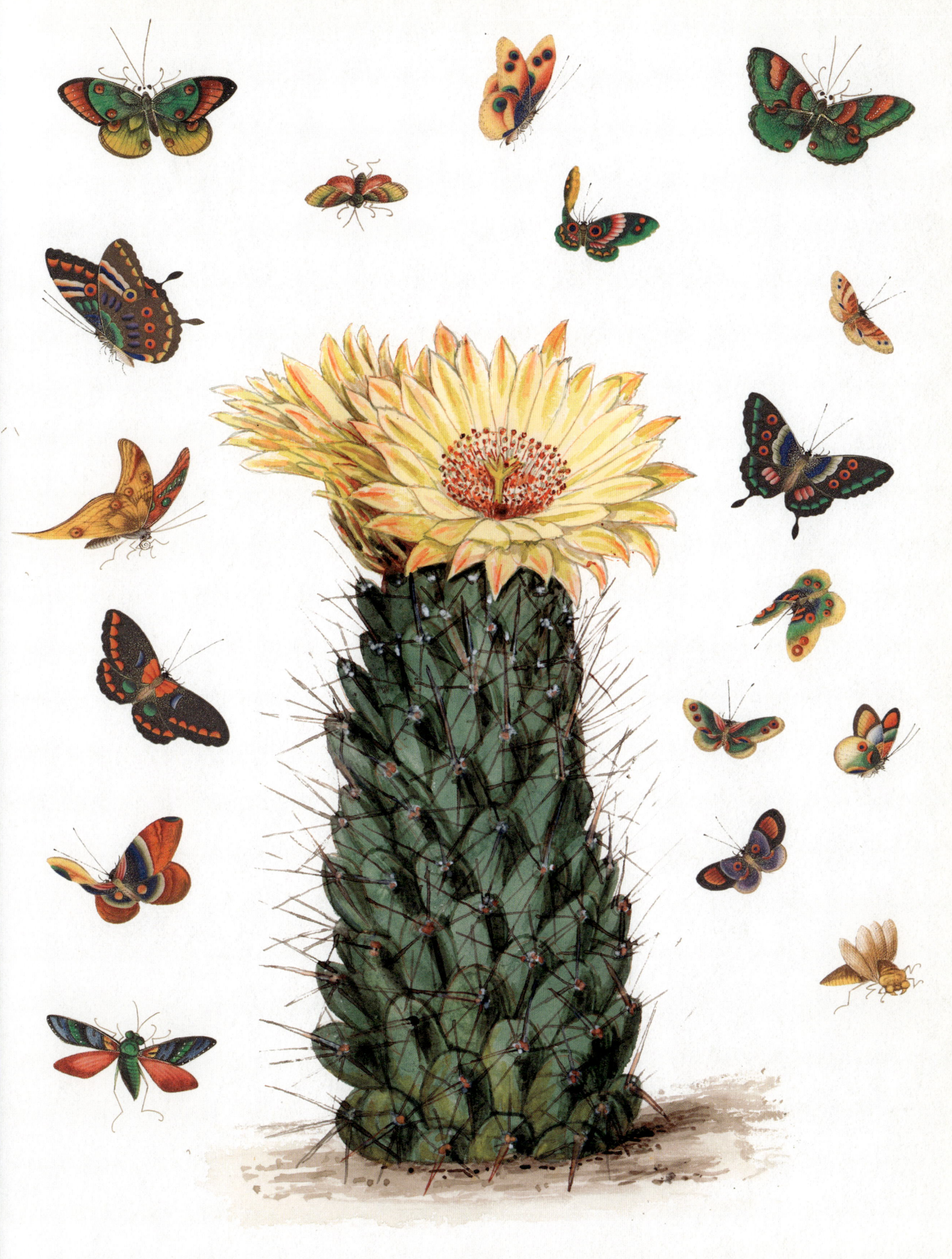

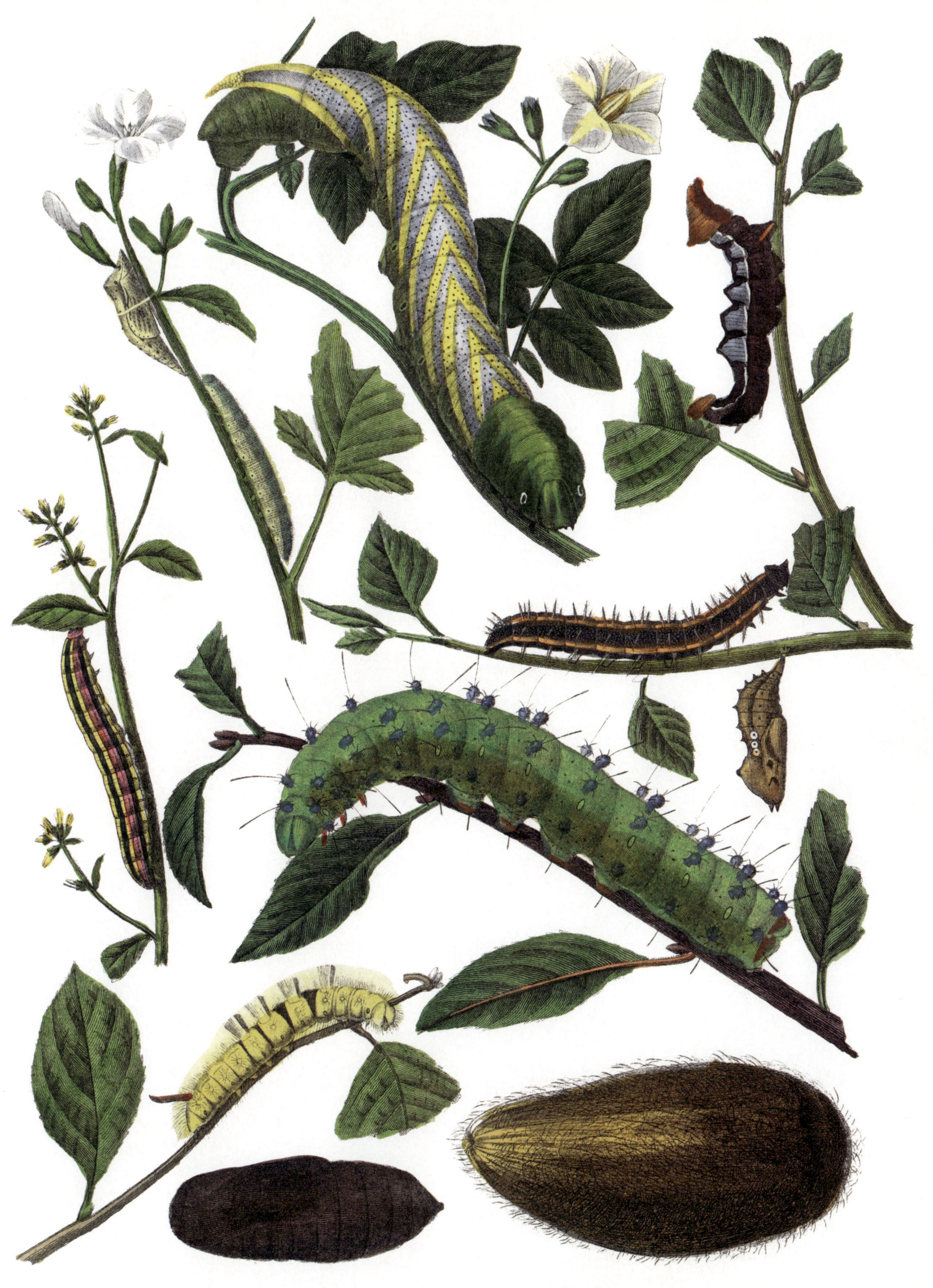

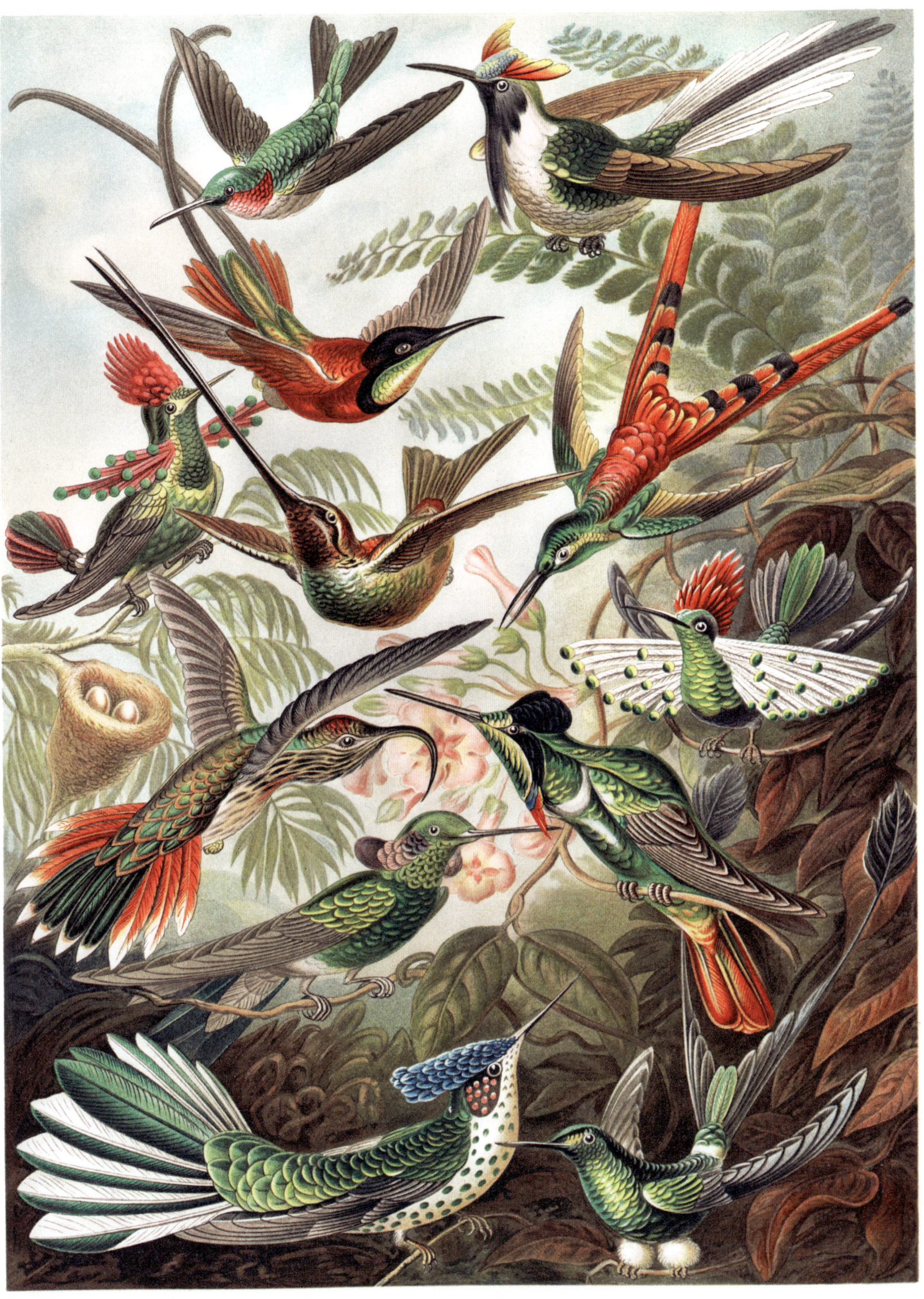

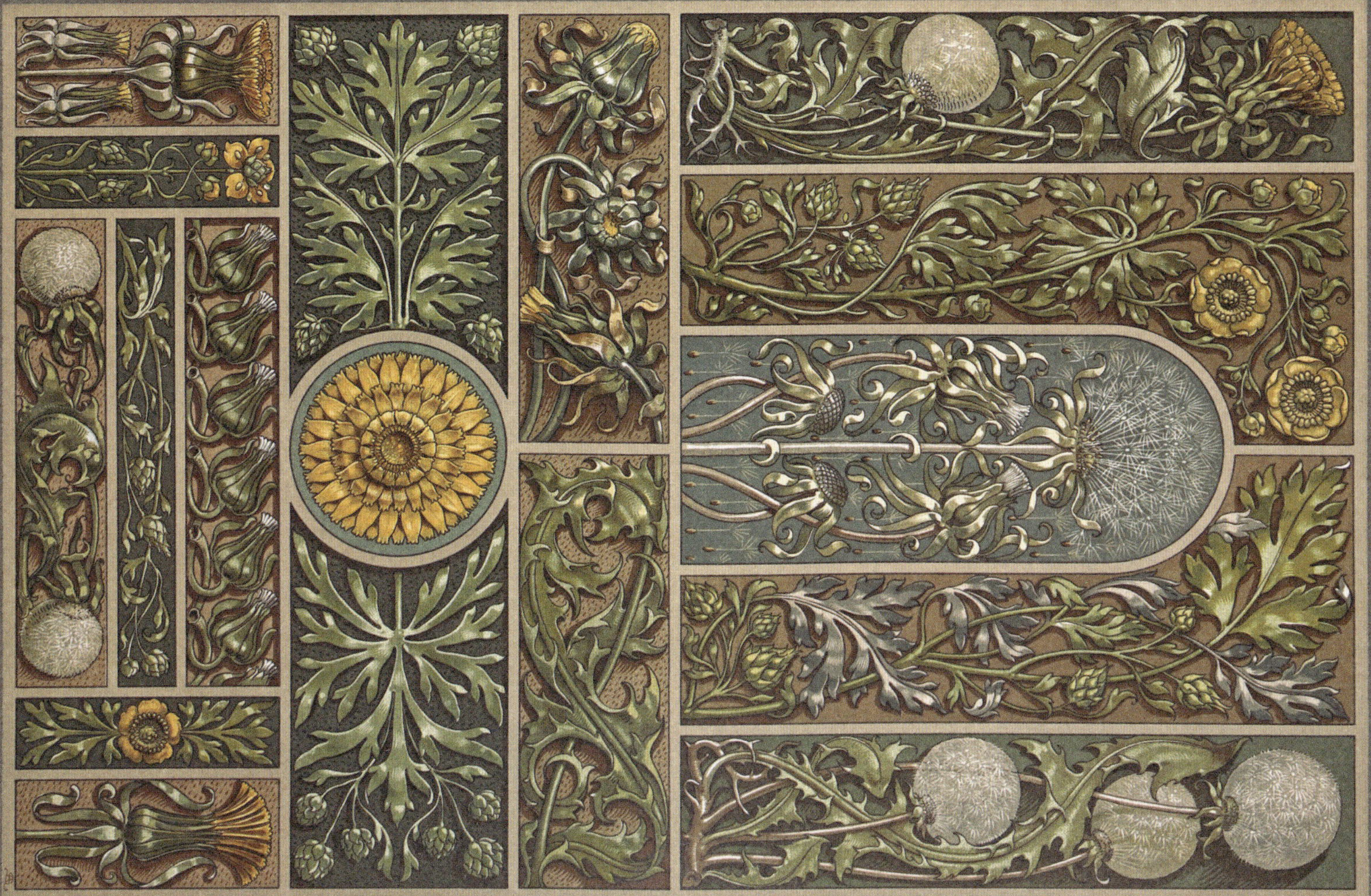

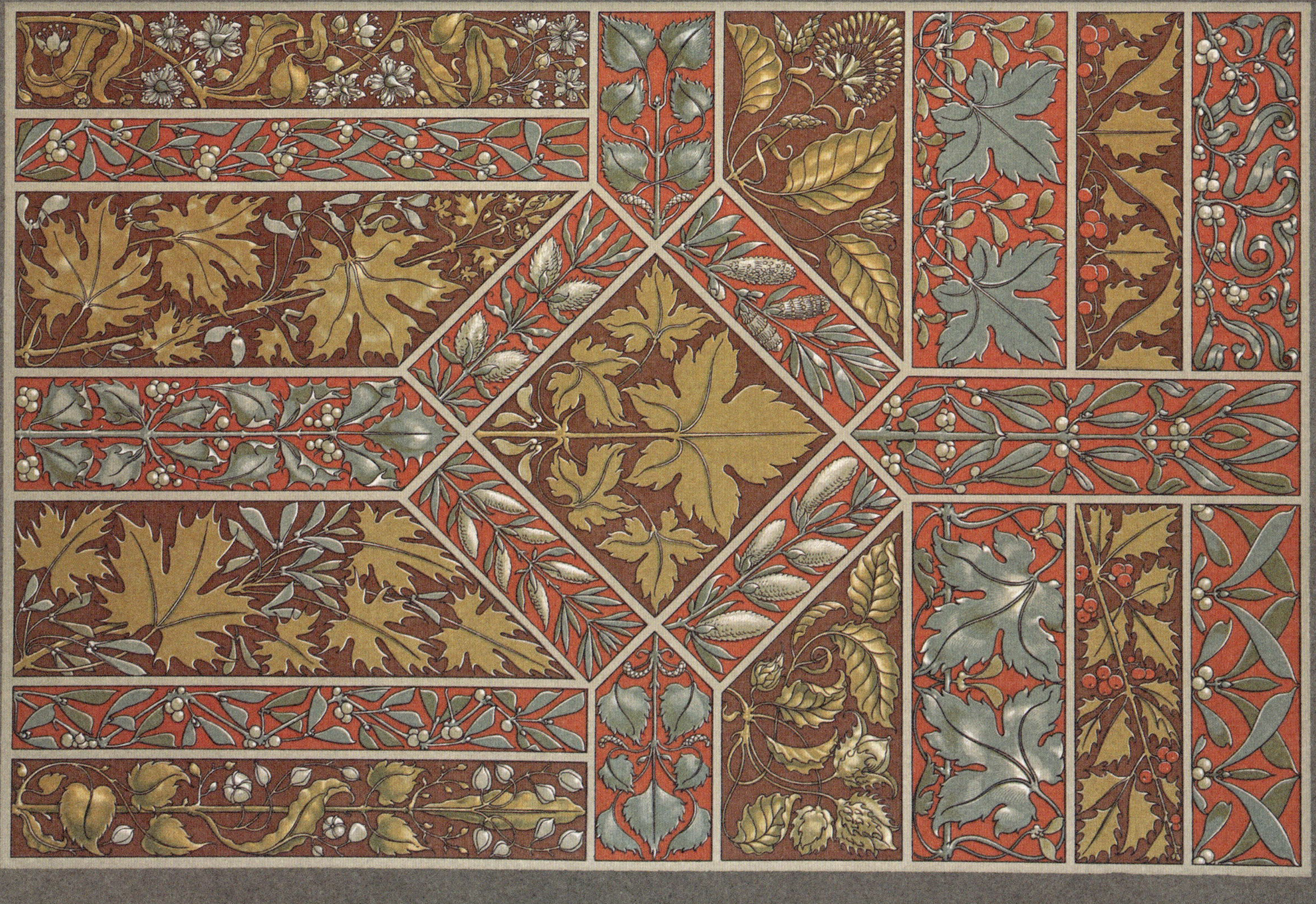

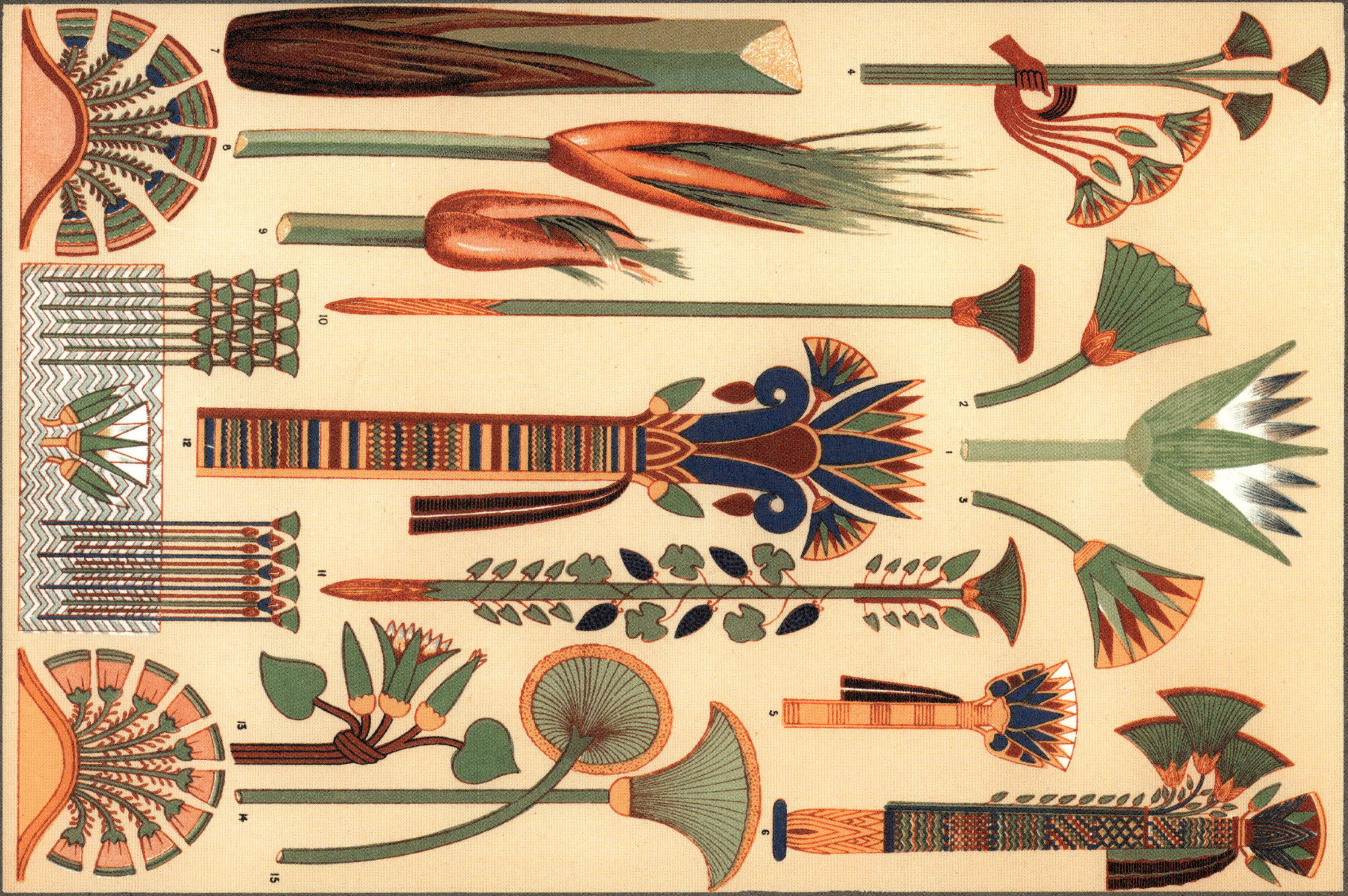

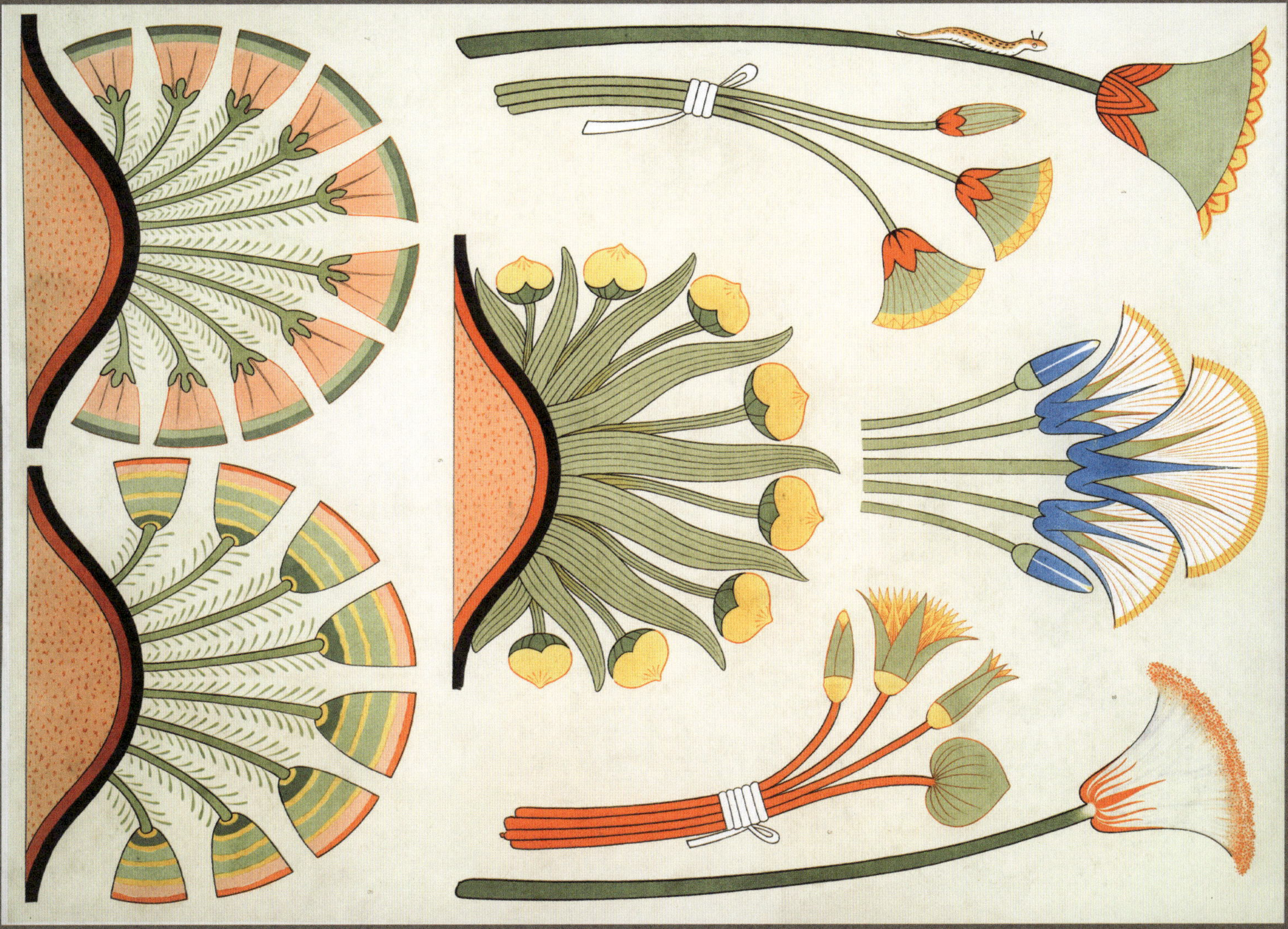

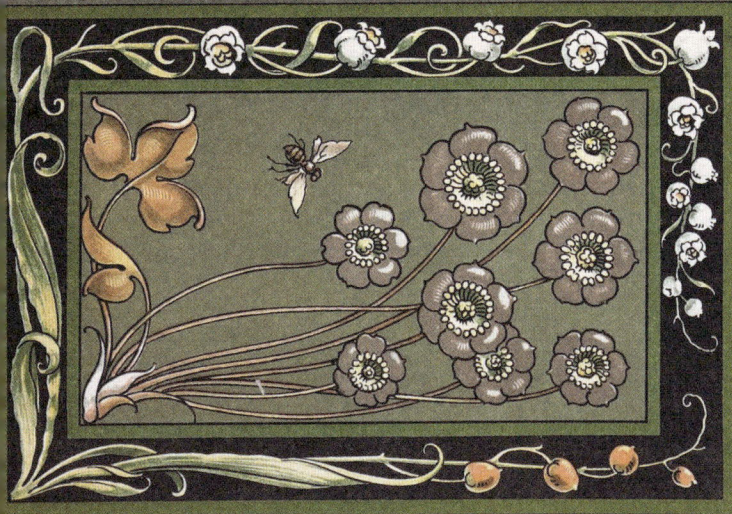
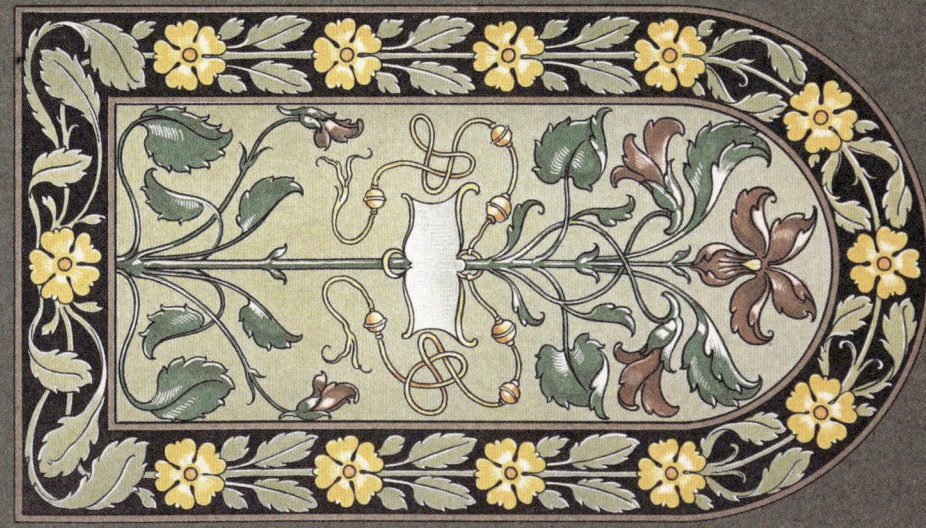

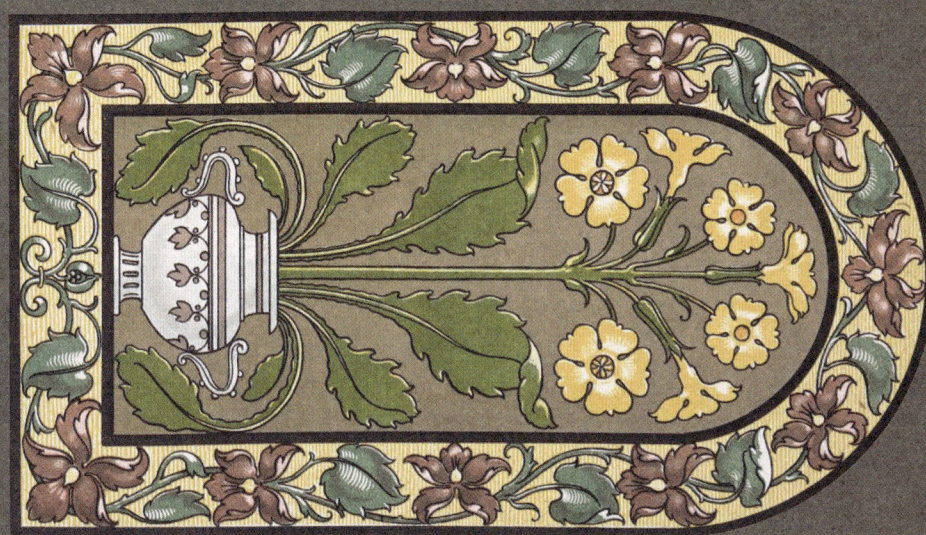
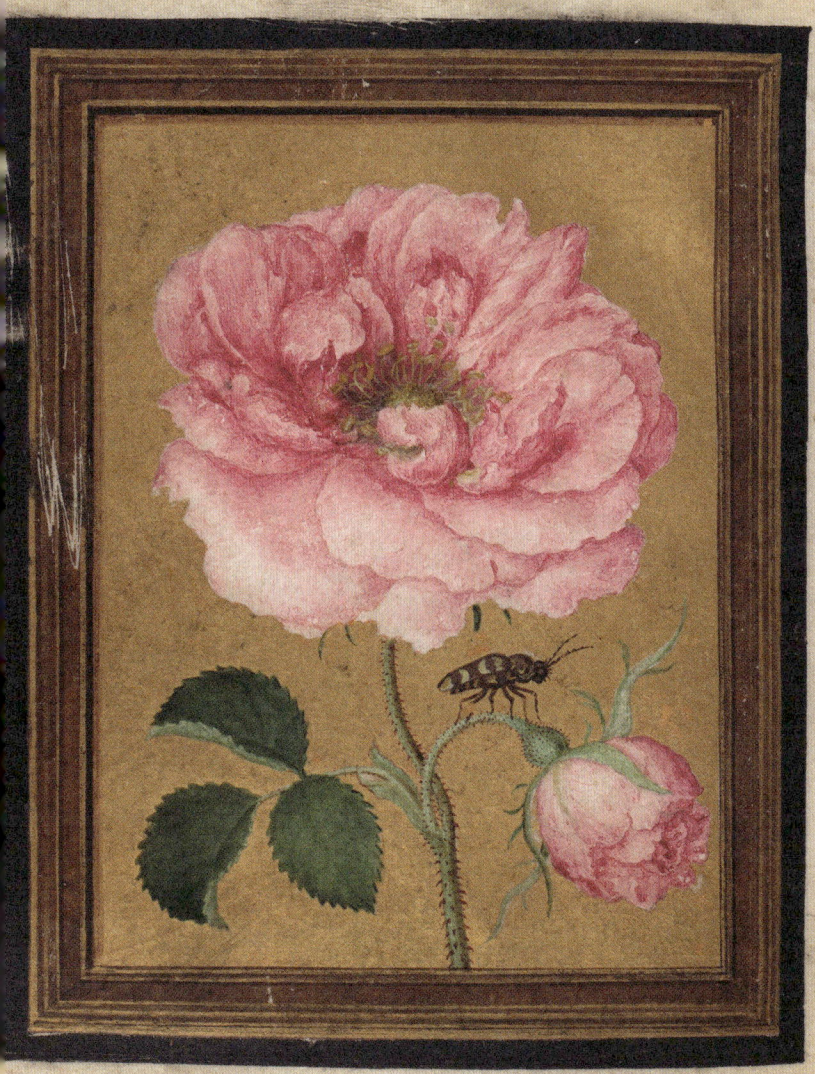
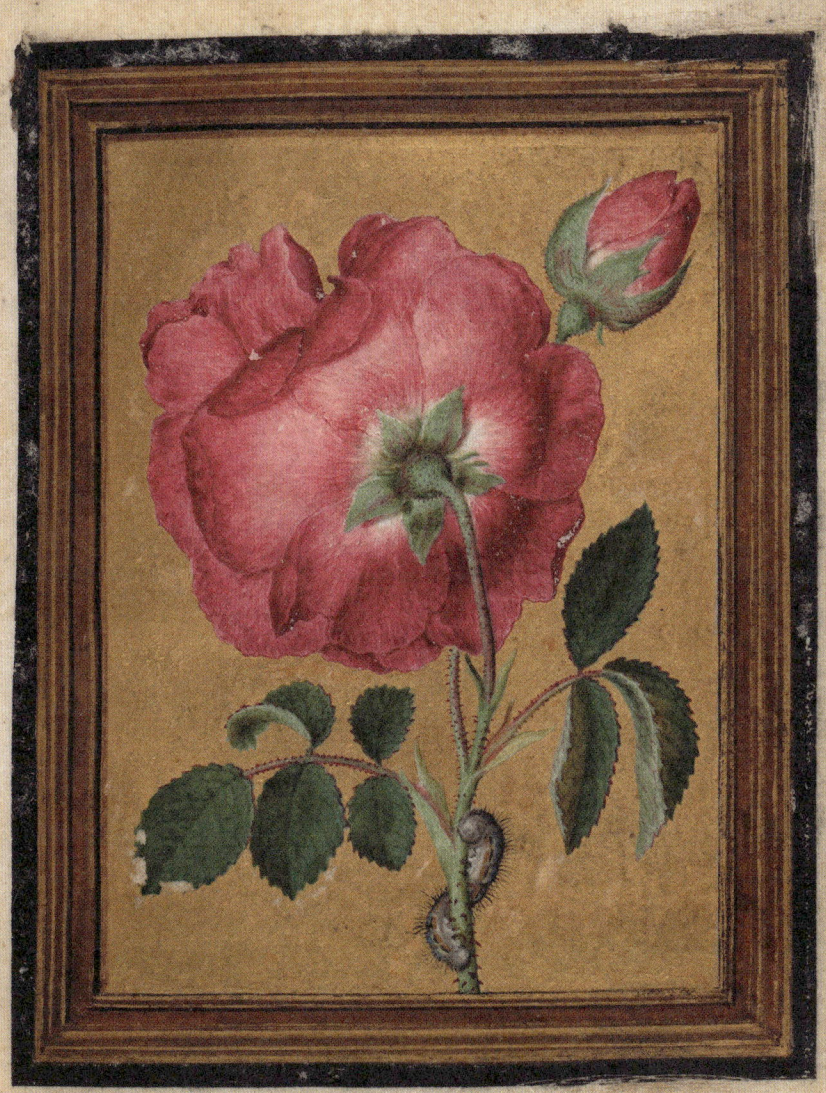

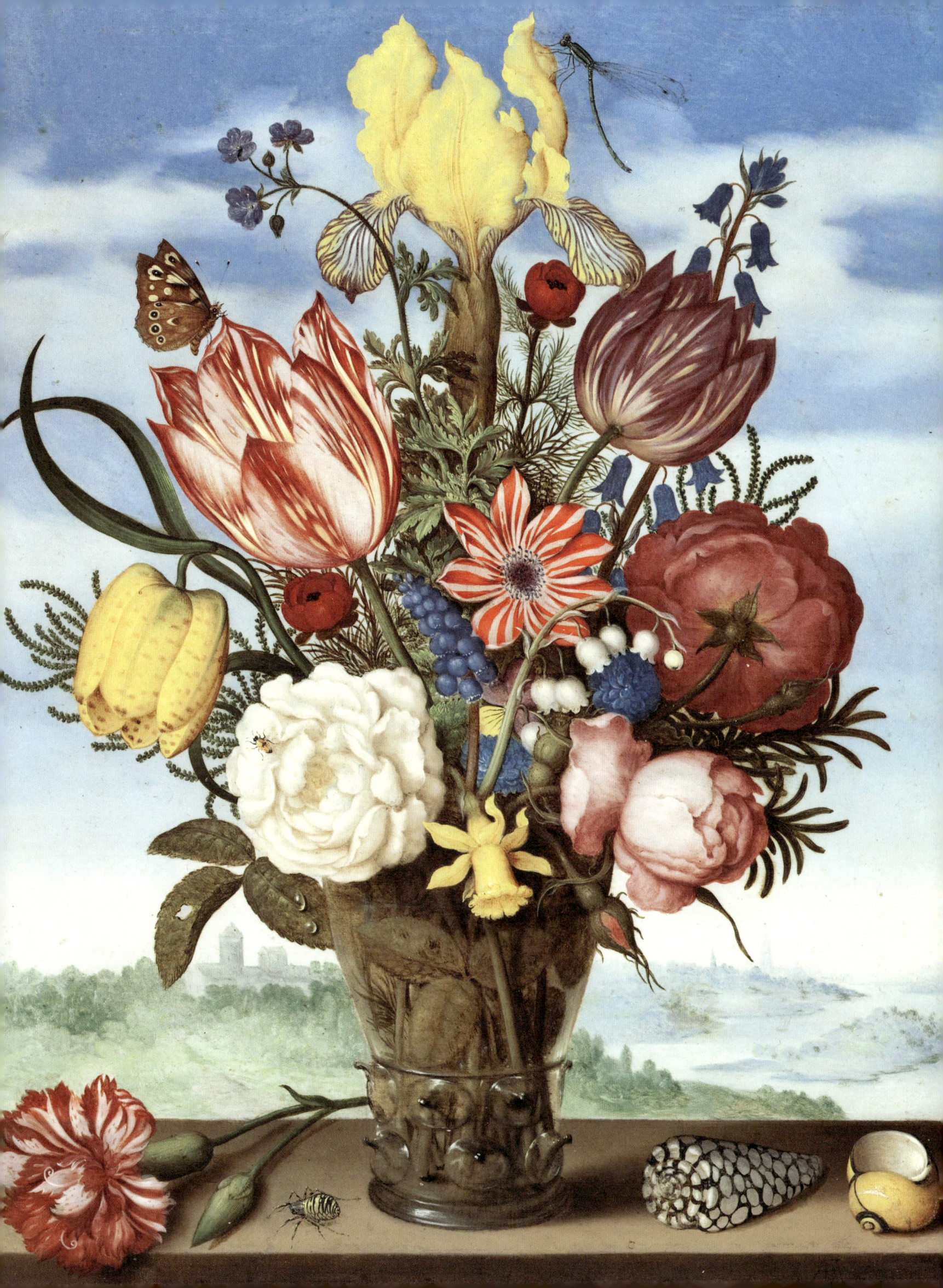

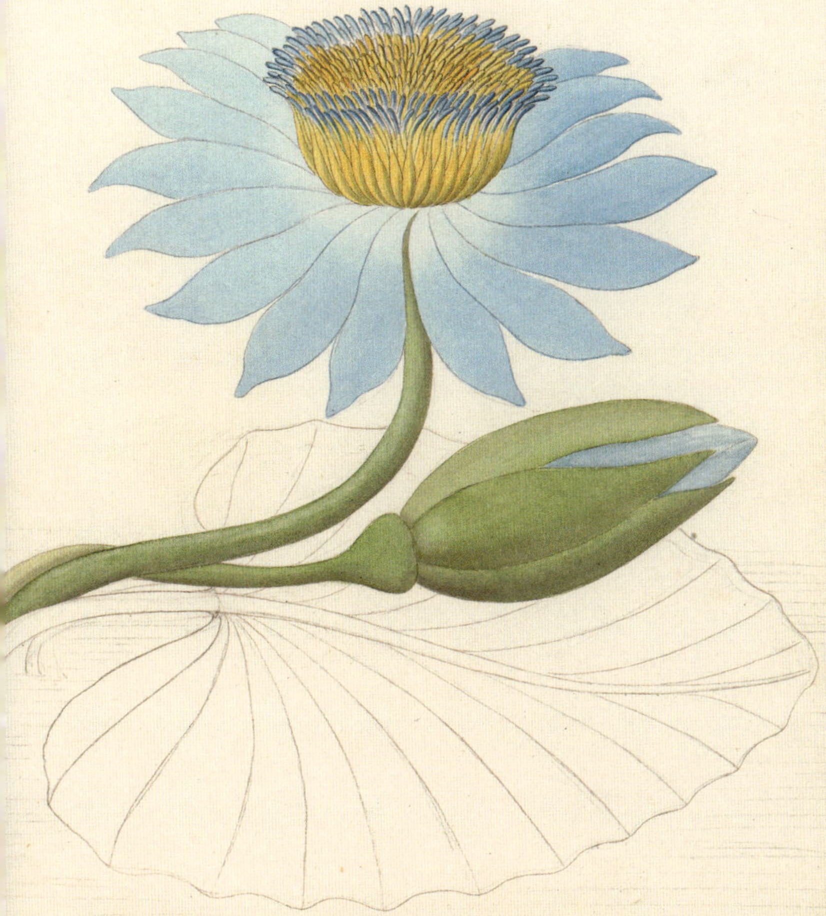

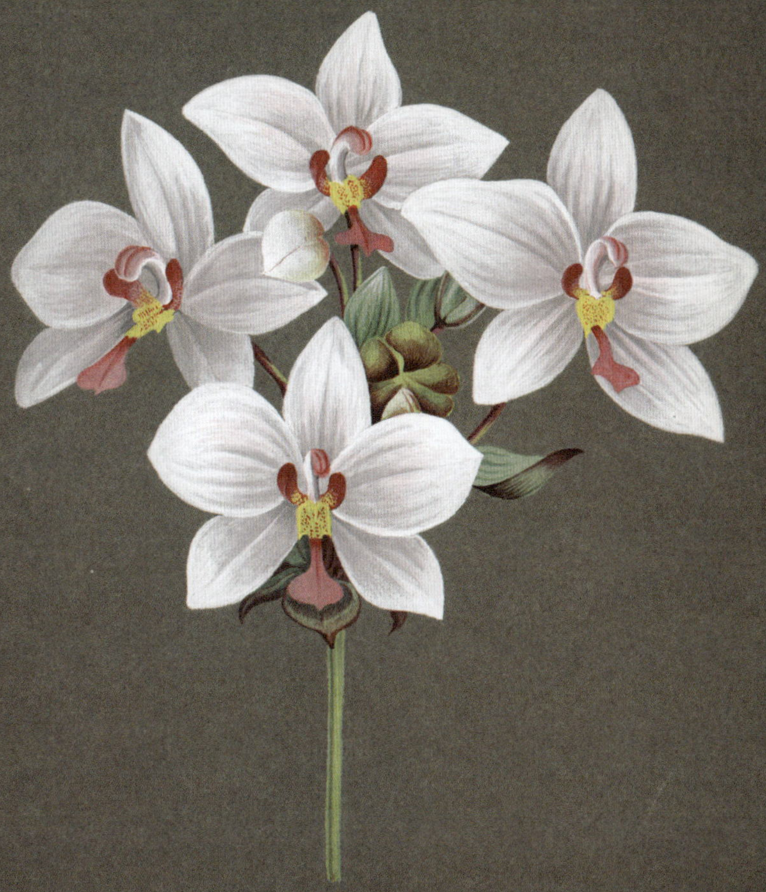

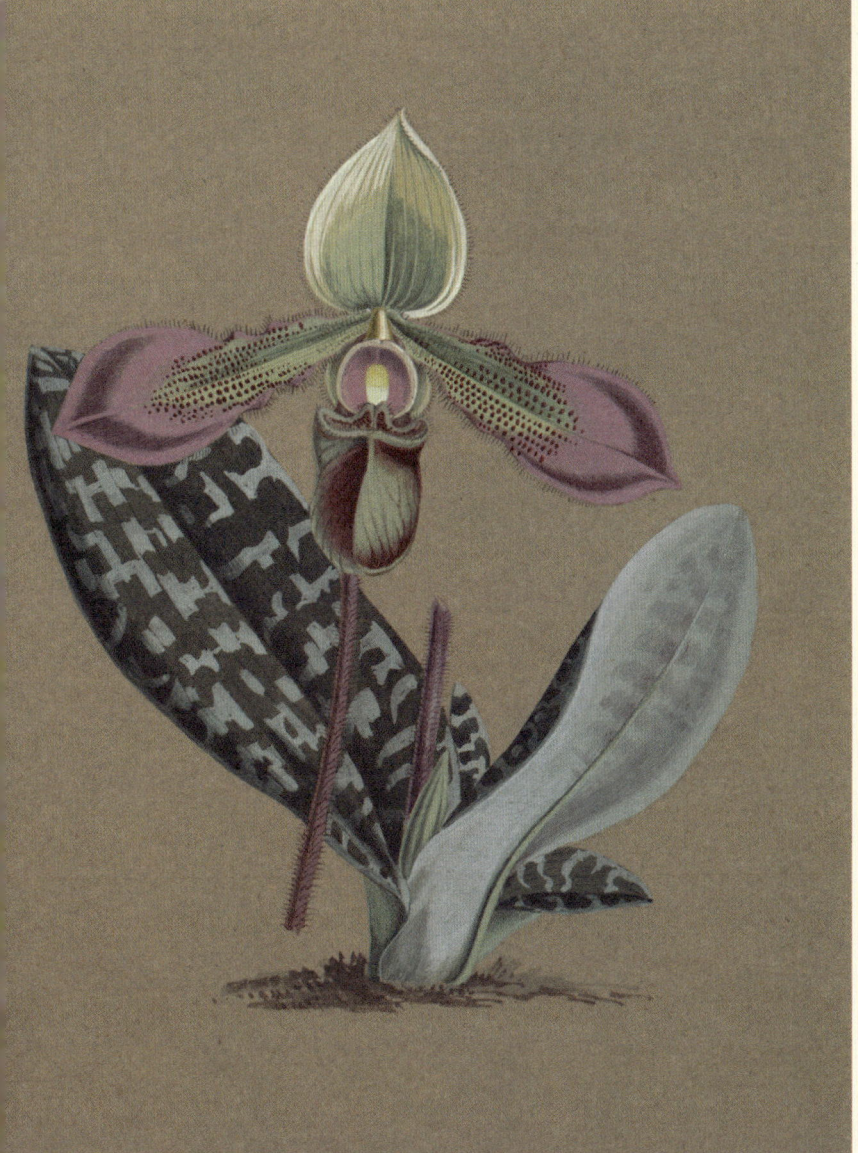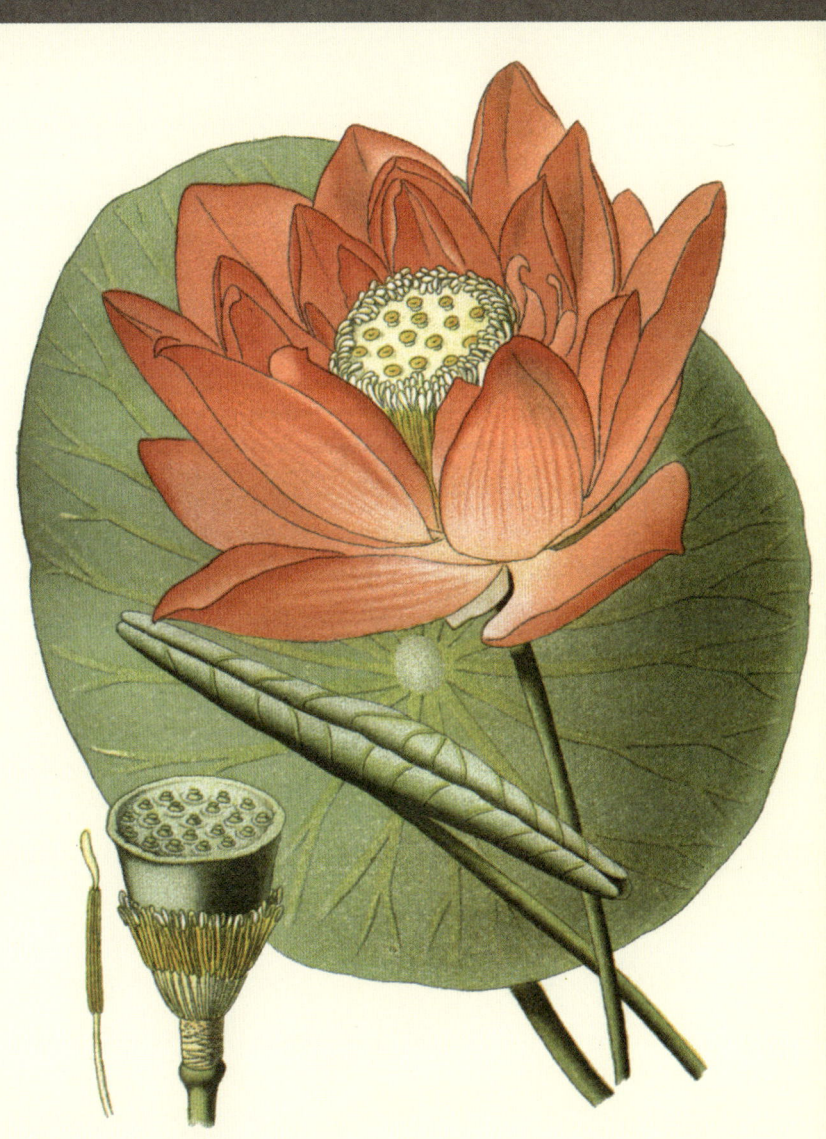

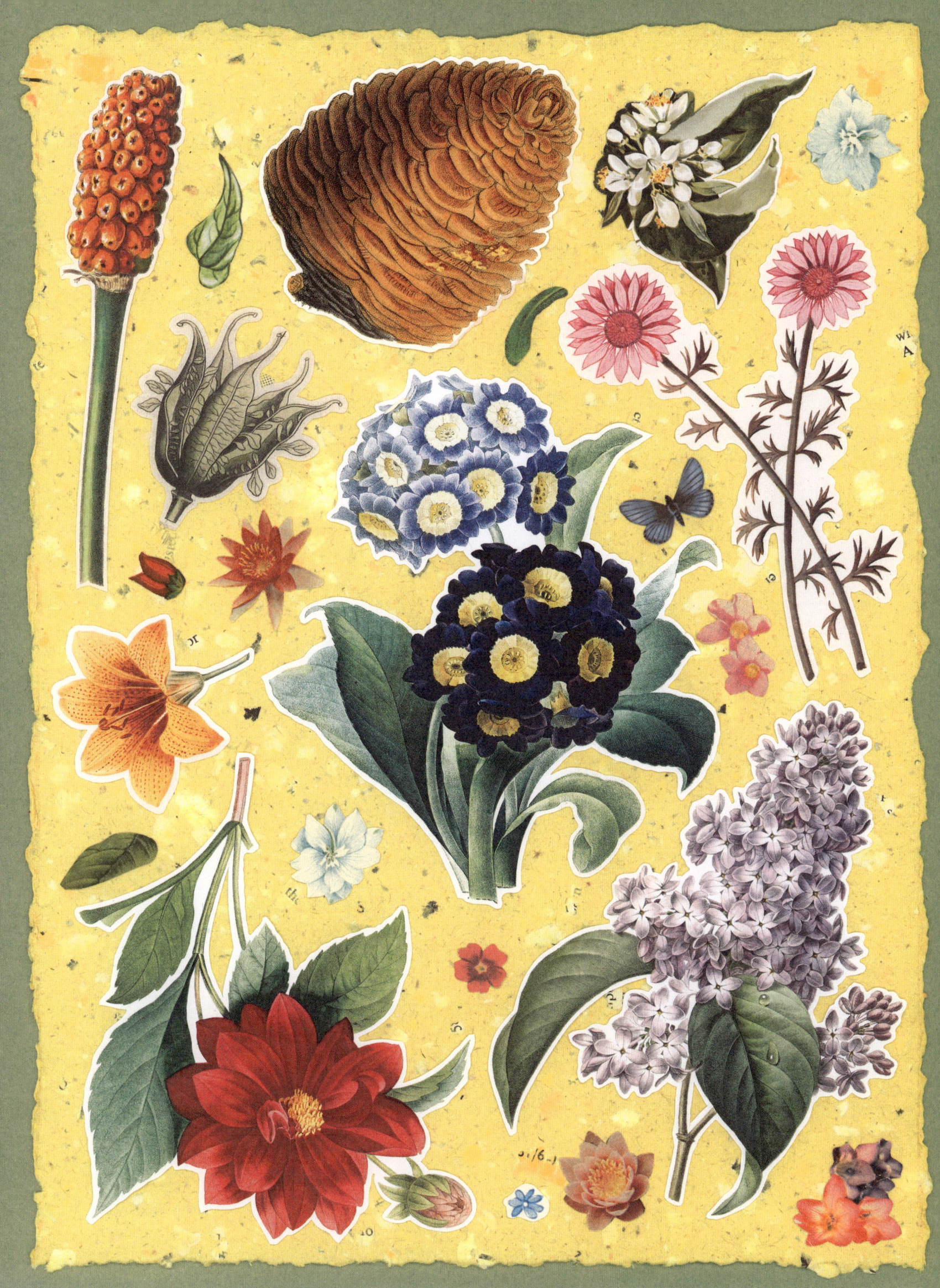

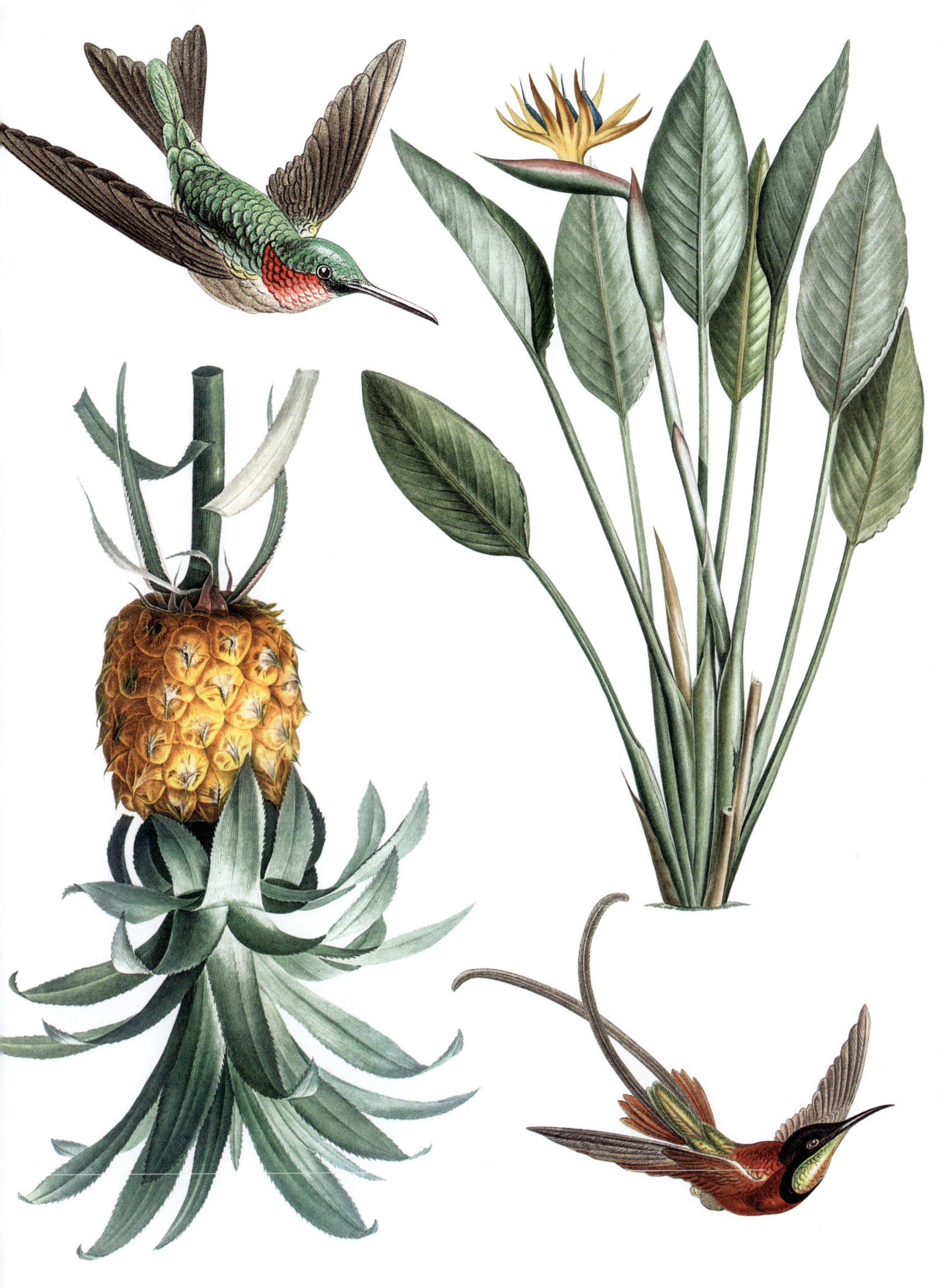

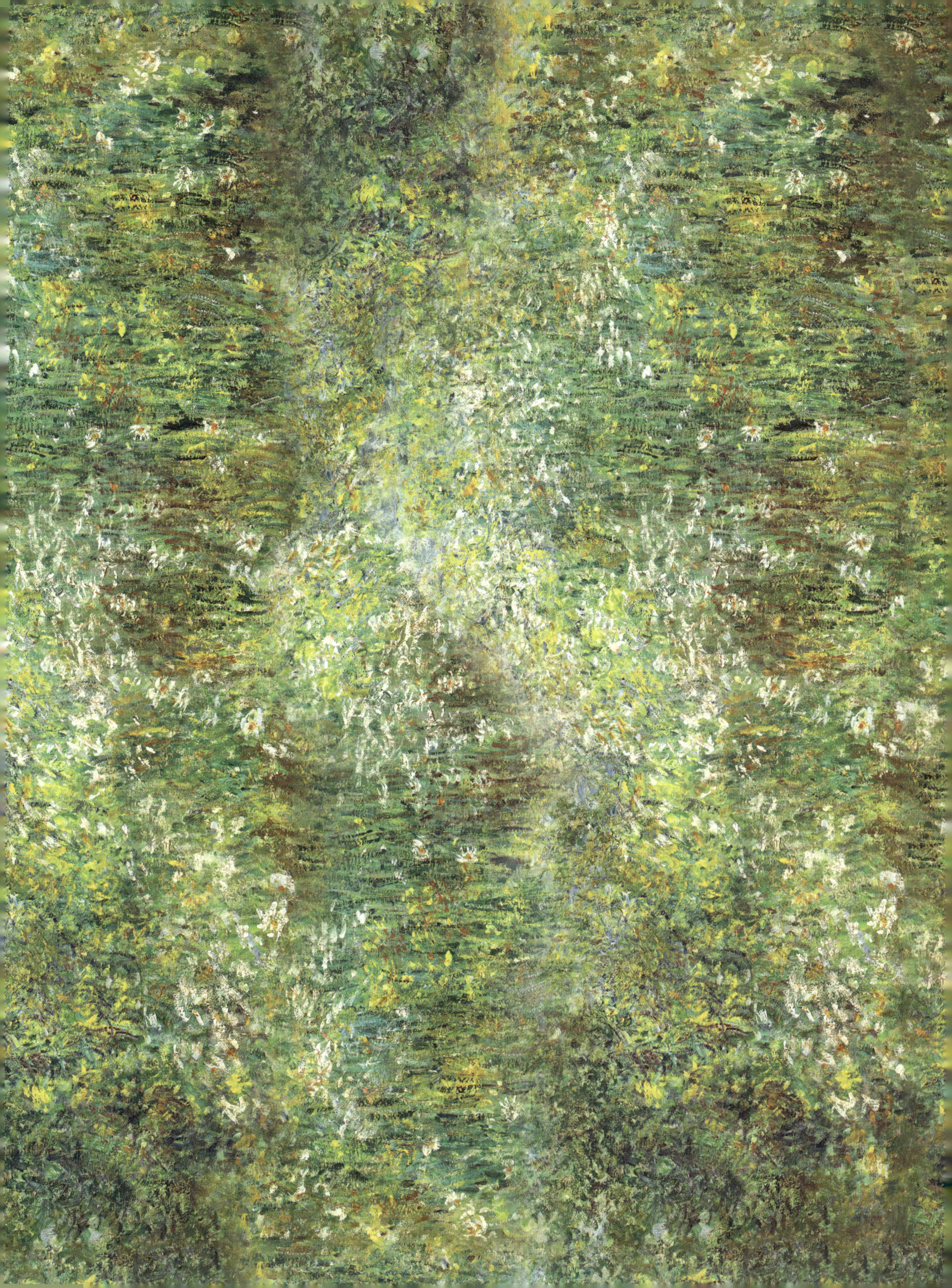

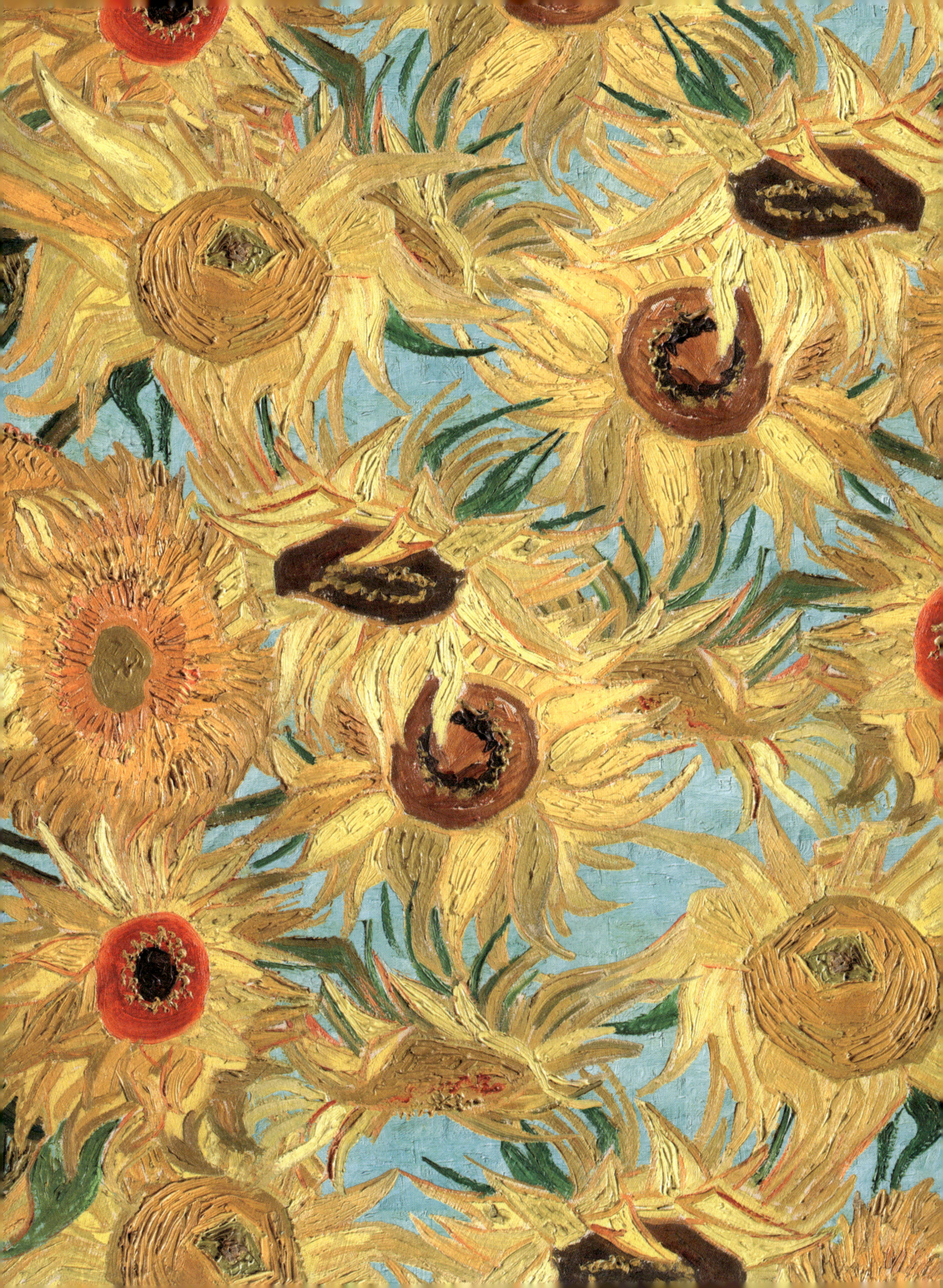

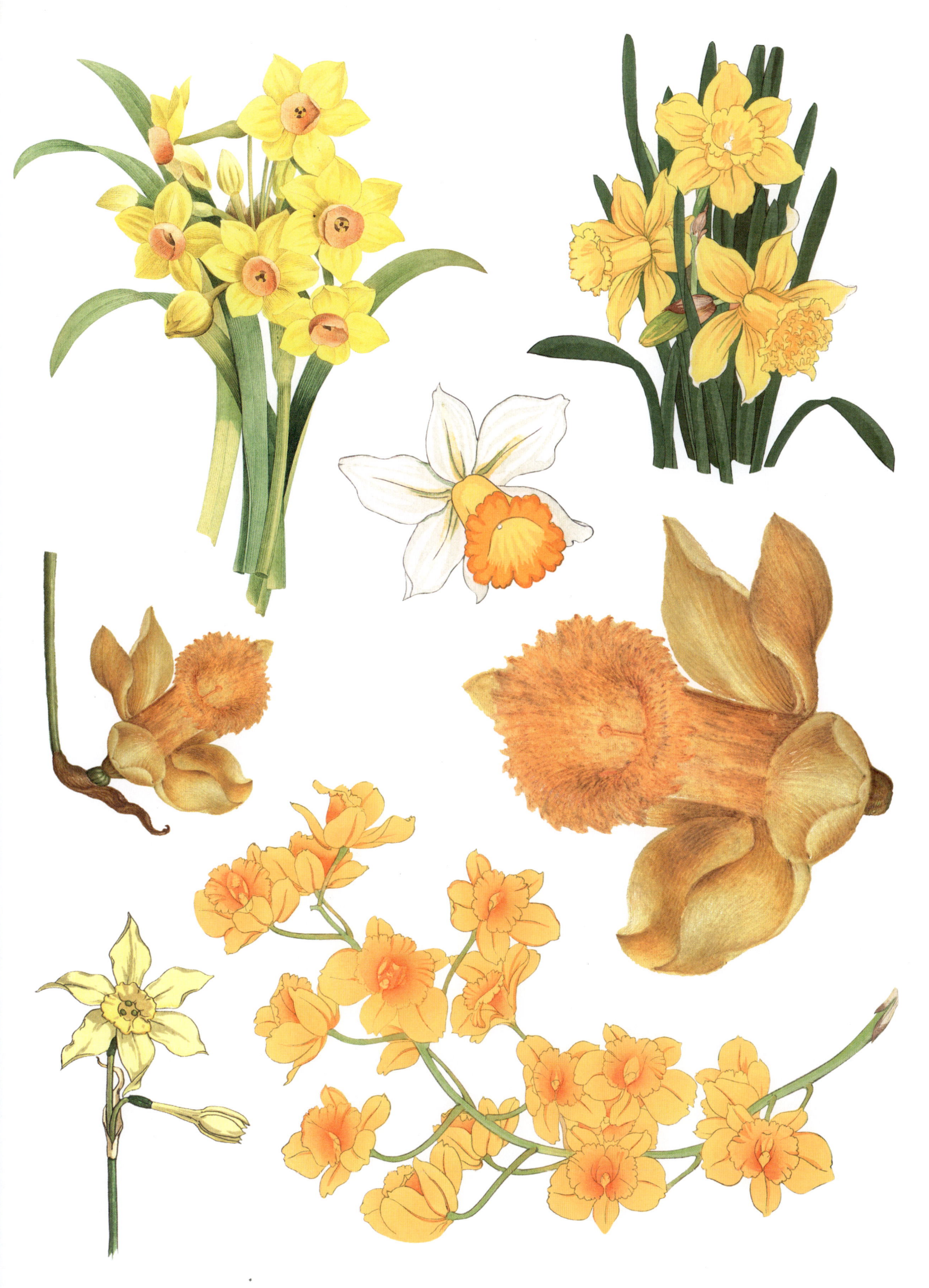

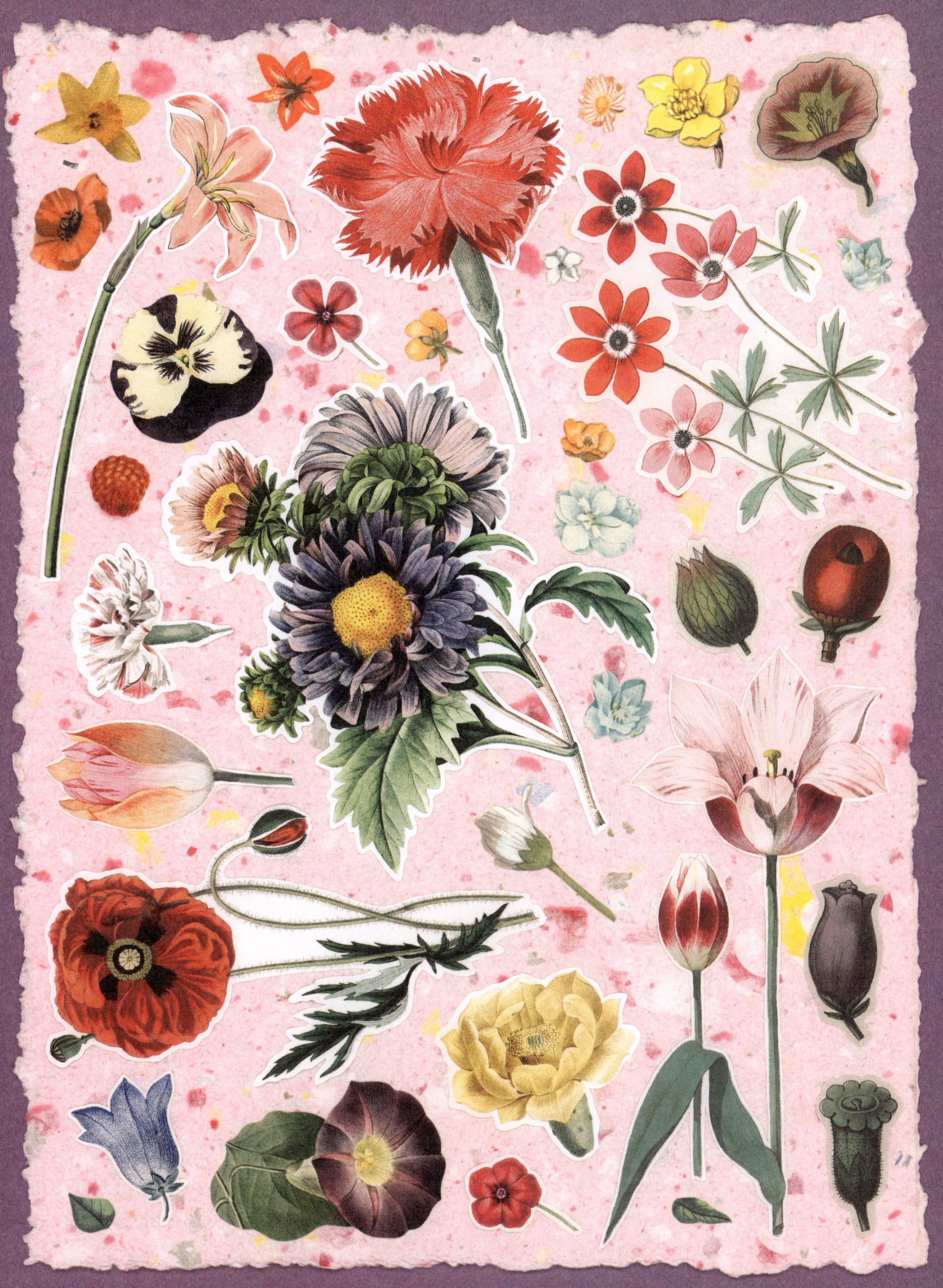

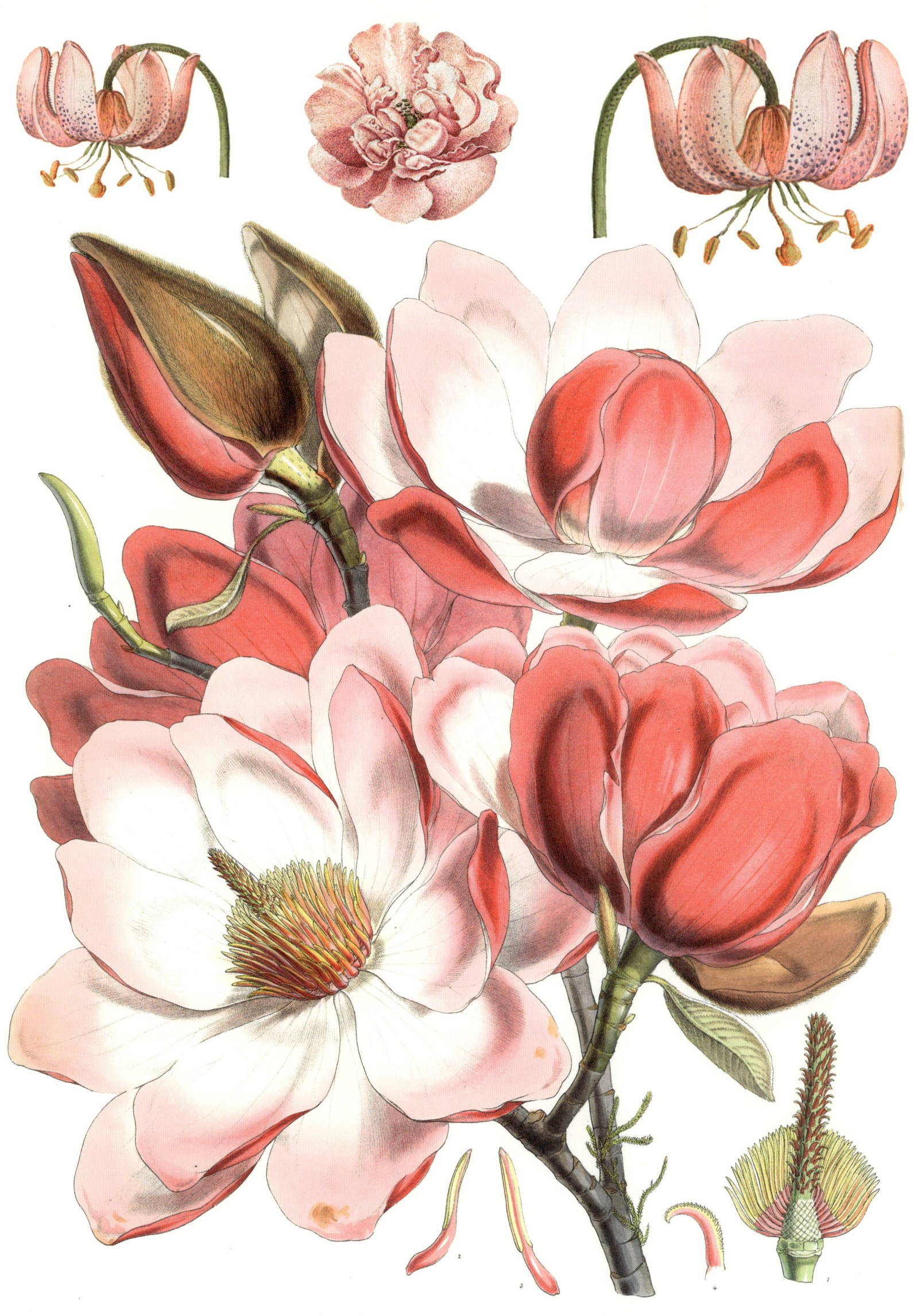

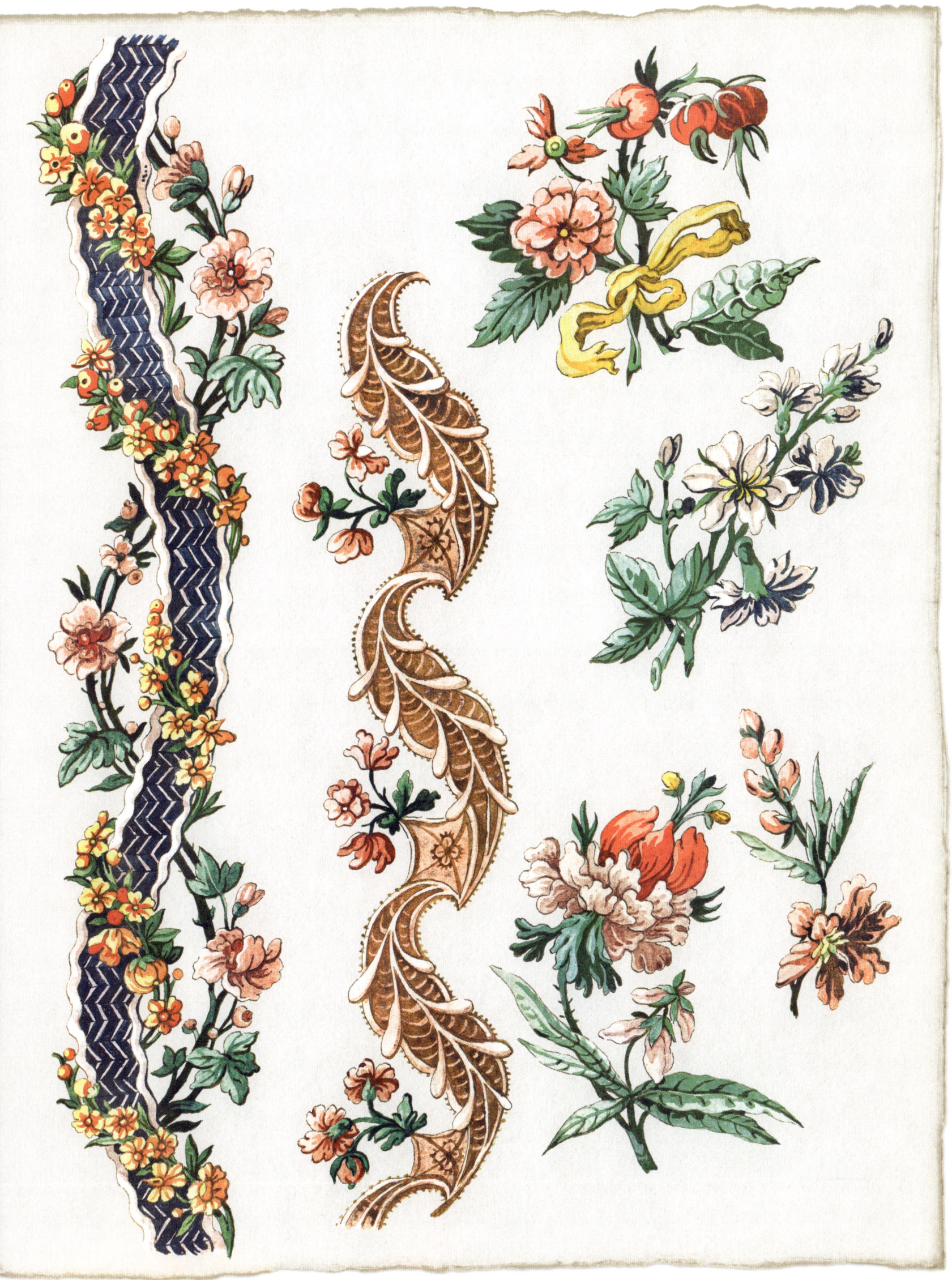

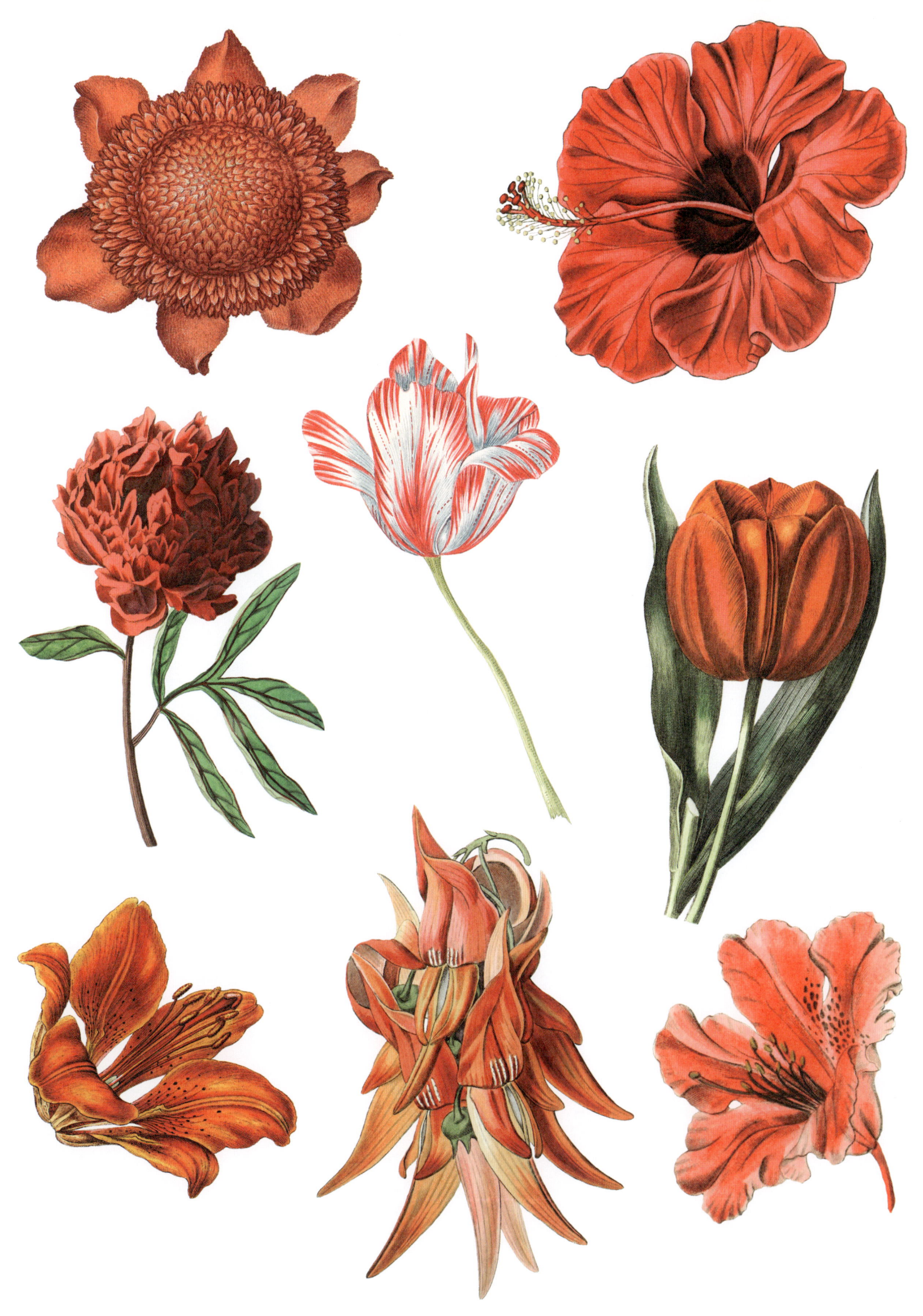

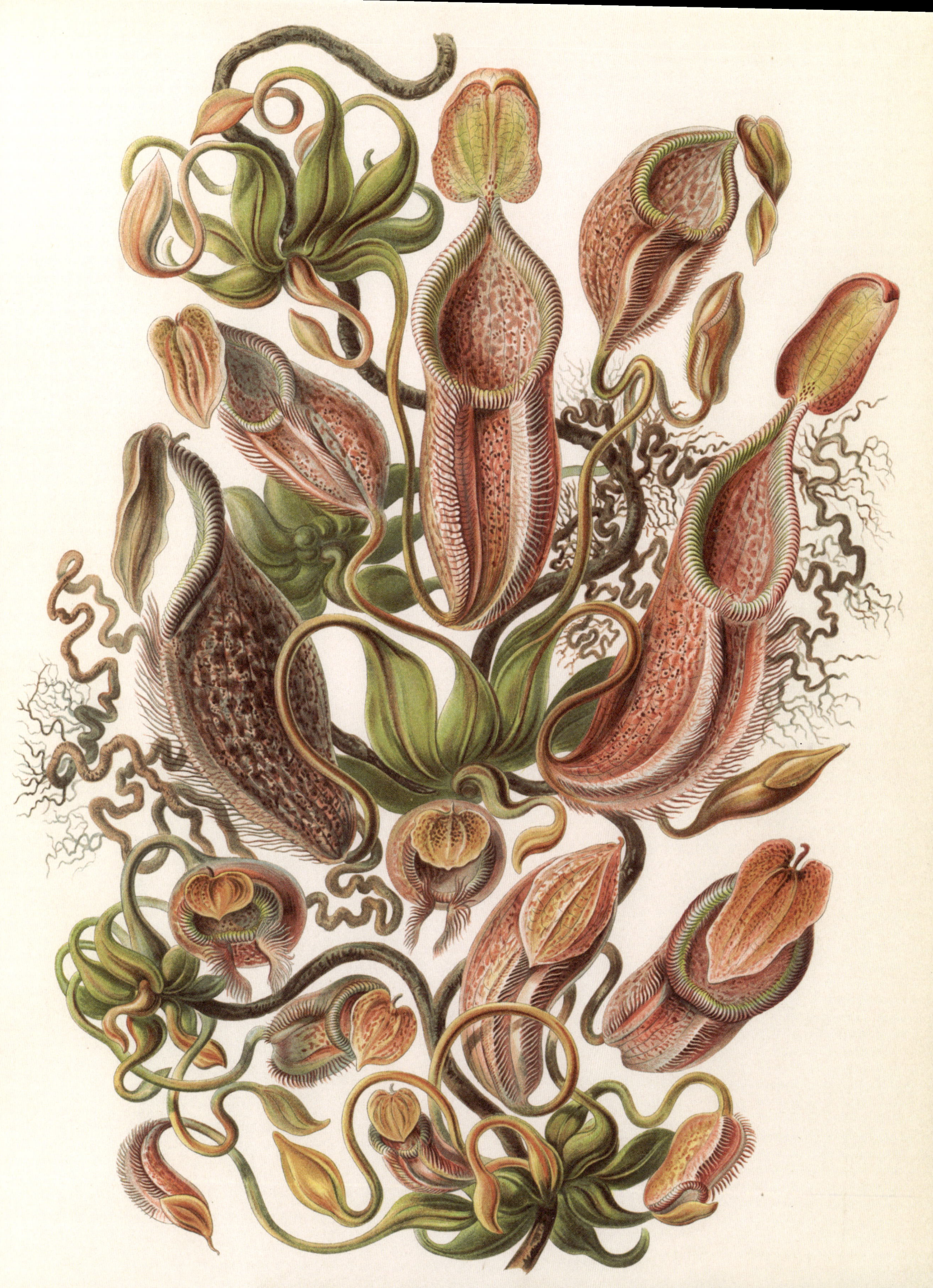

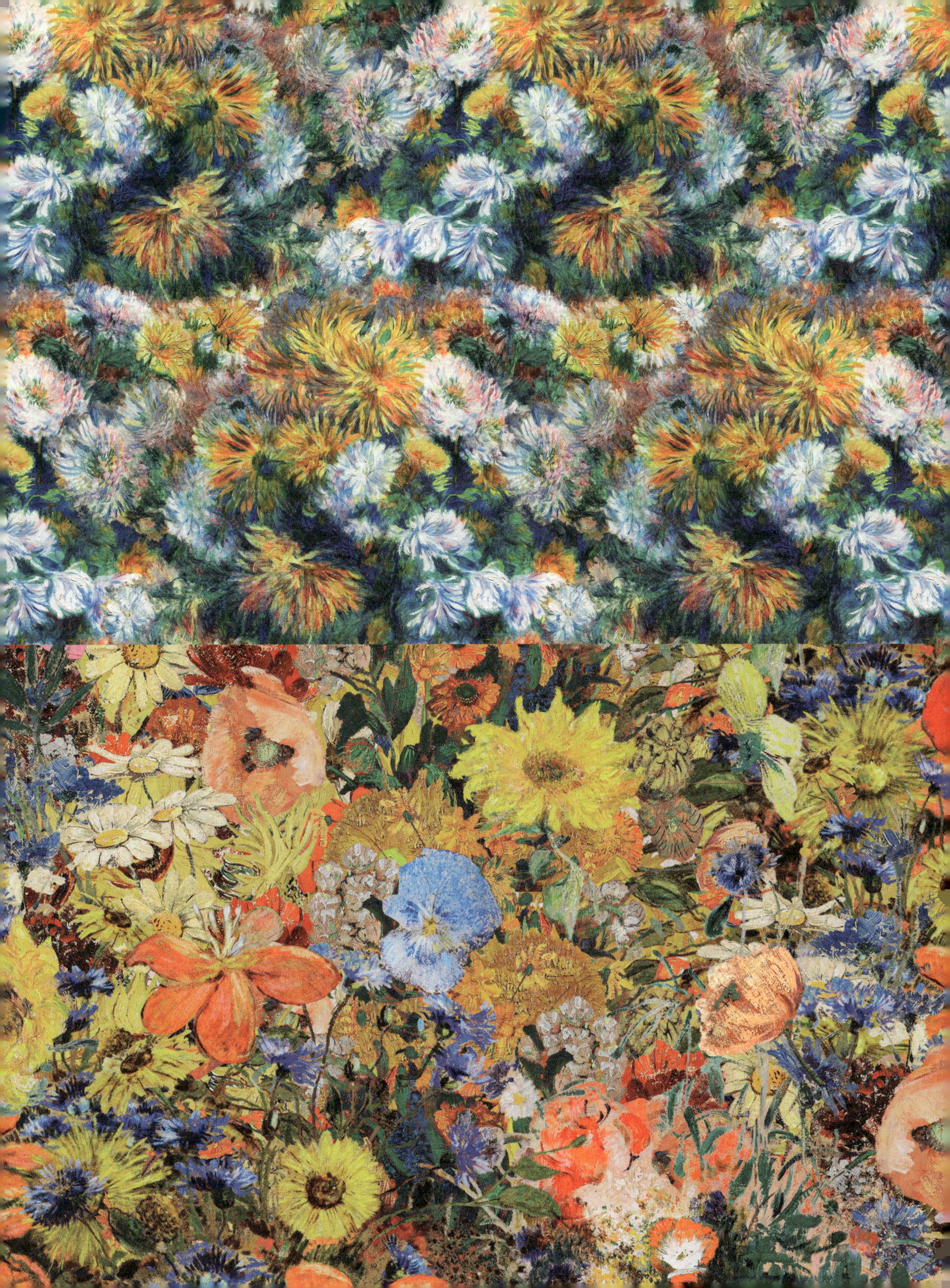

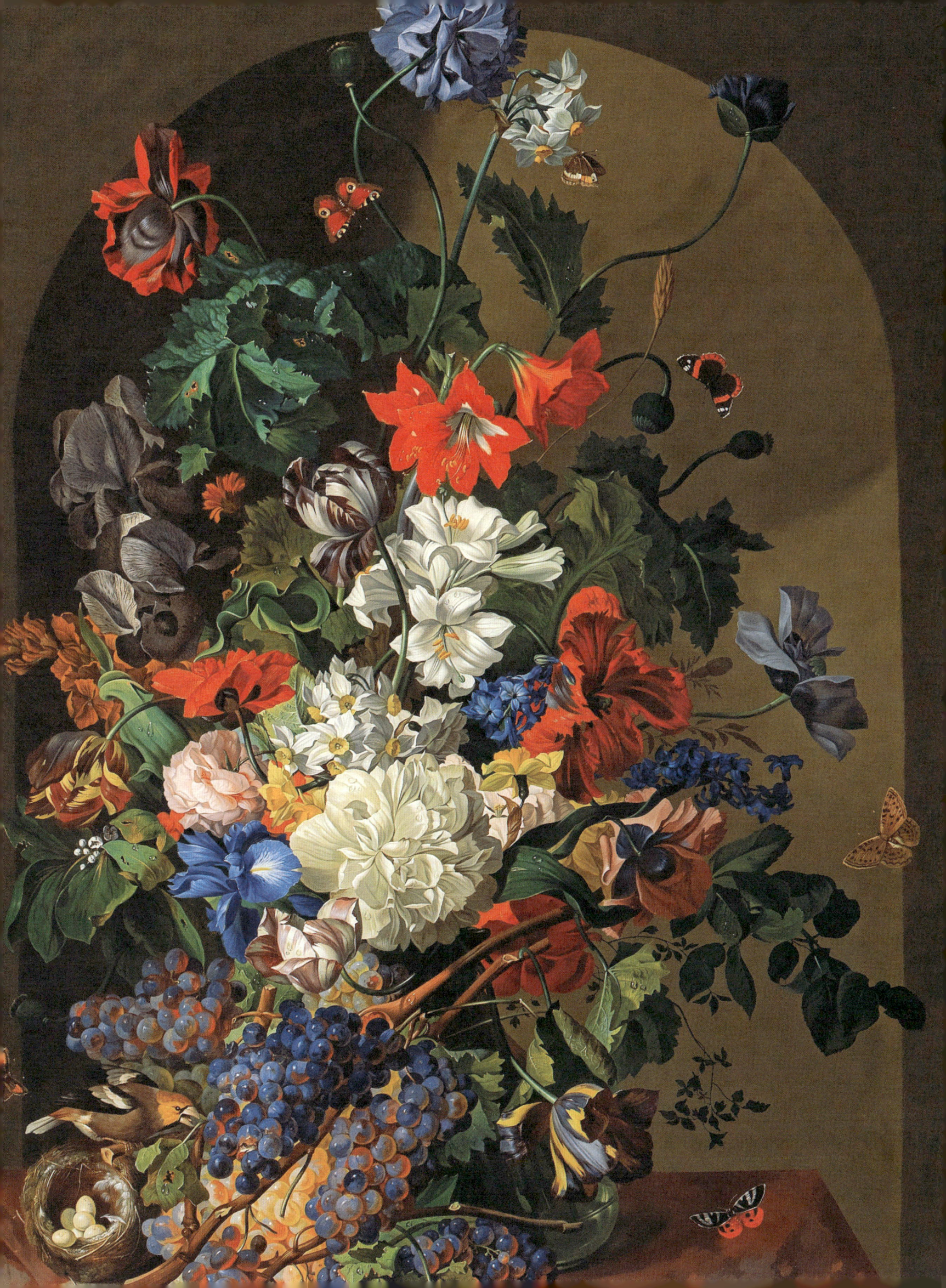

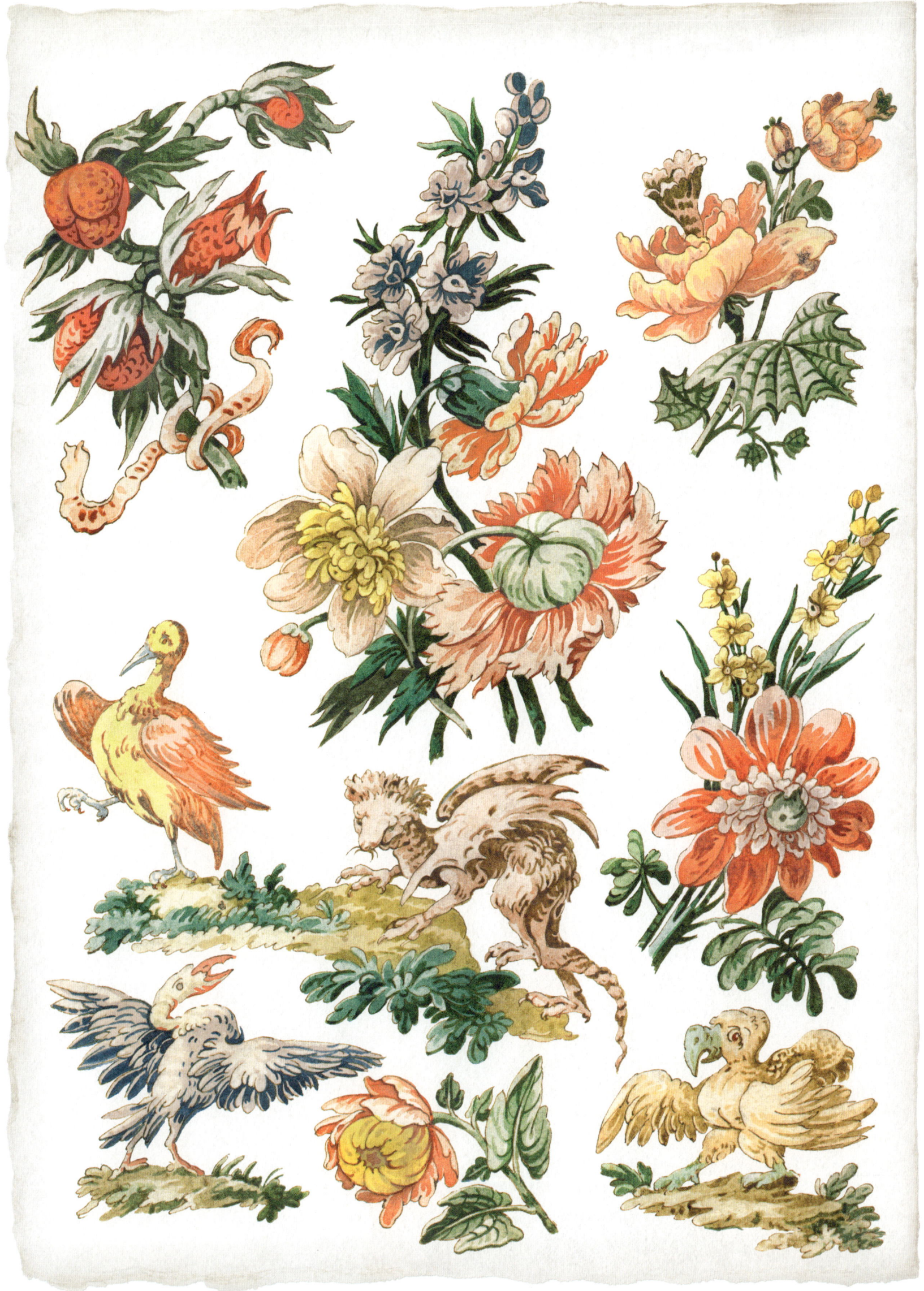

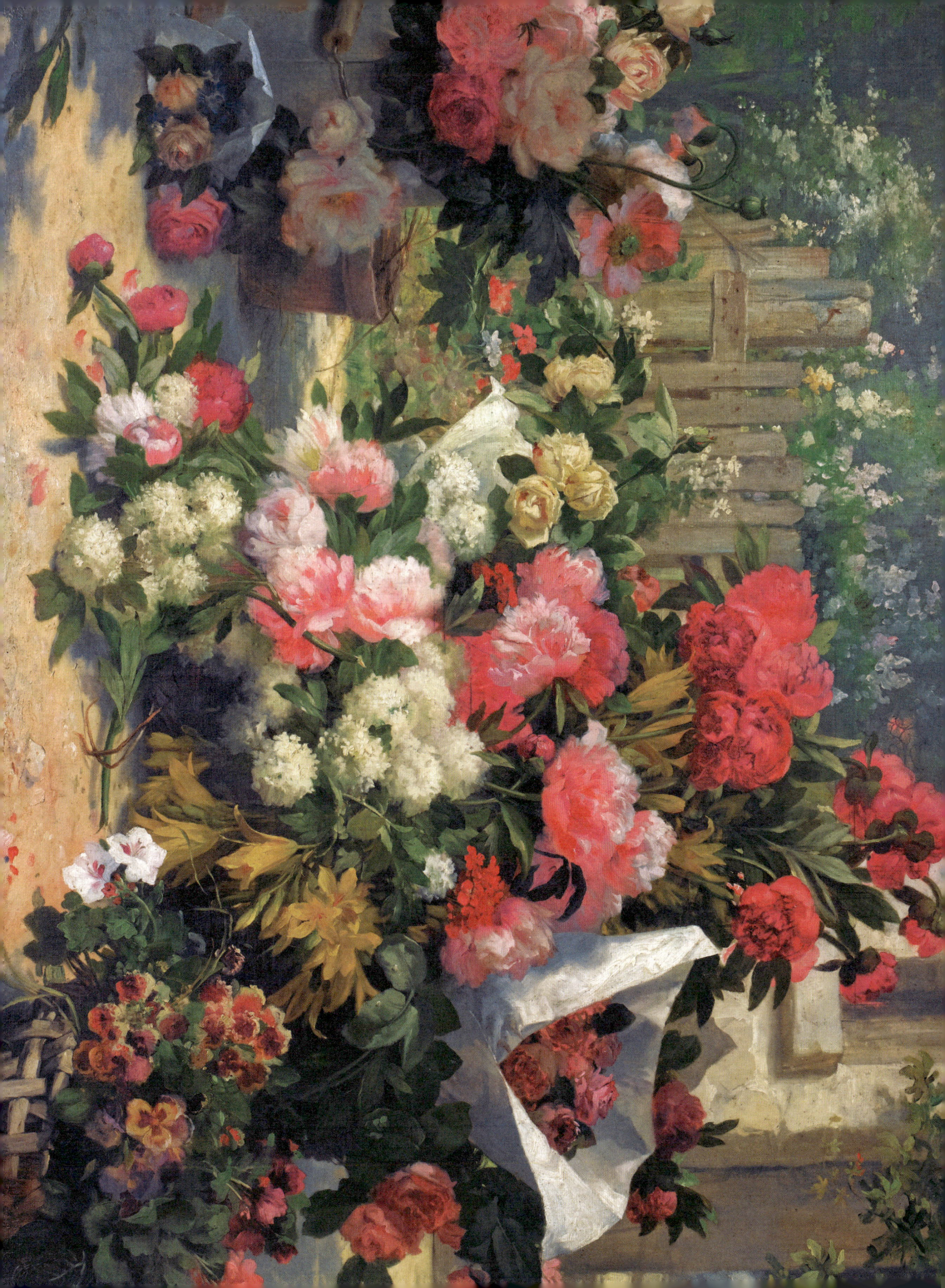

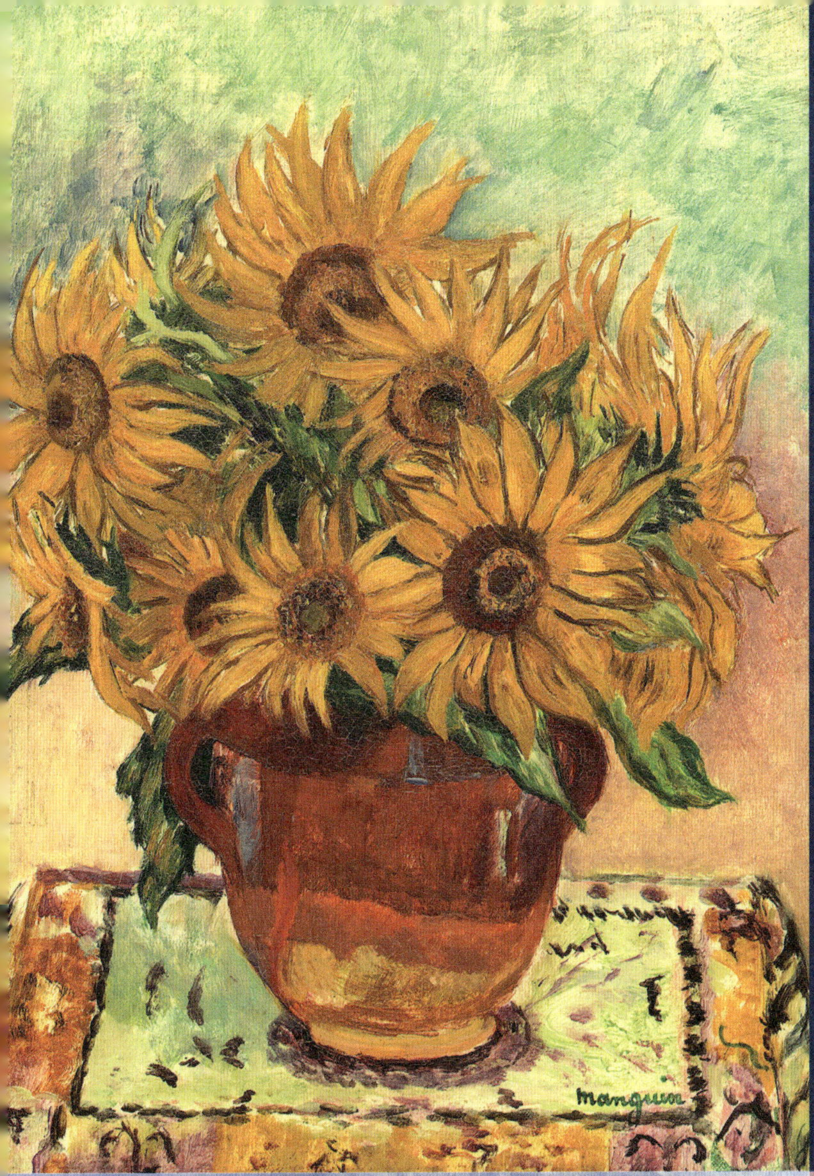

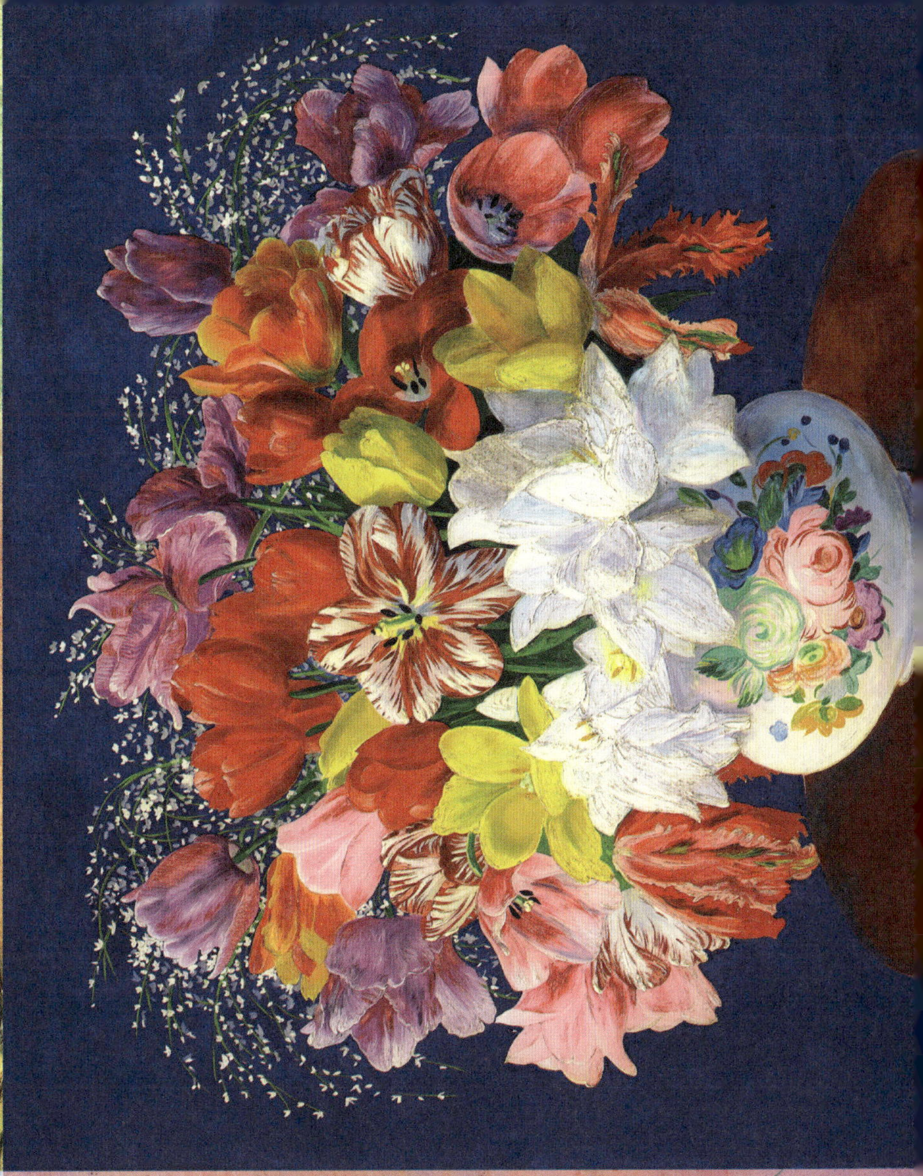

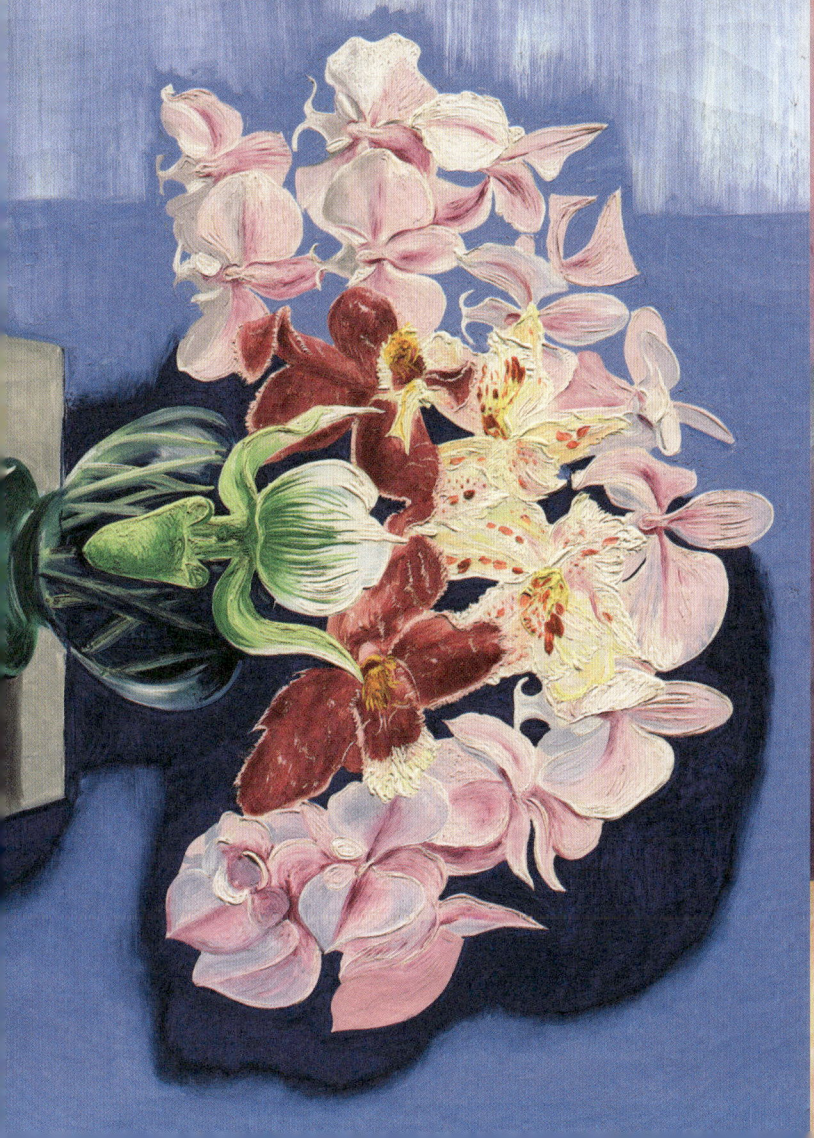
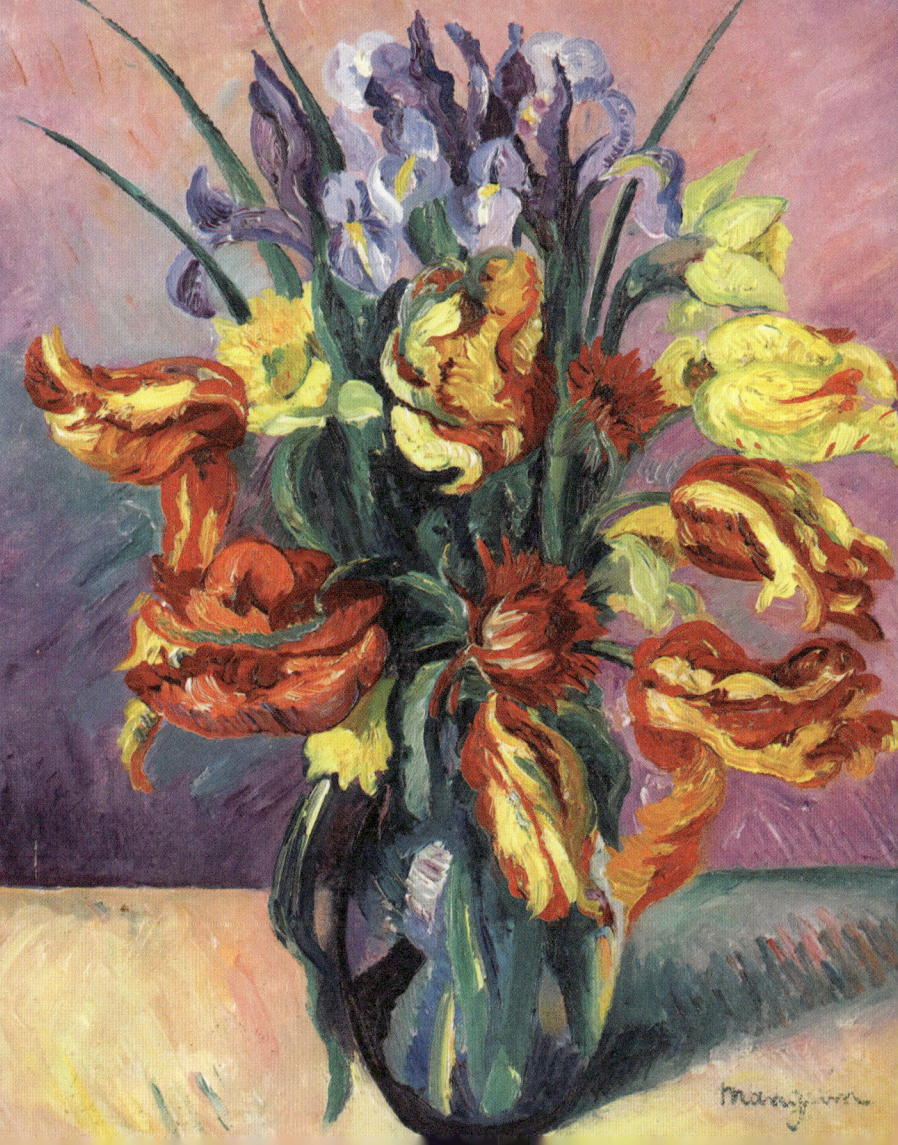

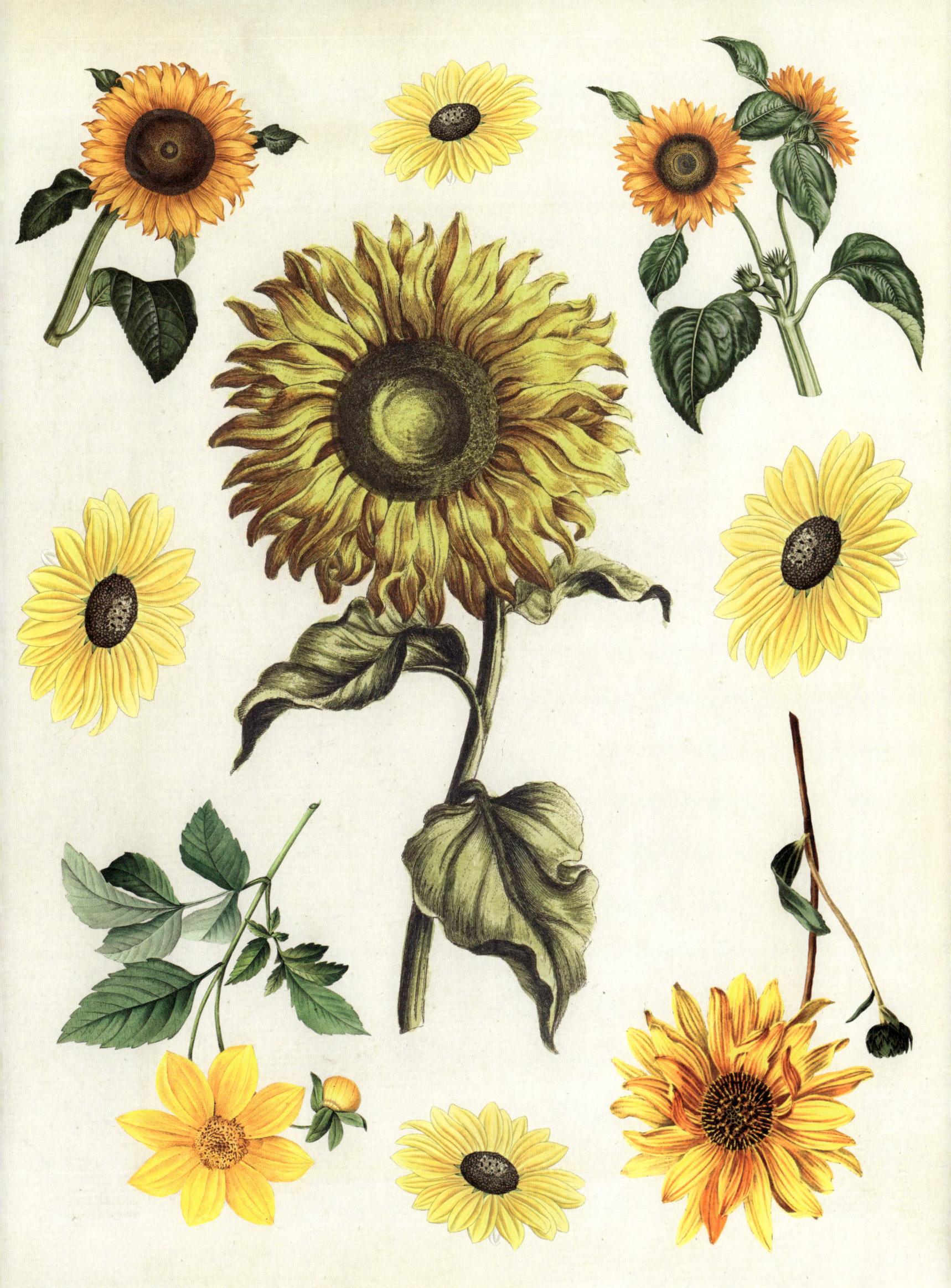

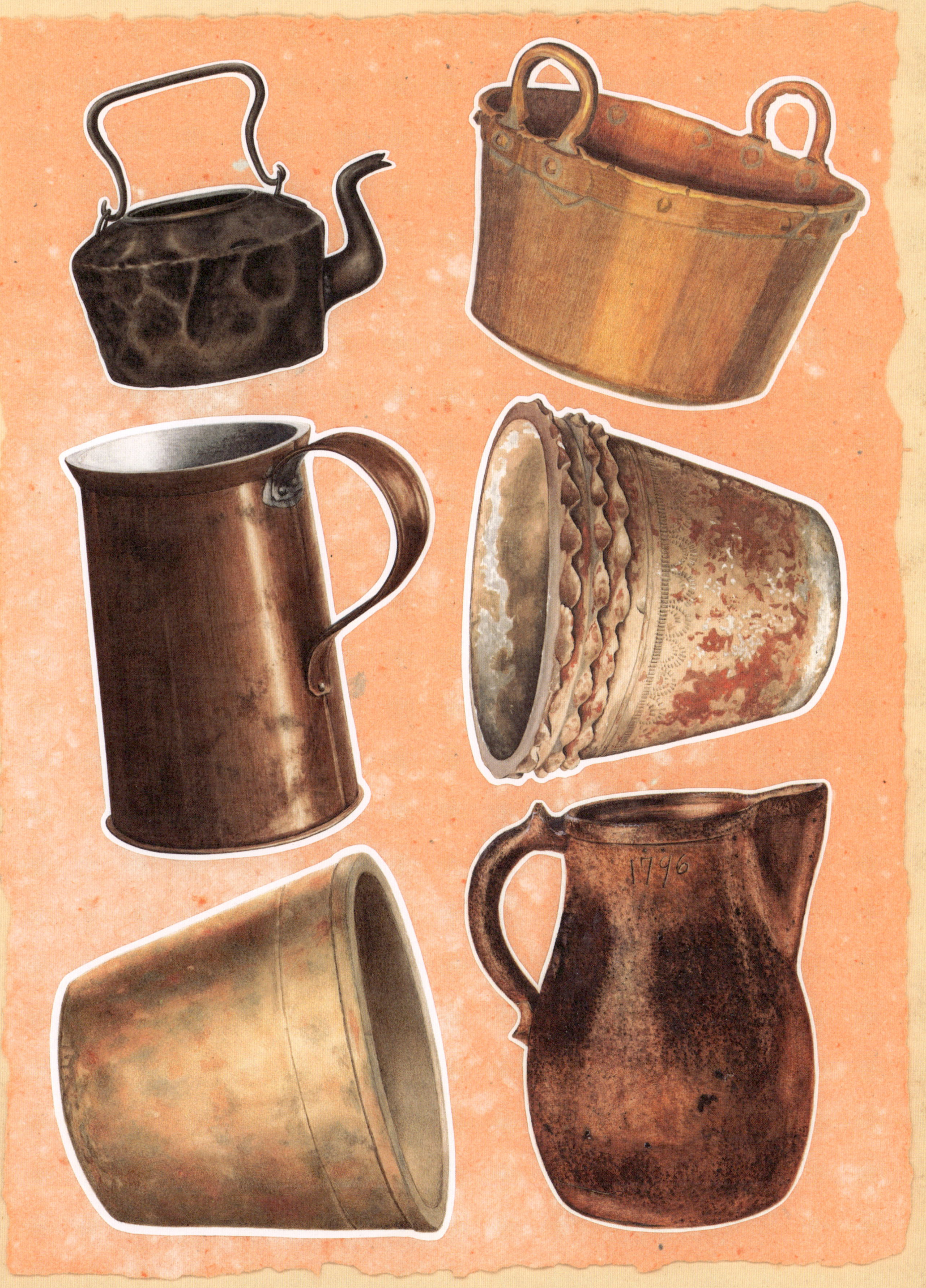

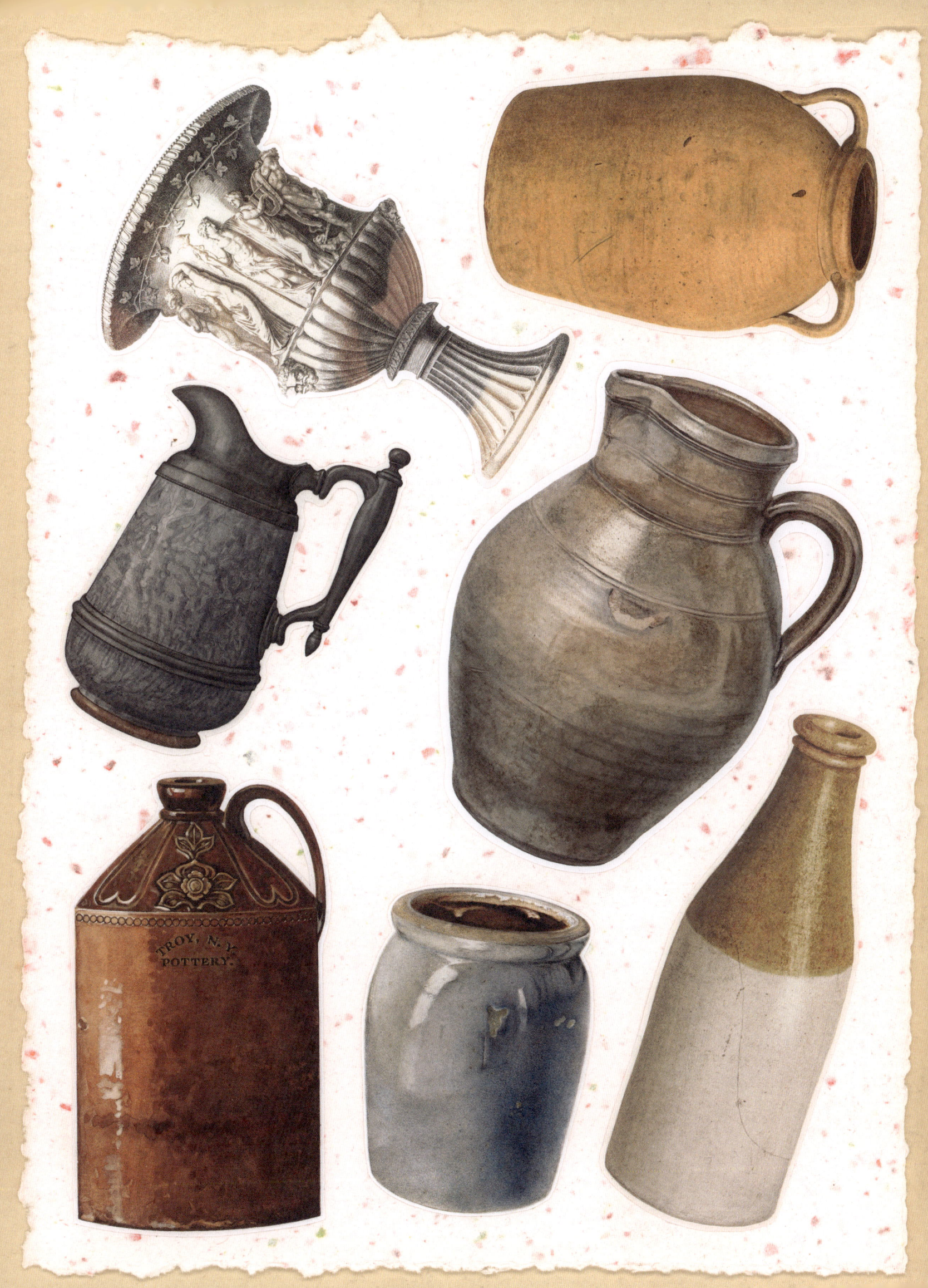

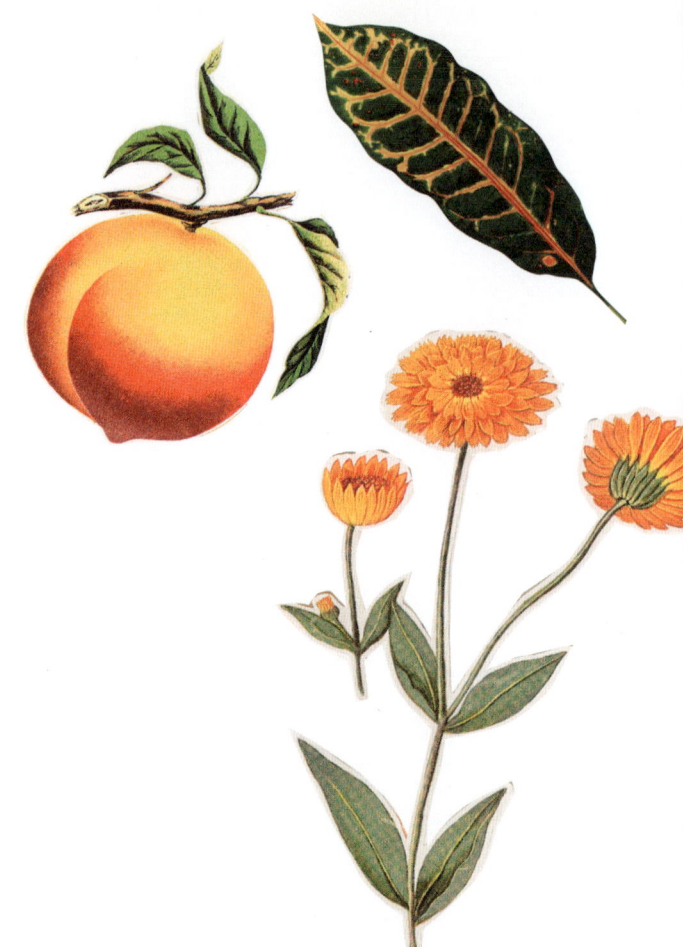

Smith Street Books

Published in 2025 by Smith Street Books
Naarm (Melbourne) | Australia
smithstreetbooks.com

ISBN: 978-1-9230-4992-5

All rights reserved. No part of this book may be reproduced or transmitted by any person or entity, in any form or by any means, electronic or mechanical, including photocopying, recording, scanning or by any storage and retrieval system, without the prior written permission of the publishers and copyright holders.

Smith Street Books respectfully acknowledges the Wurundjeri People of the Kulin Nation, who are the Traditional Owners of the land on which we work, and we pay our respects to their Elders past and present.

Copyright text © Maximillian Malone
Copyright design and photography © Smith Street Books

The moral right of the author has been asserted.

Publisher: Hannah Koelmeyer
Editor: Avery Hayes
Design & introduction layout: Susan Le
Image layout: Maximillian Malone
Introduction photography: Daniel Herrmann-Zoll
Production manager: Aisling Coughlan

Printed & bound in China by C&C Offset Printing Co., Ltd.

Book 374
10 9 8 7 6 5 4 3 2 1

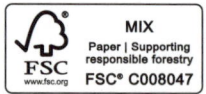